Divorce Lessons

To order additional copies, please contact us.
BookSurge, LLC
www.booksurge.com
1-866-308-6235
orders@booksurge.com

Divorce Lessons
Real Life Stories and What You Can Learn From Them

Alison Clarke-Stewart Ph.D.
and Cornelia Brentano Ph.D.

2005

Divorce Lessons

Table of Contents

To the students who shared their life stories with us

Preface

Divorce Lessons offers a comprehensive view of the entire divorce experience, based on real-life stories framed by psychological theory and enriched by sensitive and practical advice. It illuminates all facets of divorce: what risks doom some marriages from the start, what factors lead to the breakdown of dysfunctional families, what happens during the process of separation and divorce, and what short- and long-term consequences ensue. It describes these processes in a non-judgmental way and offers insights and options informed by scientific research.

In the book, adult children tell of their experiences in the front lines of the divorce wars. They candidly describe what goes on behind closed doors. They reveal in shocking detail the dynamics and secrets of family life leading to the breakdown of a marriage, and they tell of the trials of divorce and its aftermath. Yet, from these real-life tales flows a message of hope: Children and adults can and do survive the trauma of divorce. In these real-life stories are lessons that can help other divorcing—and divorced—parents and their children make better lives for themselves. The adult children of divorce who tell their stories in this book describe their experiences with such passion, such pain; it is as if we are peering into their childhood diaries. Their poignant and gripping stories touched our hearts. Until we read them, we had no inkling of the struggles these children had been through. And, we suspect, others don't either—because these true stories reveal the full spectrum of private thoughts and feelings to an extent that has not been shared before. These adult children give us their impressions of what led to their parents' problems and the demise of their families. They report details of what it is like to go through a family break-up. They describe the shock and confusion they felt when they first heard "Daddy is leaving us." "Mommy isn't coming home." They tell us in painful detail about how hard it is to leave the big house on the hill, to move to a shabby neighborhood, to be torn between two parents, to be shuttled back and forth like a piece of property, to be confused and afraid, and angry too. They tell of domestic violence and alcoholism, cruel stepmothers and abusive stepfathers, poverty and depression. Yet their stories also give countless examples of coping and surviving, of success and salvation.

We gathered these stories from hundreds of students at the University of California. For the past dozen years, we have been teaching a class titled "The Impacts of Divorce." The students in the class seem to be doing just fine. They come to class, participate in discussions, smile and laugh. They turn in term papers and pass exams. But this is a class in which more than half of the students have experienced first hand the impact of their parents' divorce. When we asked these students to share with us their family "autobiographies," the extent to which divorce had affected them—and their parents—became shockingly clear.

This was not a "research study" in the strict sense of the term. We did not set out to study the effects of divorce by selecting a sample of young people and assessing their reactions to their parents' divorce. These stories came to us as a gift, written from the heart. Although this was not a "random sample," the students who shared their life experiences with us were a large and diverse group. They reflect the make-up of the American melting pot and include students who grew up in all regions of the United States and immigrants from around the world. They ranged in age from twenty to forty-something, came from families that included the very rich and the painfully poor, and grew up in widely varied family circumstances. More important, the students' stories were consistent with the results of scientific studies, which are described in a more academic book we have written (*Divorce: Causes and Consequences,* Yale University Press, 2006).

Today, it is a matter of some controversy how detrimental divorce is for children's well-being. In most studies, researchers find that children go through a period of adjustment after their parents' divorce, but, within a couple of years, are performing well in school and getting along with other children. However, in one well-publicized, albeit much criticized, clinical study carried out by Judith Wallerstein (*The Unexpected Legacy of Divorce*), even 25 years after the divorce, many children of divorce still suffer psychologically. What the stories of the children in our book reveal is that these high-profile findings may, in fact, be capturing some of the dark realities of divorce. Even when they were doing fine in school, many of the children in the book continued to feel sad, resentful, hurt, angry, jealous, conflicted, and anxious—inside.

But the real-life stories in our book also reveal ways in which these bad feelings can be prevented or alleviated. The stories point not only to suffering but to solutions as well. Divorce doesn't have to be a catastrophe. It doesn't have to leave children scarred or scared. Adults can make children's experiences better or worse. There are lessons in these stories that can help parents as they contemplate or experience divorce, as they try to pick up the pieces and make a new life for themselves. Parents can alter their own behavior to provide a better environment for their children if they are more aware of what their children are feeling and thinking. Seeing divorce through the eyes of these children can help adults understand what their own children feel so they can be more supportive and empathic. Children of divorcing parents do not often discuss their problems openly, and their parents, absorbed in their own problems, are often not available to listen. By reading the stories and insights of the children in this book, parents will know what to expect and will better understand what their children are going through or have endured. They may also be less likely to jump into a new marriage without sober reflection, if they absorb the lessons in the book. Adolescents and young adults who experienced the disruption of their own families will learn from the book too. They will find comfort by recognizing that they are not alone in their suffering and feel reassured that they are not crazy. They may also be more cautious and informed about marriage for themselves in the future. College students and professors will find that the stories in the book illuminate the dry statistics of divorce. School teachers who wonder why their students from divorcing families act out or withdraw will find enlightenment. Individuals who simply wonder why divorce is so common in our society and want to know how divorce affects adults and children will find useful information here. We hope this book provides insights and guidance to help all people touched by divorce.

Alison Clarke-Stewart
Cornelia Brentano

Introduction: Divorce Today

In spite of the widespread coverage of divorce as a major social crisis confronting today's society, divorce has a long history. In the beginning, getting a divorce was even easier than it is today. Marriage was marked by the simplest of ceremonies—and so was divorce. It was strictly a personal decision. It was not until the Middle Ages that divorce became a serious moral issue, forbidden and condemned by the Church, and even later that it came under the control of restrictive policies enacted by national and state legislatures. After that, divorce was almost unobtainable for centuries. In the first half of the 20th century, divorce became available once again—but only with proof of the spouse's cruelty, adultery, or incompetence.

Today, divorce has come full circle; it is once again a personal decision. In 1969, with Ronald Reagan's signature on The Family Law Act, California became the first state in the union to adopt "no-fault divorce." With this new law, getting a divorce became dramatically easier. Under "no-fault" divorce proceedings, one spouse can dissolve the marriage without proving any grounds for divorce and even without obtaining the partner's consent. Decrees of "dissolution" (the new, more neutral word for divorce) are now granted on the basis of "irreconcilable differences" or when a marriage is "irretrievably broken."

All states have some form of no-fault divorce, and social attitudes toward divorce have become more accepting. Divorce has also become more common. After no-fault divorce was instituted, the number of divorces granted increased every year until 1980. Since then, the frequency of divorce has leveled off to about four divorces for every thousand people in the U.S. This still amounts to over a million divorces annually. Couples who marry today have roughly a 50 percent risk that their marriage will fail.

Divorce may be quicker and easier to get than it was a hundred years ago, but it is still not easy for the people going through it. The roots of the struggle often begin long before the divorce, in marriages that were mistakes from the beginning. We begin our story with a look at these marriages.

1
Poor Choices, No Control: The High-Risk Marriage

Sometimes it's obvious to everyone—except perhaps the bride and groom—even before a couple marries that their marriage isn't likely to last. Sometimes a marriage starts to fall apart almost as soon as it begins. When researchers compare couples who stay married with those who divorce, they find that relationships ending in divorce have certain "risk" characteristics in common. They often follow short courtships or premarital pregnancies. Frequently, the couple is young or in a hurry. Often the husband and wife come from different backgrounds— they belong to different social groups, are of different races, or practice different religions. Sometimes, the couple's parents were divorced and the couple lacked role models for what stable relationships look like. Additional risk factors for divorce include the presence of children at the time of marriage, a great deal of stress because of pressures from work or family or lack of money, alcohol abuse, or infidelity. All of these conditions can put the marriage at risk for divorce. Three quarters of our students described their divorced parents' marriages as being affected by one or more of these risk factors.

Lucy Schumacher

My parents were eighteen years old when they got married. They were young and in love and they vowed with all their naive hearts to be together "'til death do us part." But it was not to be. They were from two different worlds. My mom's upbringing in a white, Protestant, middle-class family taught her that it was her obligation to be a good wife and mother. Until then, she was chaste, waiting for her prince charming. My dad, on the other hand, born in Hawaii to a Japanese mother and a Caucasian father, grew up a flower child of the '60s. He experimented sexually and dated frequently. His relationships were brief. When he was sixteen, he got a girl pregnant, but she gave the baby up for adoption. He moved on. The next year, his senior year of high school, he started dating my mother.

High school graduation catapulted them to the next life stage. All their friends were going their separate ways. Some were being called to Vietnam, some were going to college, some were getting married. My parents joined the group getting married. My dad took a job as a mechanic and my mom became a stay-at-home wife.

They shared the popular dream of having the perfect family, and they began working on that perfect family right away. Two months after the wedding, my mother became pregnant. Unfortunately, she had a miscarriage, and this tragedy put a tremendous stress on their relationship. She was terrified of getting pregnant again. My dad thought that her fear of pregnancy and their different upbringings made them sexually incompatible. He began having an affair before their six-month anniversary. To make matters worse, his mistress, Robin, got pregnant.

Most women would have left my dad then and there, but my mother took her vows seriously. She gave him a second chance. Six months after Robin gave birth to my half-brother Dennis, my mother decided to try getting pregnant again. My dad wanted a family, so she was going to give him one. Almost immediately, she got pregnant with me. They were twenty years old when they had their first baby, and they both believed that this baby would save their marriage. This was a lot to expect from a small child.

After my birth everything was perfect again—for a little while. They had a daughter and, part-time, they had a son. My dad always loved being with us children when we were young. He was a good father to Dennis and me. When Dennis was almost two years old, his mother told my parents to keep him because she could not handle being a mother. My mother took Dennis in and raised him as her own. Now, she had two children under the age of two. Aside from sporadic visits with his real mother, my mother was his mother.

A year later, my parents were having problems again. My father's answer to a troubled marriage was to have another child. My sister Gail was born the next year. Now my parents were twenty-three years old and had three children under the age of four. My dad worked full-time to support the family and my mom stayed home to raise us. Dad worked late hours, at least that's what he told her. In reality, he began having another affair. This time it was with Peggi. Peggi was also married and was a friend of my mother's. In fact, they were close friends. She appears in many of the photos taken at my parents' wedding. Peggi had just had her first child and was also having marital problems. They kept the affair secret for a long time, but my father's hours became more and more irregular. I was only four years old at the time, but I remember that he was never home. When my mother would try to reach him, she could never find him. My parents went through ten more roller-coaster years of constant lies and suspicions, admissions of cheating, heartbreak and tears, promises, followed by more cheating. When I was fifteen, my mother finally asked for a divorce.

The breakup of this couple was highly predictable. From the outset, they had more than three strikes against them: they were young; they came from different backgrounds; they had a short courtship; and they started having children right away. To top it off, their reason for marrying was the poorest reason possible: they didn't know what else to do with their lives. The choices they made before and during the marriage led to high levels of stress. His habitual sexual exploits were a red flag from the beginning, flagrantly displayed even before their first child was conceived. Right after his new wife had a miscarriage, he fathered a child in an extramarital relationship. To follow this cheating with creating a child was hardly sensible. To attempt a year later to salvage this fledgling relationship with yet another child, a strategy that already didn't work the first time was downright foolish.

Because of their young age and their short courtship this husband and wife knew neither themselves nor each other. They were not prepared for life, much less for the tremendous commitments of marriage and child rearing. Like many young people, they were chasing the dream of the "perfect family." Their traditional values—man as breadwinner, wife as homemaker—helped little in their development as individuals or as a couple. Not knowing what felt right for them because they lacked life experience, they clung to clichés like the notion that a baby would save their failing marriage. But the early arrival of babies—including one from an extramarital affair—only compounded the emotional and financial pressures. The added emotional and financial burdens, the constant frustrations, the sense of betrayal, and the lack of time and resources ultimately led to the marriage breakup.

Marrying Too Young

Marrying young is one of the primary causes of divorce. Individuals who are under eighteen when they marry are three times as likely to divorce as those who are in their twenty's. In fact, age is the best predictor of divorce during the first five years of marriage. The most important reason that these marriages fail is that at this age young people are still developing. They are likely to change more than older couples and the husband and wife may change in different directions. Young couples also tend to view marriage naively and romantically and to focus on physical expressions of togetherness. Rarely do they fully understand the broader meaning of marriage with its implications for a long-term social, emotional, and material commitment. They make important life decisions, like marriage and starting a family, impulsively and impatiently. Many act as if they had no time to lose, as if life would end at twenty-five. Young people also are not as psychologically and emotionally mature and therefore they are less able to solve the problems and tolerate the difficulties that inevitably accompany the attempt to live together as one. They have not had the life experience that allows them to anticipate these issues and when they run into unexpected difficulties, they do not have the maturity and the skills to resolve them.

The following story provides another illustration of how marrying young and naive starts the marriage off on the wrong foot.

Naoko Russell

My parents graduated together as "high school sweethearts." Shortly after, at the ripe old ages of seventeen (my mom) and eighteen (my dad), they married. They were in love (or so they thought), but unfortunately, they had no plans for the future. Neither was heading to college right away, and neither had any solid career goals. They got married because they didn't want to go on living at home, they weren't brave enough to live alone, and their families wouldn't let them just live together. The morning after the wedding, my father put his feet up on the easy chair to watch sports—something he had never done before. It was as if he was trying to fit into the role his father played, because he was unsure of what a "married man" was supposed to do. I think his behavior that day demonstrated that he was not ready for the commitment he had just made. In a way, my parents' marriage was over before it began.

Very young couples do not yet have a clear sense of who they are and who they want to be, which leaves them generally unprepared for the complex challenges and frustrations that come with being uneducated, having no stable and satisfying employment, and becoming a family. To cope with a world full of uncertainties, they cling rigidly to stereotyped images of what a husband or a wife should be, regardless of whether those images fit their personalities or their circumstances. They play at being grown up the way this student's parents did, each falling into patterns they learned from their own parents or on TV. They think that these behaviors are the "thing to do." The husband becomes the breadwinner, the boss, and the wife is locked into a traditional role of housekeeping, child rearing, and dependency. Neither has a chance to find out who he or she is as an individual, what he or she wants in life, and how he or she handles life. Before they know the answers to these questions they assume obligations with no way out. This pattern of "mindless marrying" was repeated time and again in our students' stories.

Kristin Sanders
My parents got married when my dad was twenty and my mother was eighteen. Because they were so young, neither of them had a lot going for them as individuals. My mom got pregnant right away and my dad had to give up his dream of going to law school because he needed to work to support them. He felt cheated and resentful.

Suzanne Knowles
My parents got married when my mom was nineteen and my dad was twenty-one. My mom can't even remember why they got married. She thinks it must have been like a contagious disease. All her friends were getting married and she did too. She and my father never talked about their goals and dreams for the future. Right after they married, my mom got pregnant. Within four years she

had three little girls. She looks back now in disbelief, realizing that they never discussed anything important. Birth control was never even mentioned. They didn't discuss how many kids they wanted. The marriage and the children just happened.

These students were among many who described their parents as young and naive when they married and entered the parent trap. In the last student's story, her mother described it like a contagious disease, something that just "happened" to her. Her most important life decision was made while she was feverish, and afterward she couldn't remember how it all came about.

Marrying Too Soon

But it was not just young couples whose marriages failed. Marrying too soon—at any age—was a risk factor for divorce. A short courtship makes for spouses who do not know each other well, and, if they did, they would probably not have married each other. Among our students' parents, 82 percent had known each other for less than three years. An extreme case of marrying too soon is described in the following story.

Wendy Farran

My parents married two weeks after meeting on a student trip to Europe, and I was born nine months later. There were problems from day one. My dad's parents hated my mom, and they made that very clear. Mom felt that Dad was never loyal to her on these occasions, and she soon discovered that they could not communicate about this or any other issue. But although they were unhappy, my mom did not feel that she could leave the marriage. She had no work experience and was afraid that if they got divorced she would not get custody of me because my dad threatened to have her declared an "unfit mother." By then he was a lawyer, and he and his wealthy parents had all the money they needed for a nasty court battle. Today, the one thing my parents agree on is that if they had dated longer and known each other better, they would never have married.

Wendy's parents spent twenty years together even though they didn't like each other. There is a good chance that a lengthy courtship would have revealed their incompatibilities and saved them twenty years of grief.

Marrying Pregnant

It is estimated that one quarter of first brides are pregnant or already have children when they marry, and this, too, is a predictor of divorce. As many as half of the women who are pregnant when they marry are divorced only four years later, according to demographers. Among our students' mothers who got divorced, one-fifth were pregnant when they married. The reason that premarital pregnancy is a risk factor is that the pregnancy itself and the birth and presence of a young child create enormous stress early in the relationship. Premarital pregnancies often are accompanied by other risk factors, such as parental opposition and economic difficulties. In addition, having a child pressures husband and wife to fulfill instantly and simultaneously two new roles: the role of a spouse and the role of a parent. Either one of these roles requires a great deal of adjustment, and adjustment takes time. Only after having successfully made the adjustment to couplehood is a person secure enough to take on the more demanding role of being a parent. The demands of struggling with a new relationship, childbirth, and child rearing prove to be too much for most couples. By definition, instant families have little time for the preparation of family life. Premarital pregnancies also often lead to marriages that otherwise would not have happened. A woman who is about to be a mother may enter a marriage more hastily than one who is not.

Martina Nunez
    When my mother married the first time, she was seventeen years young and five months pregnant.

Eighteen months later came a second child, and another year later she was separated. She was barely twenty years old, divorced with two small children, and no money. About four years later she met her soon-to-be second husband. They married six months after they had me—mainly because she was pregnant again. She was married to this man for less than a year before the problems began. So both of my mom's marriages started with an unplanned pregnancy and both ended soon after the babies were born.

As in this student's story, premarital pregnancies often start a cycle of unsuccessful marriages and divorces. But it is not only women who fall into the premarital pregnancy trap. A man may decide to marry out of a sense of obligation or because he feels pressured by the woman or their families. Rather than taking a premarital pregnancy as a wake-up call and beginning to think more carefully about how to proceed, couples tend to cope with their anxieties by taking drastic steps. Many men take the pregnancy to be a symbol of their commitment, passion, virility, or adulthood and, therefore, do what they believe is right; they marry the girl. Even if they are terrified by the prospect of having a baby, they rarely have the mental resources to sit back and develop rational and practical solutions. What seems "right" though, often turns out to be wrong—a further misstep that seals their future.

An additional explanation for the adverse effects of a premarital pregnancy is that it deviates from the socially expected course of life events. Social norms lead us to expect a more conservative path, where childbirth follows marriage and family and economic circumstances support child rearing. As a consequence of deviating from this ideal path, premarital pregnancy often causes anxiety and frustration. One of the spouses often resents the other or the baby for what they have done to him or her.

Sarah Beller

My mother was twenty-one when she came to the United States. She was here on a student visa attending secretarial school. One night while she was out dancing with her girlfriends she met my father. Sparks flew. They had only been dating a few months when my mother became pregnant with me. Neither of them wanted to get married, but they found themselves in a difficult situation. My father tried to make my mother get an abortion, but she refused. He then felt the only thing to do was to get married. This forced him to take on responsibilities at a time he had intended to conquer the world. Instead of continuing his education, he found himself working two jobs to make ends meet and waking up several times a night to a crying baby. The drastic change of his plan led him to feel bitter toward his new wife.

There is a real basis for such sentiments. Beginning marriage with a baby leads to financial pressures and poor job opportunities because couples often do not complete their education. Because they take on jobs that pay the bills rather than jobs that interest them, they have fewer career opportunities and less satisfaction in the long run. The discontentment that grows out of such decisions is not limited to the intellectual dissatisfaction associated with lowered career choices. Long-term financial problems are another consequence that also affects the marital relationship adversely.

Stephanie Conaway

When my parents met, my mom already had a son, Paul, from her first marriage. Two months later, she became pregnant with me. They quickly married. Dad did not earn enough from his job at the chemical company to take care of us, so, to earn extra money, he got a part-time job working for a janitorial service. He worked very hard and was extremely tired. The stress took its toll. He was really irritable, especially with Paul. My mother resented his demands and hated the way he treated her son. This tension kept building, corroding their relationship.

Lacking Support

When couples get married, it is common for them to "leave home." They move away from their families and their communities. They move for educational and financial reasons, for better employment and housing opportunities, or just because they are "starting out" on a new life. These moves typically mean saying "good-bye" to family and friends. Embarking on a new marriage without support from these people also can put a marriage at risk. A number of our students' stories revealed that this was a risk factor in their parents' marriages.

> Allison Rodgers
>
> When my dad was accepted to the University of Denver, my parents decided to get married and move there. After he graduated, we moved to California. Each move took them farther away from their families who lived on the East Coast.

With the loss of close friends and family comes a new feeling. loneliness.

> Diana Denman
>
> My mother had moved out of state to get married, so she did not have many friends. Because of her lack of friends, she did not have anyone to talk to about her feelings of loneliness. Taking care of the house, the children, and a very demanding husband did not leave her much free time to venture out and make her own friends.

Lack of support from family and friends or their outright opposition to the relationship has been related to marital instability in research studies and also appeared in our students' stories. The adjustment to the relationship and, especially for young people, the additional demands of becoming established economically, heighten the need for support. During stressful situations people need support in three areas: material resources, emotional support, and information. It is common for young couples to receive some form of material support from their parents. Parents pay for the wedding, buy housewares, help with mortgage payments, buy baby clothes, and so on. Parents and friends also provide emotional support. They reassure the person that he or she is loved and valued. A person in stress often needs or seeks advice from family or friends in areas ranging from the intimate to the mundane to the complex—how to deal with a partner's bad habits, how to cook a certain meal, how to go house shopping. Support helps people cope with stress. On the other hand, isolation from family and friends not only deprives the individual of much needed support but becomes a source of stress in itself.

Naoko Russell

My mom received absolutely no support from her mother, who herself had been married more times than is worth mentioning. Her lack of family support caused strain on my parents' marriage from the beginning. There was no trusted and experienced person she could ask for advice. My dad was really close to his family and this made her feel even more isolated. If there was a problem, he always had his family on his side. Any problem wasn't just between the two of them; it felt like 'them' against her.

Family and friends' direct opposition to the relationship is even worse than the lack of support. It undermines the relationship and exacerbates marital difficulties. Little wonder the marriages described by the following students didn't survive.

Wendy Farran

Early on in their marriage, my parents experienced tensions because of my dad's parents. My mother came from a lower middle-class background, and her wealthy in-laws accused her of being a gold digger. They refused to support the new couple financially. In dire straits, my parents had to depend on her poorer family and the pension from her dead father to survive. A year into the marriage, my dad's mother began meddling and trying to set up her son with other, more "suitable" women. She often showed up at their house and caused scenes. But worst of all, any time there was trouble, usually caused by his mother, my dad did not defend or speak up for my mother. My mother was incredibly hurt by his disloyalty and was never able to overcome that pain.

Amanthi Chandra

When my father divorced his wife and married my mother, the families on both sides opposed the marriage. My maternal grandmother warned my mother not to marry my father because she didn't think they were a good match. He was eleven years older, had been married and had children, and both of them were very headstrong and uncompromising. My headstrong mother, of course, did not heed her mother's advice. My dad's family never even recognized my mother as his wife. Their friends were also against their relationship and cut off contact after my parents married. It was very difficult to start out with no support from friends or family.

Marrying Without Role Models

As children and adolescents, we learn from our parents how to interact with other adults. If we do not have well-functioning role models to demonstrate healthy and harmonious interactions between husband and wife, we are penalized, and when we marry we have to figure out how to interact with our spouse by trial and error. Often this leads to mistakes, as in the following story:

Rachel Hall

My mother's parents divorced when she was only a young girl and she was raised by an unloving stepfather. My father's mother died when he was an adolescent. In both their families, fights were common. So, although neither of them verbalized it, my mom and dad decided not to have turmoil of any kind in their marriage. It was an unspoken rule that they would not argue. They never talked, discussed problems, or disagreed. There were never any arguments to clear the air. There were no ups and downs, so there was no room for change, improvement, or growth. They kept everything inside, and their marriage just died. When I was ten, my mom told my dad she was moving out. He was dumbstruck. They had never dealt with their problems, so in his eyes, the marriage was going all right. All of the problems had built up for years because of their inability or unwillingness to recognize, acknowledge, and work on their problems.

Research shows that divorce is "intergenerational." If parents divorce, their children are more likely to divorce, too. Coming from a "broken home" affects your perceptions of what a marital relationship is like and increases your willingness to end an unsatisfactory relationship. People whose parents divorced have a more positive view of divorce because they have experienced it, and their lack of positive role models leaves them ill equipped for the complex demands of a marriage. The experience of family dysfunction may create faulty expectations of the marital relationship and have long-lasting consequences.

Coming from Different Worlds

The more different husband and wife are, the more likely they are to divorce. When husband and wife come from different social, economic, educational, religious, or ethnic backgrounds, they are more likely to divorce than couples that share these characteristics. Couples from different backgrounds have less in common and find it more difficult to formulate and practice shared values. Their differences in upbringing may lead to fundamental clashes. For example, the religious education of their children, as well as to differences regarding everyday trivia. Many of our students described such incompatibilities between their parents.

Esther Santiago

My father is a Greek American and my mother is Mexican. My father has a B.A. in Real Estate from USC; my mother only went to the eighth grade. My father is not religious; my mother is a strong Catholic. My father is a quiet man; my mother is very outgoing. I don't know how they ever got along, because they were always so different. They had different views about everything—how to spend money, how to raise children, how to worship, what to eat, what to wear... I think they loved each other, but it wasn't enough to keep their marriage afloat.

Sarah Bellei

My parents came from very different backgrounds, culturally and economically. Dad was born and raised in East Germany. They had very little to eat, and as a little boy he had to steal to get food. He often went to bed hungry. At age sixteen, he went into an apprenticeship as an auto mechanic, and in 1975, he came to the U.S. to escape the mandatory military draft in Germany and to make a better life for himself. Mom, on the other hand, had a privileged and sheltered childhood. She came from an upper-class family and had grown up in an exclusive neighborhood of Lima, Peru. She was accustomed to private schools, chauffeurs, and servants who made her bed and prepared her food. Her weekends were filled with parties and going out to eat and to the movies with friends and family. Vacations were spent at the country club and the beach house. For Dad, hard work was his life. For Mom, hard work was something relegated to the lower classes, something she was above doing. Dad was street smart and knew the ways of the world. Mom was educated, but knew little of the world. During their marriage, my dad did extremely well in business. He built up a German auto repair shop and invested the profits wisely. By the time he was thirty-five, he owned several car repair shops, ocean-view property in Malibu, an apartment building, a trailer park, and a small shopping center. But because of their basic and profound differences, even with this material success, their marriage failed.

Couples are also more likely to divorce if they are different in other ways—if they are of widely disparate ages, if their values, plans, hopes, and dreams are different, if their intelligence levels are different, if their expectations of marriage are different, if they express emotions in opposite ways. These kinds of differences led to divorce in the following student's family.

Paul Woo
    After they got married, my parents left China and immigrated to Paris. My dad was twelve years older than my mother, and he had a difficult time adjusting to the new culture and his loss of status. Mom was much more energetic and flexible. She did all she could to find work and to learn French at night school. Soon she was doing better than my father in every aspect. She had such grand dreams. As a teenager, having scored at the ninety-eighth percentile on the Taiwan college entrance exams, she was primed for success. My father, on the other hand, had been a farmer and didn't want to hear about her high-flying plans. Instead of being proud of her, he took her progress as an insult.

Marrying on Shaky Ground
    There are also personal qualities and demographic characteristics that make divorce more likely. One such quality is the inability to make a commitment and stick to it. People who drop out of high school or college have the highest rate of divorce (60%); people who complete a college education

are least likely to divorce (40%). The reason these high school and college dropouts are more likely to divorce is not just that they have lower levels of education and income. When a person does not complete an educational program that he or she has started, this reflects a lack of commitment and follow-through that may later also affect marital instability.

Clarissa Cambridge

The way I see it, my father was basically an impulsive kid trapped in the body of a 200-pound man. He had flunked out of high school (too boring), had taken a bunch of college courses which he usually didn't finish (also too boring), and at the age of twenty-nine had not held a job for longer than three months (his bosses were stupid or didn't appreciate his potential).

Another quality that predicts divorce is lack of commitment to a religion.

Stephanie Conaway

Religion was a sore spot in my parents' relationship. Not only did my dad refuse to go to church with my mother, he resented her going. He really hated the fact that she was the church secretary. Over the years, they got into many arguments and he made jokes about her religion and the people she went to church with. He also resented the time her church responsibilities took away from her helping him with the business.

Divorce is less common among people who belong to a religious denomination and are active in religious activities. Although religious people also experience marital breakdown, a religious affiliation counteracts divorce in a number of ways: couples are less likely to marry very young, to marry in haste (after all they want a nice big wedding in the church), or to be pregnant before marrying. They may have received premarital counseling through their church that may help them to better evaluate their decision to marry. These factors contribute to a more sound decision in the first place. Beyond this, religious beliefs and active involvement tend to exert significant external pressures to stay married, to focus on the life-long commitment that was pledged more so than on individual fulfillment. Obviously, as the foregoing student's story indicates, when only one person has the religious commitment, it is not sufficient to protect the marriage.

Marrying in Spite of Trouble in the Relationship

Not surprisingly, getting married does not fix things that were wrong before the wedding. If the couple cannot communicate, if they do not respect each other's views, if each ignores what the other person is saying, if they deliberately avoid discussing certain topics, these are bad signs. If the husband and wife-to-be have role conflicts that stem from different expectations of how one should perform to satisfy the other or different views of what a "real man," a "real woman," a "good husband," or a "good wife" should be, this, too, spells problems. Issues with intimacy and problems being open, honest, and vulnerable with the other without the fear of being violated in some way before the marriage will come to haunt the couple during the marriage. Lack of commitment to the marriage or a profound sense of hurt or betrayal before the marriage, the result of fights, lying, violence, broken promises, or a coerced abortion, are also strong predictors of divorce—because the emotional fallout from these problems lingers on. A number of our students reported that their parents' marriages were plagued with problems from the beginning, problems that should have warned them away from the marriage.

Tracey Sanchez

My parents' relationship was rocky from the start. Even when they were engaged, they fought viciously. Once my mom threw her ring at my dad because she had caught him lying about his ex-girlfriends. A number of times, they broke up. But eventually, they got married anyway. After the wedding, their problems continued. In fact, their problems were never solved.

Wendy Farran
My dad's infidelity started before he and my mom were married, and it never stopped. When my mom confronted him, he swore he would never do it again. But he did do it again—and again. To teach him a lesson, my mom did the same to him. He was furious. To retaliate, he got another woman pregnant. Even then, my mother couldn't leave him. I don't know what she was waiting for all those years. They just kept on making the same mistakes over and over.

In this last student's story, there were blatant problems before the marriage, but still they married. Why would anybody in their right mind marry under such circumstances? The answer lies in the sense of loss that is created through such violations. Romantic partners not only view each other as the source of their pain, they also see the other as the only possible cure. Only the originator of the pain can take the pain away. Wendy's mother was waiting for her husband to change, to fully commit to her and thereby take away all the pain of the past. That day apparently never came, and after twenty years of marriage this couple divorced.

Marrying for the Wrong Reasons
There are many "wrong" reasons that people get married—to have a big wedding, to have sex readily available, to prove to your parents that you can do what you want, to demonstrate your commitment to your partner. Some couples marry because they think it is the "proper" thing to do. More commonly, though, people marry because they expect it will provide an escape from a dreary and unhappy life, a cure for loneliness and isolation, a solution to their psychological problems. These people would do better seeing a therapist.

Many of our students described such maladaptive reasons for their parents' marriage.

> Yolanda Sandoval
> My dad proposed to my mother because he was sad and lonely. His mom had just passed away, and he wanted the comfort of a woman in his life. My mother accepted because she was fed up with her life. Her parents were so strict and she was miserable at home.

The idea that marriage can fill a void in your life is not uncommon. Many people wish to escape the pains of the past and search for safety and security in another person and in marriage.

> Stephanie Conaway
> My mother was twenty-one with a two-year-old son when she met my father. She had just moved to California and didn't know anyone there. She earned next to nothing as a bank teller and her little boy was growing fast. When she met my dad, he took care of her. That was what she wanted—someone to take care of her, someone who would love her and provide a home for her and her son. She did not love him. She felt needy and dependent. She had been in love with her son's father, but he wouldn't marry her, so she married my father on the rebound.

In this sad story, an abandoned woman with child was looking for somebody to take care of her. Her choice to marry was not based on mutual love and respect. Instead, it filled her need to be cared for. However, starting a marriage in despair is not a good basis for a long-lasting relationship. Marriage is no cure for low self-esteem.

Another factor that compelled our students' parents to marry was pressure from other people. In our culture, this kind of pressure occurs most commonly when there is a premarital pregnancy, as in the following story:

Elizabeth Harrison

My mother met my father at the grocery store where they both worked. Initially, she felt attracted to him because he was quiet and seemed "mysterious." But they never did anything exciting together. When they dated, they either watched television together or she watched him play guitar with his band in the garage. She was not really in love with him, but she liked the idea of having a boyfriend. When she got pregnant, my dad wanted her to have an abortion, but Mom knew she could never do that. Her priest and her parents would never approve. Her parents offered them free rent if my dad would marry her, continue to go to college, and work part-time. And so they tied the knot. As Mom walked down the aisle, she knew she was doing the wrong thing—but it was too late to back out. The marriage started to go sour on their honeymoon at the Beverly Hilton Hotel, when my dad used the time to study for his final exams.

Another pressure that catapults couples to the altar is the threat of being separated. If one of the partners is relocating, for example, moving to a new job or going off to war, the couple may leap into marriage rather than be apart. In the following story, the man was about to move to the other side of the country.

Sandi Rodriguez

My parents met at Yale Medical School six months before my father was leaving for California for his internship. There was a lot of pressure for them to get married right away because he was leaving so soon. My mother, who was in a Master's program, didn't want to transfer schools unless there was some promise of permanence in the relationship. Also, they had both been raised in traditional, religious families, so if they were going to move to California together, they felt they had better be married.

The pressure to marry builds when several "wrong reasons" combine. In the following story, the bride didn't want to be the only "old maid" among her friends and her family's approval helped her to overlook the fact that she liked the idea of being married more than she liked her future spouse.

Diana Denman

My mother was raised to marry a rich man, have children, and be taken care of by her husband. After she graduated from college, she felt a lot of pressure to get married. She was beginning to be considered an "old maid" because most of her friends were getting married. The timing was great when she met my father. Her friends and family considered him a "good catch," and she was strongly influenced by them. Although she was excited to have him as a boyfriend, she wasn't sure that she loved him. She never really felt at ease with him, and his interests were different from hers. Often she didn't know what to say to him, and she wasn't really interested in what he had to say. Her doubts about marrying him were pushed aside by her family's approval, though, and she went ahead with the wedding. Boy, was that a mistake!

Often, couples just think that marrying is the thing to do when you grow up. They marry without much conviction or commitment. They simply can't think of anything else or anything better to do with their lives. Marriage becomes an escape from the necessity of taking responsibility for one's life. Couples who marry for the wrong reasons are likely to experience a change of heart and to have their illusion end in divorce.

Not the Marrying Kind

Are there divorce prone personalities? Are some types of people simply poor marriage risks? Research reveals that divorce is more likely for individuals who are self-centered, critical, and stubborn. Several of our students described their divorced parents in these terms. One student described her father in the following way:

Roxie Levine

My father is a very domineering and manipulative person. He is totally self-centered. What he says goes. He has no appreciation of others' ideas, feelings and plans. He always lived his life how he wanted, regardless of how it affected the rest of us. I can't remember a single time when he genuinely tried to accommodate to anybody else's wishes. If we got to do what was important to us, it was because he didn't care or because he wanted to do it himself. We never got to do anything that he wasn't up for. Instead, we constantly did things that he wanted to do even when nobody else in the family did. He never moved an inch for anybody. I can't imagine what my mother saw in him. I don't know how she put up with him for eighteen years.

Alcoholics, gamblers, and people with criminal tendencies don't make good marriage material either.

Clarissa Cambridge

The one thing that got my father's full attention was the racetrack. And being the wheeling and dealing kind of guy he was, he always knew a way to come up with the money for his gambling habit—selling stolen merchandise, forging checks, taking money from my mother's account, borrowing money and never repaying it. When my mom realized that he had forged her signature on a check, he smooth talked her into forgiving him. He claimed some friend had screwed him and as soon as the scumbag friend gave him the money he would repay her. But he never repaid anything and he continued to take money from her account, each time coming up with a new story to explain the situation. He talked my mother into opening a business with him, which was going to fix all their financial problems. He explained to her that it was necessary to put the business in her name because he had bad credit. Six months later my mother owed $700,000 and had multiple lawsuits against her. The day she filed for divorce, she also filed for bankruptcy.

Marrying after Divorce

Popular myth has it that remarriage is a tool for fixing "broken homes." However, the divorce rate for second marriages even higher than the divorce rate for first marriages. Why? Among other reasons, people who have been through a divorce and survived it are more likely to view divorce as a practical solution to a problem. Thus, having been married before is another risk factor for divorce. In the following story, the mother had already experienced divorce and realized that it is a very possible outcome of marriage.

Lindsay Schoonhoven

When my parents married, Mom was twenty-seven years old and had a six-year-old daughter, Judy, from a previous marriage. This was Mom's third marriage. Dad was twenty-four and this was his first marriage. They were very much in love. Dad even wanted to adopt Judy. But Mom did not want that because she was worried that in case they divorced she would have a custody battle on her hands.

This mother's decision not to let her third husband adopt her daughter was a practical one. She knew that divorce and custody fights were part of the marriage game, and she wanted to avoid at least some of these problems.

Risk Factors after Marrying

Other conditions that develop after marriage can also contribute to an increased risk for divorce. When the wife gets pregnant and a child is born in the first year after the wedding, when the couple experiences a great deal of stress because of pressures from work or family, when the husband or wife abuses alcohol, or when one of them is unfaithful, these conditions, too, can precipitate problems in the marriage and put the marriage at risk for divorce.

Pregnancy Early in the Marriage

We have already discussed how being pregnant or having a baby at the time of the marriage is a risk factor for divorce. But even when the couple waits until after the wedding to start a family, if they don't wait long enough, this too is risky. Pregnancy, childbirth, and raising a young child present formidable physical, emotional, and financial challenges. But the enormous stress of having a baby is often not anticipated because having a baby is one of the most romanticized phenomena in our culture. Notions of becoming a "real family" and images of cute babies in designer outfits pervade popular thinking and account for many pregnancies early in the marriage. The burdens of having and raising a child, however, are sobering. The couple faces demands that are difficult to meet within a relationship that is undergoing major adjustments and has not yet stabilized. Before undertaking the life-long commitment of rearing children with another person—thereby becoming forever joined to each other—a couple should have had the opportunity to firmly establish their couplehood. They should have weathered many different and challenging circumstances together to test their weaknesses and strengths as a couple. Their weak spots should be resolved before the arrival of children. The following story portrays how the stress of a pregnancy early in the marriage leads to further stress in the relationship and further poor choices.

Masayasu Lawrence

At first their marriage was so romantic. They had no money, no food. They were living in the heart of Greenwich Village, and, like all of their friends, they were artists. They were into civil disobedience, demonstrating,

> and each other. A week before their first anniversary I was
> born. After my birth, my mother quit her job to take care
> of me. My dad continued to struggle as a photographer
> to make ends meet for this family of three. The following
> year, my sister was born, and two months later my parents
> separated. Dad told Mom in a fight that he wasn't happy
> with us children. We got on his nerves and he couldn't
> focus on his work. His career was going down the drain
> because he had this constant pressure of having three
> dependants. Then he stopped coming home. He told
> Mom things weren't working out.

The stress resulting from two early pregnancies taxed this couple's limited resources. Although before the children's births having no food and no money seemed romantic, after their births it was a burden. The stress resulting from one poor decision seems to have led right into the next problem, producing ever more stress. As is common, the mother quit her job to take care of the baby and this made money even tighter. The father, now more under pressure as the sole breadwinner, focused more on his work. The children interfered with his focus. When his frustration level rose, he retreated—leaving wife and children on welfare.

Forgetting the Marriage Vows

Infidelity is a cause of marital breakup in at least one quarter of all divorces. The roots of these extramarital affairs may lie in our biology. Sociobiologists tell us that our biological natures urge men to leave their wives after having one child, so that they can increase the genetic variability of their offspring, and that urge women to find a mate who will best provide for the welfare of their children. The prime age for divorce is when people are in their twenties and thirties—they are in their child-bearing years and there are lots of alternative mates available. In fact, being exposed to more people of the opposite sex adds to the likelihood that a person will get divorced: people whose occupations involve traveling and other ways of meeting new potential mates are more likely to divorce than people who work in the same old office year after year. When infidelity occurs, couples often struggle to hold on to the marriage. But despite their attempts to put their relationships back together, these couples typically end up in divorce court—eventually. This was clearly the case for the following student.

Denise Leblanc

The first year they were married, my mom found a birthday card to my father from a girlfriend. She suspected he was cheating, but she pushed it out of her mind. She didn't want to consider a divorce. After nine years of sitting up late waiting for him to come home, however, she reached the end of her rope. She waited up one night until 4:00 am while he was out with some girl. She just couldn't take it anymore. She deserved better. She wanted a divorce. When she told him, he was outraged, but he agreed to move out. After a couple of months, they began dating each other again. He promised her a new life and no more cheating, and they moved to a new city. Each year she kept hoping that things would improve, but in the back of her mind, she always suspected he was with other women. Whenever they were together, she wondered who else he had been with. Finally she could no longer live in a dream world. My father's cheating got another woman pregnant. My mom was devastated. Yet even through this nightmare she was willing to work things out. She demanded that they go for counseling and that he stop seeing the other woman. The counseling lasted for one month, and my dad continued to see the other woman. He claimed he wasn't in love with her, but he would not break off the relationship. My mom made him go get an HIV test. The final straw was when she came home and heard him telling his girlfriend that the results of the blood test were negative. She was crushed that he didn't care enough about her to tell her first. He had taken everything that was sacred to her. He was

having a baby with another woman and couldn't care less
that he had broken our family apart.

Lack of Money

Another factor that increases the risk of divorce is
being poor. Poverty is accompanied by a host of negative
ramifications that strain marital relations. Lack of money
can lead to arguments, and arguments can lead to lack of
respect, and lack of respect can precipitate further problems.
The couple's intimacy is jeopardized, the acerbity of the
arguments increases and may escalate into physical violence.
This is what happened in the next story.

Thuy Ngoc
With dreams of success, my parents came to the
United States. They came with nothing but their clothes
and their kids. We moved in with my mom's sister in a
little apartment. My father couldn't find work right away
and my parents started to fight. They would argue about
everything, but most of all about money. Then my dad got
a job with a shipping firm in Long Beach. Although this
was 100 miles away, he didn't feel that he could turn the
job down. To save money, he went to live with his parents
and his seven siblings in a shabby old house closer to his
new work. He would come visit us every other week, but
it wasn't the same. To make matters worse, my mother
worked the day shift as a nurse while my dad worked the
night shift at his job. They rarely saw each other. When
they did, it seemed as if all hell broke loose. There would
be yelling, tantrums, hitting, things flying, and worst of
all sobbing, in the single room shared by my parents, my
two brothers, and me.

When the stress level rises in a relationship, the problems
in the relationship go up, too. And worse, if the problems
between the couple increase, so does the stress. If couples
neglect to carefully negotiate stressful times, they may

become caught in a downhill spiral. This was the experience described by the next student.

Judd Michaelson

Because both my parents were going to school they didn't have much money. So my dad pushed my mom into dropping out of school and getting a job so he could continue his education. The deal was that after he graduated he would support the family and my mom would stop working. So Mom left college and continued to work until I was born. Then, my dad, being a macho kind of guy, insisted that she stop working to stay home with me. This is when things started getting difficult for everyone. The money situation was driving my mom crazy. They never had money to buy new clothes, to go out, or do anything at all. They basically just sat at home for an entire year without doing anything. My dad continued to refuse to let my mom work, even when they had problems paying the bills. They had endless arguments. My dad began to drink to overcome his depression and my mom began to withdraw.

Instability

Instability is another factor that increases a couple's stress level. The stresses of moving to a new community, taking a new job, losing a job, losing income, adding family members, or losing one are other conditions that tip the scales toward divorce. The following story displays a family's downward trajectory caused by instability. Frequent moves led to unsteady work and income. This, in turn, led to the separation of the family. The separation of the family led to constant fighting between the couple, and the constant fighting led to infidelity and drinking which led to divorce.

John Klinger

My family moved to Minnesota in 1990 to get away from the fast pace of Southern California and the smog. But the economy in Minnesota was poor, and so the next year they moved back to California, where the economy was on the rise. My parents hoped that this would be the start of a new life. At that point, they were both stressed out, money was scarce, and they began to fight. They dragged on like this for five years. Then everything really began to fall apart. My father quit working as a mechanic and started a mail-order business. When this didn't work, he went to work in Riverside, five hours away from home. He would drive down every Sunday to work and live with his parents. On Fridays, he would drive back home to spend the weekend with us. He hated all the driving. He got really irritable. My mother hated the fact that her husband was never there. She felt she carried all the responsibility for the household and the children. This made her really irritable. By then, my parents fought constantly when he was home, and when he was gone, they fought on the phone. Because of all the fighting, my father started drinking and staying out at bars until two or three o'clock in the morning. Sometimes he wouldn't come home at all. Then my mother found out that he was seeing another woman.

The culmination of stress factors is clearly demonstrated in this student's story. One stressful situation begets another, leading to ever-poorer decision-making, an escalation of stress, and, finally, the breaking point.

The Stress of Unemployment

Unemployment is another risk factor, because it threatens not only the couple's economic security but also each partner's individual security and the implicit expectations each spouse has of the marriage. Unemployment is threatening to the man's self-worth and is often associated with decreases in money and sexual activity and increases in depression, alcohol consumption, and fighting for both husband and wife.

Traditional gender socialization suggests that men will be the main providers and women will stay home with the children. Despite women's advances in the workforce, these expectations still prevail. Thus, an unemployed man is not living up to the unspoken expectations each spouse holds. Unemployed men are likely to feel inadequate in their role as providers, while their wives, who were taught that they were going to be taken care of as long as they did their jobs as wives and mothers, may get confused, frustrated, and angry. In this time of vulnerability, new expectations arise. The unemployed spouse is supposed to do his best to quickly find a new job. He is not supposed to feel depressed, fatigued, or angry. Otherwise normal activities, such as playing golf or going out with friends, take on a different meaning in times of unemployment. A wife may feel that her husband is not doing enough to get a job and that he is wasting his time on trivial activities rather than the job search. He, in turn, may feel that she is overly critical, unsupportive, and unloving. Communication tends to become strained and psychological pressures rise. Unemployment becomes especially taxing when other basic factors are not the way they should be. In the following story, the couple was at risk from the start because of their young ages, basic incompatibilities, and an early pregnancy—but their problems escalated when the husband lost his job.

Gerry Schonfeld

At the tender ages of eighteen and twenty-two, my parents made the decision to get married and spend the rest of their lives together. It was the biggest mistake each of them ever made. Things went along pretty well for the first two years. They were both working and they made enough to live on. Then a baby was born, and my mother quit work to stay home with her. Unfortunately, not long after, my father was laid off from his job. They decided that my mother should go back to work to pay the bills. But to everyone's surprise, before she could find a job, my mother got pregnant again. Now, my parents were very distressed, because they had no jobs and no health insurance. How were they going to survive? My dad stuck to his guns that my mom should be the one to find a job. They began to fight a lot. She was angry at him and resentful. Why should she go back to work when she was pregnant? He became withdrawn and started drinking. She went to work and hated it. Eventually, after a few years, my dad started a new job and things got better. But I think their relationship never recovered from the stress and the bad feelings that arose during that time. Their relationship had taken a downhill course that could only end in divorce.

Could it be that this mother's second pregnancy was no accident? Even if there was not much conscious thought involved, there is a good chance that on an unconscious level the pregnancy was a means to enforce the original deal: that the mother would stay at home and be the caretaker. Having another baby underscored the husband's obligation to find work and provide for his family. It is hardly surprising that this woman became angry when she had to go back to work even though she was pregnant.

The Stress of Work
But it's not just being unemployed that is stressful. Having a job can be stressful, too. The pressure on men to excel in competitive work or educational environments and the demand that they provide adequately for their wife and children can create enormous psychological strain. Many men have difficulty handling the demands of work and family at the same time. The following excerpt shows how the stress resulting from the husband's educational demands had a detrimental effect on the couple's relationship.

Judd Michaelson
When my father started veterinary school, my parents' relationship took a nosedive. The pressure of going to school changed my dad. He would go to classes all day and study half of the night. When he was at home,

he was so stressed out about school and money he would drink himself to sleep. Sometimes he got so drunk he would threaten to kill himself. It got to the point that my mom really believed he was serious. On numerous occasions he would pull out his gun in front of us and leave the house. He would get in his car and drive away. We never knew until the next day if he had actually killed himself. My mom tried to get him to go to counseling but he wouldn't. He thought psychologists were quacks and only sissies went to therapy. Finally, my mom decided that if he wouldn't go to counseling, they had to separate.

Another stressful condition that increases the probability of divorce is when the wife is working too. Researchers have found that the more hours the wife works, the higher is the probability of divorce. The following story describes a common phenomenon: marital problems begin when the wife goes back to work.

Lindsay Schoonhoven
    Before the marriage, my mom had been working as a secretary for an airline. After nine years of married life she had the opportunity to become a flight attendant. She and my dad agreed that this was a good idea. Although she would be gone for three or four days at a time, she would then be home for seven days. After she became a flight attendant, though, it was incredibly stressful. Every time she left, we kids cried and cried. My dad became angry when she was away, and they would fight when she returned. What made it worse was that my dad's family disapproved of her job. My grandfather was, of course, siding with my dad and made rude comments to other family members about her being "out with pilots" and "neglecting her family." This hurt my mom, and their marriage deteriorated from there.

In this case, the wife's work led to additional stress, upset children, an angry husband, and a hostile extended family.

Illness and Death

Other stressors that can be enormously taxing on a marriage are the illness or death of a loved one. If the couple has a child who is chronically ill or handicapped, this can contribute to a divorce, even if it occurs after the marriage is established. Researchers have found that couples who have a child with a physical handicap are much more likely to divorce than couples with healthy children. Sometimes, during the course of a marriage, one of the spouses becomes seriously ill and the vow to stand by each other in sickness and in health is put to the test.

Lauren Gordon

Eight years after my parents married, my mother was diagnosed with kidney failure. What followed was months of dialysis, never-ending trips to the hospital, and a kidney transplant. Luckily, she came out of the whole ordeal in good shape—she was one of the hospital's "star patients." But after my mom's long illness, my dad dropped a bomb. He told my mom that he had met someone else. He said that most of their marriage had been marred by my mom's illness. For one thing, their sex life had stopped. He didn't want to spend the rest of his life surrounded by sickness, and she wasn't the person he had married anymore. He needed a fresh start.

Other times, the emotional strain of caring or grieving for a loved one becomes a drain on the marriage.

Sandi Rodriguez

For five years, my mother spent a great deal of time in northern California caring for her brother, who was being treated for leukemia and who eventually died at the age of twenty-eight. My mother was deeply depressed by his death. She then discovered that during her long absences from home my father found himself an apartment and a girlfriend, and when we came back to Southern California he announced that he was leaving.

Illness and death are times of great need and heightened vulnerability. They increase the demands for mutual support and caring. But spouses are not always able or willing to give what is needed.

Brad Dawson

When my maternal grandfather died, my parents were going through a marital crisis. They went to Texas together for the funeral. But this placed even more stress on them, and they fought even more than they had before. My dad wanted to use the time away from home to discuss their problems. My mom couldn't believe he kept pounding his issues when she had just lost her dad. She needed his support and wanted to lean on him and feel his love and comfort, but he continued his verbal assaults. She was alternately depressed or angry. Two weeks after they came home, they decided to get a divorce.

Of course, not everybody who marries young, or has an illness in the family will divorce. But being "at risk" means that if any or several of these risk factors described in this chapter are present, the couple is more likely to divorce. Being aware of these risks can help a couple be more cautious. As with everything else in life: the less prepared you are for a task, the more likely you are to fail. It's just like climbing a mountain. You are more likely to get hurt or not return from your adventure if you wear slippery shoes, ignore an oncoming storm, lack adequate food and water supplies, and start in an unknown area at night without a compass. There are of course always the few lucky ones who return from mountain climbing despite having ventured out with the wrong shoes or the wrong equipment. But you get the idea: by ignoring certain safety rules, you are putting yourself at a high risk.

Lessons to Be Learned

Reviewing the real-life experiences of the people described in this chapter makes it almost obvious that much of the pain that results from derailing one's life path could have been prevented if people had made better choices early on...before they married, before they got pregnant, and yes, even before they threw themselves into "love" or what they thought was love. Acting impulsively and creating a domino effect of crises was—in hindsight—the downfall of these women and men and ultimately a life-long liability for their children. So what are the lessons to be learned?

1. Think before you act. Couples contemplating marriage should think long and hard before they take the leap. Why do you want to get married? Think about it! Can you come up with good reasons? Most people can't. Reasons like "I'm in love"; I don't want to be alone"; "I want to have sex regularly"; even, "I have always wanted a big wedding" are clearly not very good reasons to get married. Love and passion may be fleeting; loneliness is found in marriage too; and marrying for sex or for a big wedding party reflects an immaturity that certainly will fray the marriage. Couples should take their time to think about why they want to get married. They should talk about what they expect out of marriage. How do you expect your life to change for better or for worse after marriage? What do you expect from each other? What are your needs for a lover, a co-parent, and a life-partner? It may be helpful to write the answers to these questions down. This will allow the couple to reflect upon them and to add further thoughts.

It is also helpful to make a list of what you ideally want in a spouse; compare it with what you think you truly need. Try a different angle: write down what you can tolerate in a marital partner (for example, quirks, annoying habits or frustrating weaknesses, different views and tastes); compare this to what you absolutely cannot tolerate (for example, dishonesty, competitiveness, self-righteousness, impulsiveness, coercion, violence). How does your partner fit into these four categories, your ideals, your real needs, your tolerances, and the unacceptable? At the same time, think about what you offer as a marital partner. Which of your personal traits, needs, or weaknesses might make it difficult for a marital partner? What skills or qualities do you have that will help you and your spouse manage well together? As romantic and passionate as it may seem to decide to get married on the spur of the moment, there is nothing romantic about being unhappily married or about getting divorced. Therefore, lesson number one is: think long and hard before you marry.

2. Don't rush into marriage. The second lesson is that individuals should postpone marriage until they have an education, a job, money in the bank—and a suitable person to marry. There is no need to make all of life's most important decisions before the age of twenty-five. Chances are that you are going to live at least for another fifty years; so there is no need to rush. By their late twenties, people have a clearer sense of who they are and what they want out of life. You really do not want to spend the rest of your life—like the parents in these stories—fixing mistakes you made in youthful immaturity. And you really do not want to have your children suffer for decades from the legacy of your poor decisions. If a sudden desire to marry overcomes you—at any age—ask yourself "Why the rush? What am I avoiding by marrying right now?" Again, it may be helpful to write the answers down and take time to reflect on them.

3. Don't marry for the wrong reasons. Here are some bad reasons to get married: You have been going together and it feels like you should take "the next step." The wedding is already planned. Your parents approve (or disapprove) of him or her. Getting married is your childhood dream. You are rebounding from another relationship. You need somebody to pay your bills. You want independence from your parents. You want an identity. Your relationship is stale. You are afraid of being lonely. Your relationship is insecure or turbulent and you want to force a commitment. You're expecting a baby … None of these "reasons" provides a firm basis for a lifetime commitment. Marriage is not a quick fix for relationship troubles or loneliness, financial problems or identity issues. If people enter a marriage to escape these kinds of problems, the risk is great that their problems are worse after they get married.

4. Know your future spouse well. Couples should follow this rule: Marry someone you want by your side if you were stranded on a desolated island for a long, long time. Marry someone who is your best friend, a competent partner for all occasions, a person you can completely relax with, a person who is supportive of you and your goals, and a person you can get excited about. Marriage is challenging enough with the right person, but it is torturous with the wrong person. Therefore, embrace lengthy courtship. It is essential to marry someone you know well, someone you have seen under stress. It is better to marry a person who is kind and generous under the worst of circumstances than one who is sexy, good-looking, and fun in the best circumstances. Figure out before you get married whether you can resolve disagreements. Can you argue without taking each other apart? Does he get mean? Is she vengeful? You need to know this before you marry—and avoid it! Find out about your future spouse's past. Get to know his or her friends. Do you like your sweetheart in company just as much as when it's just the two of you? Is he still kind, caring, and supportive of you when in the company of his friends? Listen to the anecdotes about your beloved's less endearing qualities. Ask about the fate of prior relationships. Tales of blame and hatred are a warning signal. If your beloved's prior relationships involved mainly "evil, stupid, mean, deceptive, manipulative, self-centered bitches/jerks" you should be seriously concerned. Chances are that your honey has no insight into his or her relationships and does not take any responsibility for past choices and outcomes. You have no reason to believe that the relationship with you would be any different. Keep your eyes wide open. Don't be caught with a spouse who has a history of verbal and physical abuse, prior restraining orders, domestic violence convictions, or non-payment of child support. Many such misdeeds may be documented in public records in the courthouse.

Finally, get to know your future spouse's family. They are going to be your family, too, and, even more important, they are going to be your children's family. Do not think that relatives are unimportant and that you will not have much contact with them—even if they live far away, even if your spouse currently does not like them, and even if there has been no contact before. Blood ties are powerful, and people tend to gravitate back toward their kin as they get older. Your children will spend time and important events with these people and will view them as family. These relatives are also the people who may be raising your children in case you die. Make sure you like them and can get along with them and that you truly value and respect them and they truly value and respect you.

5. Learn to deal with stress. Even couples who start off with their stars in alignment can run into difficult times—stresses brought on by an illness, death in the family, sudden unemployment, financial loss, or an unexpected pregnancy. Everyone experiences crises at some time. The lesson is to make sure that life does not become a series of crises, and that your own actions do not contribute to new problems. If you find yourself in a stressful situation, simplify your life and set priorities. Focus your energy on those aspects of your life that are critical for survival. Be careful not to compound your problems by creating new ones. For example, if your relationship is troubled, don't have a baby to fix the relationship. Minimize stress through better planning. For example, don't buy a new house, lease a new car, and take a new job—all at the same time. Stay away from activities that provide a momentary escape from your woes—like drinking and cheating—but that lead to long-term problems. Remain faithful and loyal to your spouse especially during the tough times. Take the time to review your values, your goals, and your actions. Do your actions match your values and goals? If not, consider how you need to change your behavior to bring yourself back onto the path you truly want to be on in the long run. Everyone slips at times; but those who ultimately have a successful life always get back on target.

If stress is unavoidable, acknowledge the situation and together with your spouse develop a plan to deal with the problems. Work together to get through the tough times. Discuss your needs—don't just wait for your spouse to read your mind. Discuss your finances and make joint decisions. Avoid debt—it creates major stress in your life and in your marriage. Keep yourself healthy and fit. It is not enough to just stay alive—you need to do all you can to maintain your energy, confidence, and positive outlook. Read up on how to cope better, how to manage your time and finances better, and how to communicate more effectively. Do not be shy about asking family, friends, and professionals for advice, inspiration, or tangible help. However, beware of idle complaining to family and friends.

Heeding these "safety instructions" will save you from losing the best years of your life to a series of crises and heartaches.

2

We're Married, But I Don't Really Like You: The Mismatched Couple

Marriages also fail when husband and wife are simply incompatible. Some couples are just poor matches. The husband and wife have different expectations and goals for their relationship and life in general. They do not understand each other and do not feel understood. Their needs are so different that there is no hope that the spouse can ever meet them. Some of these couples were never compatible, even in the beginning. Other couples start out close but gradually drift apart to occupy two different worlds—usually, the husband occupies the world of work, the wife, the world of children. About 40 percent of our students' parents were "mismatched couples." Maybe the most perplexing aspect of these relationships was how long they lasted. Despite mutual unhappiness, these mismatched marriages continued year after year. On average, they lasted nineteen years!

Why do people who are generally unhappy with each other stay together for so long? Apparently, there is little conscious choice involved; it just happens. Just as the couples in "high risk" marriages do not consciously choose the wrong partner, mismatched couples do not consciously choose to be miserable for many years. They just can't seem to get unstuck. They are the victims of strong social and religious pressures to stay married ("Just tough it out"), of their own hopes ("I want this to work"), fears ("I can't make it on my own"), guilt ("A divorce would destroy the family"), and pain ("I'll be lonely if I divorce"). These pressures blur their vision of the relationship. For a long time, they cannot see the full extent of the many ways in which their relationship is not working. They can't see how they are each contributing to their marital malaise. They delude themselves that things will get better. The following story illustrates the complexity of the issues involved in the marriage of a mismatched couple.

Sandra Hayward

My parents were married for twenty-five years. They had many things in common. They were both Caucasian, middle class and Protestant. My father is a minister and an author and he was president of a large organization for the homeless. He has his master's degree in theology. My mother is a marriage and family counselor. They had four daughters, of which I am the youngest. But underneath the facade of education and religion, helping people and raising children, my parents had problems. Over the years the pressure of these problems kept building and finally erupted.

Three years into their marriage, my father revealed to my mother that he had an addiction to pornography. My mother felt shocked and betrayed, but because of her religious beliefs, leaving was not an option. She thought my father needed some kind of therapy—after all, she was a therapist—but he would not go. He told her that if she thought his fascination with pornography was a problem, it was her problem. She also had trouble accepting his habit of giving away her things to the needy. He said that if she thought this was wrong, that was her problem, too. They couldn't discuss these issues and come to an understanding, so their problems remained unresolved. My mother became so frustrated with my dad for ignoring her thoughts and feelings that eventually she stopped sharing them.

My parents also disagreed about the most fundamental issues of marriage—money management and child rearing. My mother was scrupulous and punctual about bill paying; my father didn't care about paying bills on time, and some bills he simply chose not to pay. My father thought it was fine to discuss their financial problems with us children; my mother did not. As parents, my mother was strict; my father, laissez faire. When Mom told us kids to clean up our room, Dad would tell us that it was no big deal and he would take us to a movie. (Guess who was our favorite parent at that moment?)

Their personalities were very different too. My mother takes a long time to process information. She likes to think about all the aspects of the situation and sort out her thoughts and feelings. My father is the opposite. He is impulsive and spontaneous and makes decisions quickly. During a conversation, my mother would usually go along with him, but after she had thought about it she would sometimes express a different opinion. He, then, would think that she had been dishonest in the initial conversation. These situations were typical in their marriage and were frustrating for both of them.

Eventually, the mounting pressure of their unresolved issues became unbearable, and my mom initiated a divorce. I believe they made the right decision to get divorced, because they were together for the wrong reasons. Both of them were in the relationship just because they needed somebody, not because they truly loved or respected each other.

This student identifies astutely a key problem that was shared by most of the mismatched couples: her parents were together for the wrong reasons. The relationships of mismatched couples seemed to be based on neediness, not love or respect for each other. They felt a void in their lives and they plugged each other into this void hoping to fill the emptiness. But when this did not still their needs, they became resentful, angry, and eventually, depressed. Most of their married years were miserable, but they were stuck in a rut and could not initiate a change. With each day of misery, they resented each other more and grew angrier.

Tracey Sanchez

My father and mother met just after the Vietnam War. The world looked down at anyone who fought in the war and my dad felt very isolated from his friends and society. He just couldn't fit in anymore after what he had experienced. My mother felt just as lonely. They instantly locked onto each other. It was like a new beginning. At the time, of course, they thought it was love. Only much later did they realize that they were both only filling their own needs.

Their problems began right away, because they simply couldn't get along. On most issues they stood at opposite ends. At the time, they thought this was part of marriage and that it would get better. But beyond their surname, there was little they shared. Both saw things stubbornly their own ways. There was never any compromise—instead, after a disagreement, one or the other would throw in the towel and then resent it. With the passing of time, their fights only got worse. The yelling turned into screaming, and the screaming into violence. There wasn't a year that went by that they didn't seriously contemplate divorce. But my mother felt it was important to keep the marriage together so we could stay in our house, our neighborhood, and our school. Eventually, my father says, he couldn't take my mother's "bitching" anymore. He knew he had to get out. He gathered his things and, after fifteen years of marriage, he left. According to my mother, he left after eighteen years. Even on this, they can't agree.

This couple's relationship was forged out of pain. Falling in love was a "quick fix" to alleviate both the husband's and the wife's pains from the past. When a relationship is used as an escape from all the things that are wrong or missing in one's life, the strength of the "love" is more reflective of the extent of each partner's pain than the couple's true feelings for each other. The experience of the new relationship temporarily numbs their pain. But after the numbing effect wears off, and the love turns out to be an illusion, the pain steadily grows. In addition to their original problems, they now wake up every morning with a person who they don't particularly like. The pain and frustration of this realization can become very isolating because it is difficult to discuss with one's spouse— or anybody—a mistake as fundamental as this.

Mismatched spouses are so self-absorbed they cannot see beyond their own needs and expectations. They do not recognize their partner's limitations and cannot accept the fact that their partner is not the person they need. Their relationship is not a balanced "give and take"; it is "give me or else." To avoid the painful realization that they chose the wrong partner, they zero in on the spouse's flaws. They feel victimized and betrayed and react with fits of anger or stonewalling and withdrawal. They are mired in one-upmanship. Their anger and hurt keeps building, but they don't do anything about it. They are too busy blaming each other for their misery.

Symptoms of Incompatibility

Mismatched couples seem as if they are never really married. They are strangely disconnected. They resemble roommates who share the same house without much to unite them as individuals. They are neither friends nor lovers. They share few enjoyable interactions and have little respect for each other. They cannot communicate. They disagree on fundamental issues and their sex life is poor. There are few expressions of positive emotion—little affection, little playfulness, little lightheartedness—but many expressions of negative emotions—anger, blame, depression, and withdrawal. After a while, they are too hurt and frustrated to be genuinely kind to each other. Mismatched couples are joined together only by marriage, not by shared ideas and ideals, similar personal qualities, or mutually enjoyed activities.

Poor Communication

Poor communication is a common denominator among mismatched couples. Communication problems described in our students' stories were of two types. The first type was not talking about problems. The couples with this kind of communication problem turned a blind eye to the problems in their relationship. Although they knew that something was wrong in their marriage, they didn't speak up; they didn't want to rock the boat.

Melissa Shipman

One big problem in our family was lack of communication. Both my mom and dad were raised in families where you do not show any emotions or talk about your feelings—so they did not communicate or show their emotions. My mother complained about my father's unavailability but she never knew how to open up and be persistent when something was bothering her. Everyone used to think that they had a wonderful relationship because they never argued. All my dad would have to do was deepen his voice slightly, and my mother would go along. They both knew they had problems, but they ignored them.

I now realize that lack of communication is what led to the breakdown of their marriage. But when I was fourteen years old, and my parents separated, I did not understand that. I thought that I came from a perfectly fine family. Only looking back did I realize that things had not been as smooth as I thought at the time. I remember, when I was nine years old, my dad and I took a trip to Sacramento over summer vacation. We went by ourselves, and the rest of the family stayed home. I have wonderful memories about this trip. One day I was telling a friend about this trip and he asked me, "Where were your mom, sister, and brother? Why didn't they go?" All this time I had only remembered the great fun I had on the trip that I had never stopped to wonder why my mom, sister and brother weren't there. The next time I talked to my dad, I asked him, "Remember that trip to Sacramento you and I took? How come Mom, Susy and Bill stayed home?" Then Dad told me that he and my mom hadn't been getting along and had decided to take separate vacations. I was amazed. It wasn't until that moment that I realized that something was wrong with my parents' marriage years before they divorced. It is shocking to me now that I was blind to the very obvious fact that half of my family wasn't with us on this trip. Just like my parents, I had tuned out problems I couldn't deal with.

After much pent-up frustration, many mismatched couples shift into the second pattern of poor communication: the use of negative communication strategies. After swallowing their frustrations for a long time, the pain eventually erupts in one or the other partner. They blame, they fight, they cry—but nothing gets resolved. They fall back into their marriage like an old shoe—ugly but comfortable.

The following student's story presents a typical scenario. Women often cite, as a reason for not speaking up in the marriage, the fact that they thought it was part of their role as a wife to endure the problems. They have been socialized to believe that if only they behave perfectly, things will get better. So they plunge themselves into cleaning the house, cooking his favorite meal, changing their hairstyle, or losing weight. If none of this provides a solution for the underlying problems, they become angry and depressed. In this mismatched couple, the wife did her job of keeping the house, but it was hard work and she was not happy. When she tried to tell her husband, he didn't listen.

Tiffany Maurer

Our family was a traditional family, with my father the ruling patriarch. Although my mother worked, it was still her job to pick up after the kids and have dinner on the table when he came home. She did this with enthusiasm and efficiency. But after a while, it became a burden. My father traveled a lot, and when he was not away, he spent most of his time either working or playing golf. My mother felt isolated because they hardly talked and didn't see each other often. She tried to talk to him and asked for more of his attention and his time, but my father was oblivious. He acknowledged that there were some problems but, in his opinion, as a whole, the family was fine. My mother started to complain, but he didn't listen. When she started to cry, he still wouldn't listen. Then the yelling began. But the more emotional she became, the colder my father grew. The colder my father became, the more she withdrew. She felt rejected and helpless in the relationship because my father did not validate her feelings. Instead of dealing with their problems, my father spent more of his time traveling and golfing, while she spent all of her time shopping.

Husbands' lack of listening may be wives' most commonly voiced complaint. Feeling ignored, these wives increase the pitch and frequency of their complaints, which makes their husbands go completely deaf. The husband withdraws ("My wife doesn't understand me. She's nagging all the time."), and the wife becomes even angrier. Unless both make a conscious effort to be sensitive to the other, both will eventually remove themselves from the relationship, he in response to her "nagging" and she in response to his unresponsiveness.

No Respect. No Trust. No Intimacy

Respect is said to be the key ingredient of a healthy marriage. Mismatched couples are distinguished by their marked lack of respect for each other. Some couples lose respect for each other through bitter experience. Innumerable fruitless attempts to make the spouse understand their needs and wishes, thoughts and feelings lead to corrosive frustration, anger, and disrespect. Without respect, the couple cannot build trust or true intimacy. Other couples already start their relationships with little mutual respect.

> Stephanie Conaway
>   From the beginning, my parents' relationship was empty and loveless. My mom married my dad because she wanted a father for her child. But she was disappointed, because he was not a good father. She was angry all the time, and as a result could give us children only perfunctory care. She fed us and took us to school, but she did not give us affection. She did not have any affection to give. She did not feel that my father loved her or admired her or that she was in any way special to him. Before they got married, she was a conquest for him. Being Mexican, he thought it was cool to have a white girlfriend. But after they were married, he acted as if he despised her. He made stupid jokes about the things she did. He never said nice things or paid her compliments. When she made dinner, he never commented on it. When she asked whether he liked it, he would reply that he would tell her if he didn't. My mom stayed in this marriage for twenty-eight years because she was afraid to leave. She was used to raising children and keeping a household; she did not have anywhere else to go.

From the beginning, this couple had no respect for each other. They had different agendas, and in the twenty-eight years they were married, their agendas never converged.

Instead, they formed an opportunistic alliance that fueled their mutual disrespect and anger. They were each victims, tied together by their despair, and their mutual mistreatment allowed led them to slip even deeper into despondency. This ill-fated mismatch was by no means a rarity. In 70 percent of our students' stories, the parents' decision to marry seemed to be the "easy way out" of an otherwise unsatisfying life. Taking charge of one's existence and future are overwhelming tasks for many people. Inept and overwhelmed, they become passive. This deludes them, for a while, into believing that whatever is happening is not their fault but the fault of their circumstances or their spouse. Having, thus, relieved themselves of responsibility for their misery, they live a second-hand life—a life in which they are not actors but only re-actors. All their energy is spent on reacting to others rather than charting their own course and steering toward their desired destiny. Only years, and sometimes decades, later do they realize that the price for their passive reactivity was more painful than anything they could have suffered had they mustered up courage to take charge of their lives.

Sometimes lack of respect turns into outright aversion against the spouse. The person feels best when the spouse is not around and avoids physical contact.

Gerry Schonfeld

My mother knew she married the wrong man early on in their marriage. My dad had always been a homebody who loved to sit in his armchair and watch sports. He was a quiet, passive man. This was okay for a while. But then, when it was time for him to get a raise, he was afraid to talk to his boss. My mother lost respect for him. In her eyes, my father was always doing something wrong. She hoped he would change, but he never did. He remained the twenty-two-year-old she married for the entire twenty years of their marriage. My mother wanted more out of life. She was looking for a more interesting mate, someone who would offer her excitement and passion. Toward the end of their marriage, she slept on the couch because she was not able to share the same bed with a man she had come to despise.

And sometimes a spouse's aversion gets so strong that he or she can't wait to get rid of the mismatched partner.

Kristin Sanders

My father realized that he had made a mistake three weeks after he and my mother eloped to Las Vegas, but for fifteen years he stayed in an unhappy marriage. He had no difficulty with the idea of marriage-—in fact, he found being married and having a family appealing. He just didn't like it with my mother. According to him, my mother went from being dependent on her parents to being dependent on him. She never had a period when she was self-reliant; she never grew up to be a logical and competent adult. My father found her impossible to reason with. Within a short time after getting married, he had no respect for her anymore. Toward the end of the marriage, he was overwhelmed by the realization that he had wasted his life with a woman he despised.

This man's frustration and pain from having spent so much of his precious lifetime in an utterly unsatisfying relationship is palpable. Yet, like many others, he did not accept his own responsibility for creating the situation and maintaining it so long. This ill-fitting relationship was clearly not the wife's doing alone—but the husband could not see this. The fact that his own choices ruined his life was unbearable. The only way he could tolerate the thought of his "wasted life" was to blame her.

Sexual Incompatibility

Just as marriage seems to be for many an easy way out of an otherwise unsatisfying life, infidelity appears to be an easy way out of an unsatisfying marriage. Perhaps the ultimate mismatch occurs in the bedroom.

Wendy Farran

Dad resorted to affairs because, as he put it, "when life hands you a lemon, you make lemonade." According to him, my mother deserved it. She had "set the stage" for his repeated affairs because she did not fulfill him sexually. They did not have sex for over a month after their marriage, and his emotional needs and physical needs were not being satisfied. He still believes that he made the right choice to find fulfillment outside the marriage and he "would do it again in a heartbeat."

A couple's sexuality serves as a form of communication and a process of mutual reassurance, and an affirmation of love and unity. Disturbances in a couple's sexual relations may generate feelings of rejection, exploitation, or degradation. Although it often seems that infidelity has caused a couple to divorce, it is more likely that the couple's poor fit caused sexual incompatibility and that this led to infidelity. In healthy marriages, the causes of sexual problems include external stress, poor health, and sexual ignorance—and these causes tend to be temporary. Persistent sexual problems, on the other hand, may reflect the poor quality of their non-sexual interactions. It may also precipitate further difficulties in the relationship. In the following student's story, the wife understood that her husband's affair was only the outgrowth of their poor fit.

Jenny Messerman

Three years before my parents divorced, my dad joined Overeaters Anonymous. He began to go to this group more and more, until he was attending OA meetings four nights a week. He usually came home at about 11 p.m., but every few weeks he would come home at 4 a.m. He always had some excuse, such as a friend with car trouble who needed help. Dad was sponsoring a woman named Andrea at these meetings, and he was always telling my mom how hard Andrea's life was and how much she needed support because she was a single mother of three young boys. Dad and Andrea would go out for coffee after meetings. Mom thought they were just good friends. She should have known better! But although my dad's affair with Andrea was the trigger for the divorce, my mom says it was not Andrea herself who wrecked their marriage. The real problem was that she and my dad never had much in common. The first time Mom realized this was during their honeymoon. She was expecting a week filled with romance and intimacy, but all Dad wanted to do was see all the naval landmarks in the area. (By the way, Andrea now happily accompanies my dad on his excursions).

Despite repeated infidelities, couples often try to protect the marriage. This strategy is seldom effective. If the spouse knows about the other's affairs, it is almost impossible to "forgive and forget." The pain rankles and the marriage finally folds. This is what happened in the following student's family.

Lucy Schumacher
    Although there were many factors that led up to my parents' divorce, the most obvious reason was my father's infidelity. But this was only a symptom of their underlying problems. They were never sexually compatible. His high sex drive and liberal upbringing clashed with her strict religious upbringing. He wanted to experiment with sex; she viewed it as a duty. My mother grew up believing that a woman should not enjoy sex and that the only justification for intercourse was procreation. My father had an affair only six months into their marriage. They probably should have ended the marriage then, but my mother gave him a second chance. She believed it was her

duty to forgive him and to try to make the marriage work. My father must have thought that this meant infidelity was no big deal, because the next year he fathered an illegitimate child. Even after that, my mother gave him a third chance and took him back. But she never forgot. It was always in the back of her mind. I don't believe that the idea of "forgive and forget" is realistic. My mother suffered great heartache and humiliation because of my father's cheating. But it took twenty years before she filed for divorce.

Gender: Are Women and Men Mismatched?

Perhaps one reason we see so many mismatched couples is that men and women are from different planets, as the popular book title suggests. The bestseller status of John Gray's book "Men Are from Mars, Women Are from Venus" is testimony to our persistent and profound confusion about the opposite sex and our strong desire to understand and be understood by our mates. Scientists contend that our evolutionary background predisposes men and women to be different. In eons past, men were hunters, and women gatherers of food and caretakers of children. This "hunter hypothesis" would explain why males are more aggressive and have certain physical advantages. Successful hunting and survival depended on men's ability to track and attack moving animals. The hunter hypothesis also offers an explanation for why men tend to be more group oriented than women. To maximize their success in hunting, men relied on joint action in groups. During a hunt it was important to pick up nonverbal signals and cooperate without discussion. To this day, men like to congregate in groups—gangs, sports teams, with the boys at the bar—where there is little emphasis on individual bonds but a strong push for camaraderie.

The "gatherer-caretaker hypothesis" would explain why women are more likely to have emotional exchanges with one or two individuals rather than casual interactions with a group of people. Their greater emotional sensitivity may be a reason that studies consistently show that women are more affected by family problems and suffer more from depression than men. One of the salient differences between men and women is that women are more committed to marriage than men are.

Sally Salow

When my mom met my dad, she knew what she wanted. She wanted family ties and a place where roots could grow deep and solid. She dreamed of a house in the suburbs with a white picket fence. My father wasn't sure what he wanted for the rest of his life, but he liked the idea that my mom was so certain. By the time they got married, the house with the picket fence had turned into a studio apartment above a garage in a poor neighborhood in Los Angeles, but still, in my mother's mind, it was a place where they could begin to build a life together. Shortly after the wedding, two major events occurred: Mom got pregnant and Dad got himself an apartment.

Almost from the moment that they exchanged vows, marriage had felt like a yoke to my father. The very certainty that had attracted him to Mom was now the thing he was running from. The more she pushed for commitment and family responsibilities, the more he resisted. And so he insisted on having his own place—just in case. He told my mom he "needed his space." This was going to be a new version of marriage, 'his' and 'hers' apartments, while maintaining the sacred marriage bond. Of course it didn't work.

In the beginning, Dad spent the nights at their place, and, for a while, Mom remained trusting and accepting of his need to have space. But then feelings of trust turned into suspicion and doubt. My dad's lack of commitment led Mom to consider filing for divorce. But each time she announced that the relationship was over, Dad would get back in line and act like the perfect husband. Then the same dance would begin again—Dad insisting that he keep his own place and Mom insisting that he give it up and invest 100 percent in the marriage. Today they agree that his lack of commitment led to their divorce.

The lack of commitment and the ambivalent feelings toward wife and baby displayed by this man were by no means an isolated instance. Many of our students reported that their fathers had second thoughts immediately after the wedding or after the birth of a baby. They felt trapped and acted as if they had been taken hostage. In their struggle for autonomy, they often escaped into childish behaviors—pouting, throwing tantrums, playing deaf to their wife's needs and requests, and going out with the boys. These men needed a mother more than a wife—a mother who would unselfishly give them as much time as they needed to grow up, and who would remain patient, regardless of their bad behavior.

Elizabeth Harrison

My mom was pregnant when she got married and looking forward to hearing the pitter-patter of little feet around the home. But after the wedding, my dad started going to his aunt's house every day to practice with his band. Often he spent the night there. My mom was surprised, because, in the past, he had never gone out with his friends, and he had certainly never spent the night with them. She was not used to being alone and she missed him. She wrote little love notes and sneaked them into his college books. He mostly ignored them. When Mom asked him if he could come home earlier and spend more time with her, he said that his friends would laugh at him. He felt that he had to prove to them that she "didn't have him wrapped around her little finger." He did not seem to want to be with her. Being pregnant and alone most of the time made her feel depressed. When she started complaining, he told her that being married

was "living in misery" for him. Then he started going out
more and staying out longer. After I was born, my mom
became extremely depressed. Now my dad stayed out all
the time. He felt that she was trying to control his life and
she wanted him to have a steady job, make a lot of money,
buy a house right away, and cut off his interest in music
and friends. He thought he was doing nothing wrong
and resented the pressure. Her "bitching" made him feel
inadequate. Meanwhile, my mom tried to work things
out. She discussed their problems with each of their
families, hoping they could help, but they didn't want
to get involved. She didn't know what to do and began
threatening him with divorce. She hoped this would get
Dad to try harder at the marriage. But he didn't care. He
didn't even seem to care when she got so sick that she
needed to be hospitalized. Mom was angry for everything
he put her through and the fact that he did not act as if he
cared about us. Around my first birthday, she finally gave
up. She told him that she wanted a divorce and custody
of me. He said that she could have both.

The ambivalence toward family responsibilities that the
fathers in these two stories displayed may be, in part, an
attribute of males' emotional immaturity in their early adult
years. Paradoxically, young males' sex drive is strongest at a
time when few are ready to assume the responsibilities for a
baby and a wife; few are ready to "settle down." Evolutionary
theories suggest that because men were not the children's
caretakers, they had limited options in trying to ensure that
their gene pool survived, and this is why they move on and
father more children with more women, to maximize the
potential for surviving offspring.

Women, in contrast, who biologically cannot produce
nearly as many children as men, maximize the survival of their
genes by seeking security and stability to ensure that their
children have sufficient resources to survive into adulthood.
These different priorities may explain why the pairing between

older men and younger women has remained popular—
notwithstanding the frustrations that the age difference may
produce in other areas of the couple's relationship.

Our mentioning of evolutionary theories should not be
interpreted as a justification for individual irresponsibility;
rather it is presented as a possible explanation for a common
phenomenon. Problems arise because our social structures
have become far more complex than prehistoric hunter-
gatherer societies. What may have been adaptive in those times
is apparently not functional now. In our society, the exclusive
bond between a man and woman promotes the stability of the
family unit, the well-being of the children, and thereby, social
stability. As our evolutionary requirements have changed, our
behaviors need to change, too.

In some cultures, the differences between men and women
are even more extreme than in mainstream America. This
can create very challenging problems for a couple.

Juan Hernandez

My father grew up in a traditional Mexican family—
his parent's marriage lasted seventy years. He didn't even
know what divorce was when he was a kid. He now says that
the only reason that his parents' marriage endured was
that his mother was completely submissive to his father.
His father's attitude toward marriage included physical
abuse if his wife didn't please him. So when my father
and mother got married, he wanted her to give him the
impossible—the wife his mother was. He expected her
to be there for him no matter what and to tolerate his
affairs and his abusiveness. My mother, however, was too
strong willed to submit to my dad's version of marriage.
She did not come from such a traditional family and she
was more educated. Her "disobedience" got his blood
boiling. He felt challenged by her, and the only way he
knew to react was with angry and sometimes violent
displays of his manly "power." Even now, he says, "In
general, women are pretty stupid and stubborn."

Cristina Bernal

By the time she was twenty-four, my mom found herself with two small babies and a full-time job helping my dad with his contracting business. Her life was overwhelming. They did not have their own washing machine and dryer, so every week, my mom would gather all the laundry (ten loads), carry it to the car, go to the Laundromat, wash, dry, and fold the ten loads, put them back in the car, drive home, and carry ten loads of clean clothes into the house, to find my dad crashed out in front of the TV. He would not help her at all. He did not even help her carry the baskets into the house. He was lazy and she hated him in those moments. Although she was married, she always felt that she was alone. Their life together was devoid of companionship, communication, and cooperation. They had no sex life. My father lived the stereotypical male role: he brought home a paycheck and she did everything else. He never changed a diaper. He never helped with anything in the household. He did not provide adult companionship after she had spent the entire day at home with the kids. One day, another laundry day, my mom could not stop crying about the way her life was. She asked herself the classic question "Is this all there is?" It was then that she made the decision to divorce.

Different Interests, Values, Lifestyles

Beyond the conflicts inherent in uniting the two sexes, mismatched couples also wrestle with personal differences. Their troubles bespeak of few shared values, interests, and goals. In fact, they seem so different that it is unclear what they even like about each other. They appear like characters from two different plays following two different scripts. Although few couples are a precise match on all interests and ideals, in mismatched couples the differences grossly outnumber the similarities.

Sarah Beller

My parents' relationship started out passionately. In the beginning, the sex was great (my mom got pregnant with me a few months after they met), but it was not enough to sustain their relationship. Passion would sometimes flare up during their otherwise miserable marriage, but they did not have much else in common. They even differed in how they wanted to spend their free time. Mom was traditional; Dad was adventurous. She wanted to entertain at their house or go to a play; he wanted to take off with his friends to go skiing or racing. Most of my early memories are of them fighting.

As is typical for mismatched couples, this couple shared little—except in this case, sexual attraction. Fundamental differences become even more difficult to recognize when the couple share some interests on the surface. Couples are often fooled into believing that they are alike if they have the same hobby or the same taste in music. Because of this, they tend to overlook the fact that on a deeper level they still have little in common. Sharing the same hobby, the same taste in music, food, or clothing, the same political views, or a favorite TV show is not enough to build a life together. It is more important to share goals and values and have a functional way of communicating with each other. If spouses differ in their most basic goals, values, and expectations for life, they are headed toward stormy seas.

But sometimes it seems that couples do have shared goals and, still, they clash. What is happening? In all likelihood the couples' behavior does not match their stated values and goals. Their actions do not match their words or even their beliefs. Most couples can easily agree that they want a nice home, financial security, and well-mannered children. Who would want to live in a shack, be poor, and raise brats? But agreeing on such general values and goals is not sufficient insurance that all will be well. The couple may agree that they want a nice life but have different understandings of what that specifically means. They may differ in their emphases on certain goals and the behaviors necessary to attain them. They may both value security; but in everyday life, it may be more important to one of them to have an exciting lifestyle. Thus, one of them will want to save money and the other to spend it. They may both profess to valuing a comfortable home, but, to one of them, "comfortable" means casual and lived-in, whereas, to the other, it means scrupulously clean and orderly. Same goal, different definitions. Even if the couple agrees on the behaviors necessary to attain their goal, sometimes one spouse lacks the commitment and persistence to follow through. In other cases, the couples initially agree on goals, but, as life goes on and their circumstances change, the needs of one of the partners change and the other is left with a deal gone wrong.

Naoko Russell

Even though my parents shared very similar values in high school, they realized once they started growing up that the two of them were "mismatched." My dad, modeling his role after that of his own father, wanted to be the "family provider" and didn't want his wife to work. My mom had initially liked the idea of being a homemaker, but once she found herself stuck in that role she started going "stir crazy" and wanted to work, at least part time. My father insisted on their role division, although it clearly made my mother unhappy.

Although this couple agreed initially on how they would divide their roles, this division did not turn out to be satisfying to the wife—and she changed her mind. A healthy marriage would accommodate to the changing needs of each spouse. Mismatched couples, however, get stuck in their initial roles and have difficulty adjusting to changes in circumstances or needs. Couples in unhealthy relationships cling rigidly to the once agreed upon roles and react negatively to a request for change.

In the following story, the couple experienced a clash of lifestyles.

Masayasu Lawrence

My mom was on welfare, struggling to pay for the rent, the food, and the electricity, when she married my stepfather. We immediately moved into a house in a fancy neighborhood. This was a big shock, because we were a lower-class, counter-culture family from Berkeley, definitely not mainstream. My mom was a hippie who was into civil disobedience and public demonstrations. Edward, on the other hand, was upper middle class, very materialistic, and very much in charge. He was into showy things and his high-powered job. We were used to a simpler life. Mom felt that this change would make our lives "more stable." Well, life definitely became more structured. Edward was a control freak. Everyone had to eat at the same time. Strict manners were of the utmost importance. Any superficial structure was important to him. At first, this fascinated Mom because she was so laid back and without structure. But then it became oppressive. Edward controlled everything. He had a strong sense of "shoulds"—what you should look like, what you should wear, what you should eat. They started fighting a lot and Mom became really depressed. They were a total mismatch. No wonder they couldn't get along.

The pairing was doomed, because when it came down to it, the couple had nothing in common. Although on the surface they may have both searched for a stable family life, their interpretations were very different. The mother wanted stability, but what she got was control. The pain from their differences far outweighed her small gain.

Conflicting Personalities

Husbands' and wives' personality traits also can contribute to their incompatibility. Even people with "divorce prone" personalities can have successful marriages—if they are lucky enough to find their "perfect match." But unfortunately, there is no simple guide to which personality combinations will blossom and which will wither. There are too many factors that can tip the balance. For example, the pairing of a passive and a dominant spouse may be successful, if other factors work in their favor. Such a relationship may provide the passive partner with energy and direction and the dominant spouse with stabilizing peace—presuming that the husband and wife are able to respect each in spite of their differences. Another couple with these same personality traits but with different goals, additional personality clashes, or unexpected stresses may find themselves on a warpath. The passive spouse may feel oppressed, and the dominant spouse may feel bored, and each may lose respect for the other. A number of our students described their parents as having incompatible personalities.

Sarah Beller

I think the main problem with my parents' marriage was that they have completely different personalities. The only way they are alike is that they both have very strong tempers. Because they have different views on everything, their unrelenting natures made them clash ferociously. I never understood why they fell in love in the first place, because they were so different and didn't even seem to like each other. Dad was fiercely independent, strong and ambitious. I remember him saying that he was ready to "squeeze the juice out of life." Mom was his opposite— passive, waiting for things to fall into place for her, yet demanding a great deal. She expected things to happen the way she wanted and when she wanted them, but she did not make them happen. If things didn't turn out the way she wanted, she was disappointed, hurt, or angry and would start complaining. My dad did not respect my mother because of her passive attitude toward life. They regularly had violent arguments and shouted horrible things at each other. Finally, it was Dad who initiated the divorce.

Popular myth suggests that opposites attract, in reality, couples with opposite personality characteristics usually tire of their differences. They may initially be attracted to the differences, but they are not likely to stay happily married. What in the beginning seems fascinating, charming, and stimulating, in everyday life turns into a misunderstanding or nuisance, then a failure in communication, and eventually the breakdown of the relationship. The following stories portray such mismatched couples, in which opposite characteristics initially contributed to attraction and later to the relationship's demise.

Justine Reese

My mother left my father for her horseback-riding instructor when I was twelve. She felt that she had finally found her soul mate in this man. They shared a passion for horses, they loved the same music, they read the same books, and they had great sex. For a year, they carried on a secret affair, while she planned the divorce. Then immediately after the divorce was finalized, he moved in with us. That was the end of their great love. My mother was from an upper-class background; he was blue collar. She was very precise, orderly, determined, and detail oriented; he was pretty much the opposite. During their affair, she loved his relaxed way of being in the world. It was so refreshingly different from the structured life she led. Once they were living together, it was a different story. He was basically a slob. She complained that she needed to clean up after him; he complained that she was bitching. Before he moved in, she had been extremely attracted to his "manliness"; he was able to hold his own in discussions, had strong opinions, and did not give in to her whims. Later, she took this as evidence of his egocentrism. For years, we watched them scream at each other and then make up again, only to have something trivial trigger the next fight the next day.

Elena Parker

My father was soft-spoken and reserved; my mother was outgoing and vivacious. When they met at a college party, they were attracted to each other right away. My mother's liveliness appealed to my dad, and my mother thought she had found in him a sensitive and strong man who could give her the security she had been seeking. They got married, had two children, and he got a law degree and she a real estate license. Then, they discovered, their two different personalities were too different. In fact, they were simply incompatible. Being an outgoing and sociable person, my mom really enjoyed working in real estate. But my dad didn't like the idea that she was out all the time, having business lunches and dinners. He thought she dressed too provocatively. He would tell her that he wished she was ugly so he wouldn't have to be jealous.

My mom thought my dad was too uptight. She wanted an exciting, busy life. He wanted isolation. His work and his family were plenty for him. My dad was serious and logical, and he claimed my mom was only interested in the trivial. She was too emotional, talkative, and spontaneous. To him, she was like a self-centered child. Her high-energy activities were irritating and overwhelming. A typical example of their mutual misunderstanding and poor communication occurred when my mom threw a surprise party for my dad's birthday. My dad really didn't like big social events, and most definitely did not like them if he was the focus. According to my father, he made it perfectly clear that a surprise party would be the last thing he wanted. According to my mother, she thought he would enjoy it. When my dad came home and realized there was a party, he yelled at my mom right in front of the guests and started a huge argument. In his mind, the surprise party was just another example of her selfish need for entertainment. He believed that my mom knew that the party wouldn't make him happy, but she had planned it for herself.

These couples discovered that the very personality traits that initially attracted them drove them apart in the long run. Some of their different characteristics might have complemented each other; others only served to antagonize. To achieve marital success, there needs to be a harmonious interplay of many traits. Unfortunately, there is no single dimension along which one can simply match a couple. We cannot say that an extraverted person should find an extraverted partner, or that extraverts should pair up with introverts. How much of the same is enough? How much is too much? The issue is confusingly complex. There are many subtle ways in which couples need to synchronize their daily interactions. The confluence of many factors either creates a harmonious dance or constant antagonism. Consider the analogy of an orchestra. Orchestras are not made up of just two types of instruments. In the same way, we cannot fit two people on the basis of two or three traits alone. Even a good fit between two instruments is not enough to make up the orchestra. Many more instruments are needed and all must play harmoniously together to make great music.

Lessons to Be Learned

Mismatched couples are marked by their lack of genuine commitment to their spouse, basic and profound incompatibility, poor communication patterns, and a reactive way of dealing with problems and with each other. These are some of the Lessons to Be Learned from these truly miserable lives:

1. Make marriage a commitment. It is essential that if a marriage is going to last each person make a genuine commitment to the other. Each should wholeheartedly like and accept the other, knowing his or her weaknesses. Each must answer affirmatively: Are you proud of your partner even on his or her bad days? Are you at peace when together? Are you at peace when apart? Are you able to be loyal to him or her even if that conflicts with your own needs? Do you truly respect your partner? Are you ready to protect him or her? Commitment does not ask "what can that person do for me" but focuses on what one can give to the other and what one can do to enhance and sustain the relationship. Commitment is selfless but self-respecting. It does not mean always compromising one's own goals, but it does mean always taking the other person's needs and wishes into consideration.

2. Choose a compatible partner. Marriage is a team effort, so it's important to make sure both husband and wife are headed in the same direction. Develop a vision of the person who can successfully share your life and of the life you want to commit to. Writing down your criteria for a partner and for married life can prevent a lot of missteps. Choose someone with a similar socioeconomic, religious, and ethnic background. Choose someone who is sexually compatible— you'll spend one third of your married life together in bed. Discuss in detail your values, goals, and plans regarding family life, child rearing, finances, work—and everything else that is important to you. Carefully evaluate your compatibility in all these areas. Discuss concretely how to work out any differences. Don't just hope or expect that "things will work out" after you are married—they won't!

Premarital counseling can identify potential problem areas and help couples work through them or determine they are not right for each other. As the stories in this chapter suggest, it is far less painful to realize this before marriage than after. Topics discussed in counseling include communication and problem solving skills, the ability to share weaknesses and worries with a partner, money matters, mutual respect and intimacy. Counseling gives couples the opportunity to explore and resolve potential problem areas before they become problems. It also gives couples tools to make their relationship stronger.

A prenuptial agreement can precipitate a discussion of practical and ideological issues in a relationship. It is a good way of finding out more about each other's values and beliefs and discovering each other's "hot buttons." If she says, "I'll take you to the cleaners if you ever divorce me," and he says, "I'll fight you tooth and nail to keep the kids"—believe it, and find somebody else. If you can't agree on important issues during the courtship, just imagine how bad it would be to go through a divorce. And remember that the probability of your marriage lasting is a mere 50/50.

3. Probe the details of your compatibility. Before you get married be sure that you really have the same values, goals, and lifestyles. Reflect on some of the real-life examples in this chapter that show that couples, despite their mutual assurances of wanting a great relationship, a happy family life, and a nice home, were actually clueless about what these global terms concretely meant to the other. Before you marry, discuss in great detail what a "happy family life" and "great sex" mean to you in practical terms. Also explore whether your intended spouse has the mental and emotional capacity to actualize his or her professed values and beliefs. After all what people say and do are often two different things. What are your partner's "credentials" that suggest that the two of you really have the same road map and the tools to get to where you want to be? How does he interact with children? What role does she take in her family? How has she treated her exes? How financially stable is he really? Pay attention to the details.

4. Take responsibility for your life and your marriage. In the marriage, each person must take some responsibility for the way things go. It is not good to ruminate about all the "bad" things your spouse said or did. Blaming will not help; it will only drain you and make you bitter. Instead focus on what you can do to make your own life and your marriage better. You should expect disagreements in your marriage; you should expect some anger and pain. But don't cling to these negative feelings; they are not your friends. During difficult times, remember that your partner is not the enemy but the person you chose to love and live life with. Zeroing in on your spouse's flaws will not make you or the relationship better. Keep your communication at all cost open—aggression, stonewalling, and withdrawal will only worsen your problems. Instead of sitting there feeling victimized, betrayed and paralyzed, remember your commitment and do something constructive that serves the relationship. Get help if you can't find a constructive path on your own.

5. Monitor your behavior and the well-being of your relationship. Pay yourself and your marriage a visit from time to time. Pretend you are a visitor and watch how you behave and how you relate to each other. Do you share enjoyable activities? Do you respect each other and show it? Are you proud of each other? Do you openly communicate your concerns, needs, or disagreements? Or do you pretend that nothing is wrong even when you don't feel right? Do you enjoy your sex life? Do you like each other and does it show in expressions of affection, playfulness, and support? Or is there a preponderance of anger, blame, depression, and withdrawal. Do you continue to shape and share your life together? Or have you fallen into a rut? Have you drifted apart? From time to time (not every day), take the temperature of your relationship and discuss your concerns with your spouse. Express your needs, consider your spouse's needs, and devise together a plan to get back on

track. It is far easier to do this before problems have become
overwhelming and you are locked into misstep.

6. Keep practicing communication skills. Successful
couples are able to express their feelings and talk about
the things that bother them. Communication skills are
essential in marriage. Not talking about problem issues leads
to frustration, alienation, and blow-ups. It is important to
raise issues that persistently bother you and discuss them
in a civilized manner. Don't just vent, but know what you
want to achieve with the discussion. Clarify in your own
mind, or on paper, what the issues are, what each partner's
needs are, and how the problem could be solved before you
open your mouth. Stay constructive, listen to your partner's
needs and concerns, and brainstorm and problem solve
together. If you don't feel heard or understood, don't raise
the pitch and the frequency of your complaints but state
that the issue is important to you and ask your partner to
give it some thought and discuss it again another day. Make
appointments for important or difficult discussions. It is also
a good idea to meet in a public place, a favorite restaurant
or café, to have such discussions. Such meetings underscore
the importance of the discussion and help prevent irrational
outbursts. Make sure you are talking with each other, not at
each other. Establish ground rules for turn taking and adopt
a civil tone. You wouldn't roll your eyes, wouldn't constantly
interrupt, and wouldn't snort with contempt or make hostile
remarks to a valued person. Don't do it to your spouse either!
Limit the length of the discussion to about one hour to avoid
burnout. Don't expect to solve every issue in the marriage in
one session. Reschedule instead to continue the discussion.
Follow up and follow through on agreements. Jointly chose
books on communication skills and review and practice these
skills together.

Communication is not just about problems; communication
of good feelings is also important. It is important, for example,

to nurture your sexual life. Remember that a couple's sexuality is more than just sex. It is a form of communicating, nurturing, and reassuring each other. It adds playfulness and closeness and reaffirms your love and unity, and as such deserves attention, time, and care. Express your needs and be attentive to your spouse's needs. Address any sexual problems and find ways to enhance or improve your sexuality by tapping into the wealth of educational and inspirational material or find professional help.

7. Appreciate differences. Even compatible couples have differences in gender, personality, and experiences. Don't let these differences get in the way of a great marriage. If you have carefully selected a compatible partner, cherish the ways in which your differences enrich the relationship. Don't expect your partner to be, feel, and think exactly like you. Your spouse is not your clone. Besides it might be rather boring to be married to a clone. Abstain from trying to change your partner to do things the "right" way, namely your way. Refrain from patronizing your wife's weaknesses or picking on your husband's quirks. And put an end to the criticizing—it never works. Try something else—kindness, a sense of humor, and appreciation for the ways in which you complement each other.

8. Protect your relationship. It should be the couple's first priority to protect their marital relationship from bad feelings. Your spouse should not be your emotional dumpster. It is not necessary to vent each and every one of your life's frustrations at home. Don't whine and complain daily about your boss, your co-workers, your kids. Communicate honestly about major issues, but let the little things go. Also, don't complain about your spouse to others, including your children. Resolve your marital problems between the two of you. It is important not to ignore problems in your marriage; if any arise, you should talk to your spouse about how you can both improve things. But curb the complaints. You want your relationship to be brimming with good feelings, not dragged down by disagreeable ones. Behave the way you want your spouse to behave toward you. If you want your spouse to be honest, reasonable and kind—act that way.

3
Candlelight Dinners and a White Picket Fence: The "Perfect Couple"

Connie Phillips

> From the outside, my family looked like the perfect family and, indeed, for a while we were. We lived in a nice four-bedroom house. My father worked as a sales manager for a news magazine and my mother did part-time office work. During the week, we would all eat dinner together as a family, and on Sundays we all went to church. We were a very close, loving and supportive family My parents got along great and they never fought. All their friends thought they were the perfect couple and would be happily married forever.

The "perfect couple" is so sweet together—at least at first. They look perfect—at least from the outside. They have a nice home and good jobs and their children are well behaved—right up until things fall apart. Perfect couples are not necessarily happy, but it is important to them to appear happy to the outside world. The "perfect couples" differ from truly happy couples in their almost fanatical pursuit of idealized and clichéd notions of the perfect family life—without regard for any evidence to the contrary. About 15 percent of our students had parents who started out as "perfect couples."

Tiffani Leach

Our extended family viewed my parents as role models. Often one of my aunts or uncles would say, "I want to be the same kind of parent that you are." It looked like my parents handled everything just right. Their friends, too, thought my parents were the perfect couple. They always dealt with issues maturely, never arguing in public. In fact, this was something they took pride in.

Most of my parents' friends were teachers at the school where my dad worked, and my parents often had them over for dinner. My mother was a great hostess. She cooked wonderful food and created a comfortable atmosphere that made all this look easy. My father was a hero to everyone. He taught physics and computer science and in general was the "fix it" man in the community. People called him with any problems they had. We three daughters also saw him as our hero. In fact, we looked up to both of our parents and to what they'd done with the family. They were fair, easy to approach, and more like good adult friends than parents.

But right after my graduation, when everything couldn't have been better, my mom approached me and said she had something to tell me. She started crying, "I can't believe I have to tell you this.., Pop and I, we are … separating." She explained that it was not an easy decision, but it had been two years since they decided they would separate. They had been hiding all the problems in their marriage, even though they were eating them up inside. For many years, there had been a lack of physical, mental, and emotional communication. They still loved each other, but it felt more like a brother-sister relationship than a marriage. Translation: they weren't having sex. My dad had not wanted to go to counseling, and since one of his major problems was his lack of being able to say what was on his mind, my mom initiated talks about a separation. My father felt ambivalent about it because they had made a promise to each other that they were supposed to keep. But he was relieved that she had broached the topic.

A month later I had to leave for college. Within that month my mom managed to find a wonderful apartment and move in. When I came home for summer vacation, my father was treating my mom as if she were his daughter, fixing things for her, giving her money when she needed it, and making sure her computer was set up properly. One day he knocked on the door. I opened it and he stood there with a dozen roses for my mom. She began to cry and I went to my room. It turns out that it was their anniversary and my dad was just trying to make a nice gesture. But he had never bought her flowers when they were married, and the fact that he was doing it now was too much for her to handle.

Perfect marriages have great appeal. Who wouldn't want to have the perfect marriage? The promise of a perfect romance, perfect children, and a perfect life is so seductive that everybody at times engages in some of the behaviors that marked the perfect couples. However, in healthy relationships, people are able to cope with the challenges and changes of life—those resulting from external events and those from within the relationship. Perfect couples cannot do that. Effective coping requires that they acknowledge their problems, deal with them and, if necessary, transform the terms of their relationship. Perfect couples are not prepared to do this.

Profound denial and a strong aversion to overt conflict are distinguishing characteristics of perfect couples. For example, Tiffani's parents "always dealt with issues maturely, never arguing in public." The preoccupation with appearing perfect became so pervasive that these spouses did not even allow themselves to notice any problems. Perfect couples are so heavily into denial that they become expert at blaming external circumstances to rationalize their problems. Tiffani's mother never got a full-time job "because she was taking care of my two sisters and me the whole time."

Perfect couples have a high need for social approval; they want very much to be liked, to be popular, to be respected. They present to the world a picture of perfection even if that means faking it. They are so compelled to appear perfect that they try to do "all the right things" even if they are not right for them. For better or worse, they rigidly stick to idealizing marriage and family life. It is as if being a "good girl" or "good boy" is the only way they know to be accepted and liked. So they emphasize unthinkingly "playing by the rules." Tiffani's father was ambivalent about divorcing, not because he wanted to salvage the marriage but because he made a promise that he was supposed to keep. Sticking to the rules and appearing perfect, being a 'good boy,' was the only way he knew to be.

Like the marriages of mismatched couples, the marriages of perfect couples tend to last a long time. But whereas the mismatched couples are too hurt, too angry, or too passive to initiate a change, perfect couples deny or hide their growing unhappiness. They are so busy upholding the flag of happiness that it often takes decades before they crack under the cumulative impact of problems simmering beneath the surface. They keep themselves busy being PTA parents, soccer moms, little league coaches, active church members. They climb the social ladder and achieve success in work. They focus on the success of their children and gain satisfaction from their good manners: "say please", "say thank you", "say I'm sorry", "that is not nice honey", "kiss auntie", "be good." Often the break in the perfect family facade occurs only after one of the spouses experiences a change or crisis that forces them to acknowledge the hollowness of their "perfect happiness."

Perfect Beginnings

Most perfect couples started their marriages with images of perfection. Our stories contained many phrases of clichéd happiness: the "love of her life," his "dream woman," "the house with the white picket fence." Perfect couples plug each other into a pre-cut template of idealized romance and marriage. Like many of the divorced parents, the following couple magically knew that they were "meant for each other." Their descriptions of perfect encounters, passionate and "true" love, "wonderful" lives, and "many blessings" read like romance novels.

Brittany Roberts

My mother found the love of her life in a Van Nuys nightclub in 1970. She was talking to her girlfriends when a tall, dark, handsome man came up to her and asked her to dance. There was an instant spark between them. They "lit up" the dance floor, dancing all night long into the sunrise. My mom knew right away that she had found that special man in her life.

Pamela Wilson

My mother was attending San Jose State University when she met my father at a friend's party. She noticed him the moment he walked in the door. In fact, every girl did. He strode into the room—tall, strong, and with a presence that commanded attention. My mom was instantly attracted to the dark-haired, handsome college student, and he was attracted to her, too. From that night forward, they were inseparable. The final months of college were filled with long nights of conversation and passionate love. After graduation, he proposed, and a few months later she became his wife, an event she had been waiting for her entire life.

"Ideal" marriages often started with beautiful weddings.

Tiffany Maurer
    My parents' wedding was the crowning event of
their love. They were married in a beautiful ceremony
on the black sand beaches of Kona against a gorgeous
Hawaiian sunset.

Gerry Schonfeld
    The reception at my parents' wedding was incredibly
beautiful. I've seen the photos. Her parents had spent a
fortune to make her wedding a memorable event—and it
was. They were off to a spectacular start.

Everything Is Perfectly Fine, Thank You
Alas, happy beginnings and "doing all the right things"
do not guarantee satisfying marriages. The majority of the
perfect couples in our students' families were idealists wearing
blinders. They held romantically stereotyped notions of the
perfect wife or the perfect husband and the perfect family
life with the perfect house. External appearances were very
important to them. A subgroup was not romantics but rigid
role adherents. They were less concerned with being nice
than they were with being right, and they had a tendency to
spiral into abusive behaviors once their idea of perfection was
shattered. Their ideas of perfection included rigid images of
the strong husband and the devoted wife.
    Perfect couples were the least insightful of the couples
described by our students. They could not understand why
doing all the "nice" or "right" things did not produce eternal
happiness or at least a stable marriage. All perfect couples also
share a powerful urge to pretend that there are no problems
in their relationship. Even in the face of very obvious problems
they try to live "happily ever after." On the surface, they
are usually very sweet with each other. They repress harsh
feelings and harsh words because it is not nice to be hostile
and angry. Dissatisfactions are ignored. This contributes to a

marked lack of communication and impoverished intimacy. If you can only talk about happy things, and there are few happy events or pleasant shared activities to talk about, then pretty soon there is not much talk. The following student's parents lived parallel lives alongside each other rather than dealing with their problems and finding shared sources of satisfaction.

Tyler Small

Sunday was family day. All five of us would wake up bright and early, dress in our Sunday best, and head off to the Nazarene church. My father was the church treasurer; my mother was the church organist and led the choir. I was always active in the church, as a nursery attendant, youth group leader, and soloist. My younger brother involved himself in Sunday school and Christmas programs. My older sister would rather have stayed home on the telephone, but, like the rest of us, she went faithfully. We seemed the perfect Christian family. All my friends envied my close and loving family. I thought I had it all. Then, during my senior year in high school, reality hit hard. My father and my mother called me and my brother into their bedroom. We sat down on the bed, and our parents announced they were getting a divorce. I remember the exact words my father uttered as tears welled up in his eyes: "Your mother and I have decided to get a divorce." That was the first time I had seen my father cry. That night, after almost twenty years of marriage, my father gathered together his clothes and moved to an apartment.

As I look back now, I realize that there were problems all along. Although we appeared to be a close family on Sundays, in reality, we were not. We rarely spoke at the dinner table. My brother and I tucked ourselves away in our separate rooms. My father rarely spoke to my brother unless he was punishing him. My brother was jealous of the close relationship my father and I shared, and we fought constantly. My parents' relationship was also distant. After dinner, my father spent his time alone in the barn working on various hobbies, while my mother played the organ or piano. My father always went to bed at 10 o'clock while my mother stayed up watching television until 2 o'clock. The distant atmosphere in my home provided the perfect conditions for a divorce but not for a family.

Trapped in Stereotypes

Often perfect couples try to live according to the stereotypes of husband as breadwinner and head of household and mother as homemaker and caretaker of children. They believe in the fairy tale notion of the man taking care of the wife and the wife being cared for. In these couples, the woman suffers from a "Cinderella complex": she expects to meet a handsome man, marry him, and be taken care of. She does not expect or want to be an equal wage earner. This romantic vision proved to be more an idealized notion than an ideal situation in our students' families. During their marriages, their mothers' exclusive investment in the traditionally feminine tasks of child rearing and housekeeping afforded them little satisfaction and self-esteem. Their sinking self-esteem was often accompanied by increased personal dissatisfactions, depression, dependency, and demands on their husband. The following story reveals many of the underlying dissatisfactions that are produced by the relentless pursuit of the fairy tale notion of "living happily ever after."

Lynn Milstein

We were the perfect family. My parents met on a double date in college and decided a little while later to drop out of college and get married. They were young, beautiful, and my dad could make a terrific salary working for his father. They wanted to create a family and enjoy a wonderful family life. Tragically, my dad's father passed away only a year later, and he was thrust into the role of owner of a large insurance company. At the time, he did not know much about the insurance business, and he was advised to sell it. But he felt that he should keep the business in his father's honor. A year later he had lost the business. Still, my parents didn't worry too much because they had each other and they knew everything would be all right. They were blessed with a great family and friends, and soon enough Daddy went to work for one of his buddies. It was a great job but they found it economically advisable for Mom to work as well. I was two years old and they had another baby on the way. Mommy had never expected to work during her married years, but she didn't mind because she knew that it would be only temporary.

Both Mommy and Daddy continued working, she as a secretary and he as an insurance agent, until he decided that he needed a change in jobs because he felt unfulfilled. He went into the printing business and she increased her hours at work. Even when the money got tighter after he kept changing jobs, they were a very loving family and their happiness only increased as we children grew up. My brother was a very talented athlete and always the team captain, and I was an excellent student and the student president of the school. We lived in a nice middle-class area and the whole neighborhood was a sort of "family." Daddy would coach our sports while Mommy was always the "team mom" who brought homemade cookies. My parents, too, were very popular with their friends. They joined bowling and softball leagues and they would go out every weekend to nice places with all their wealthy friends.

Then all of a sudden, my parents announced that they were getting a divorce. It was a complete shock to everyone who knew them. They were an ideal couple. Everybody thought that they were just going through a "phase." But Daddy moved out and the divorce was final a year later. So, what went wrong?

Well, I guess we were not perfect. Despite their appearance as a happy couple, Dad carried with him a feeling of failure after he lost his father's business. He kept switching jobs because everywhere he felt that he wasn't competent to do the job. Then he would lie and tell my mom that he had a job, while he was sitting all day in a coffee shop. He ended up getting into some legal trouble making bad business deals with his friends. Instead of telling people that a deal fell through, he would lie and try to cover it, but he got caught in the mess. He vented his unhappiness by having fits of anger at home. Instead of helping him through his inner torment, Mom withdrew into inner torment of her own. She is a passive person and hates making waves, so she played along with his irrational outbursts. She was ashamed to discuss his lies with anyone. She was angry that she had to be the primary wage earner—because she had never expected she would need to work, she was not prepared for the role, and she hated it. But she suppressed her frustrations and kept her feelings bottled up inside her and painted a pretty picture for the world to see. She stayed in the marriage because she was afraid of change, afraid of making waves and, of course, because of the children. It was not until their twentieth year of marriage that she decided to get a divorce. When she finally got the courage to make this decision she called my dad at the office. He responded with, "Okay, if that's how you feel." He was relieved, because for a long time he had felt that there was no honesty in their relationship. She could not accept his weaknesses, so he could not trust her to help him with them. This led him to be dishonest, because he worried about not succeeding financially and not being the man she wanted him to be. I realize now that my family appeared to be perfect because of the perfect image my mother painted and because the rest of us were willing to go along with that picture. We, too, wanted to be perfect.

Like many of the perfect couples, this couple shared fairytale fantasies of life. Their unrealistic expectations and demands on life and each other left them inadequately prepared. They gave up college expecting that things would fall into place for them. They were special and, therefore, they would be happy—and nothing, not even reality, could get in their way and change their ideal vision of family bliss. They wanted nothing less than perfection: the perfect marriage, the perfect children, the perfect social life. Anything not perfect was ignored. It is as if they lived their lives blindfolded and only the brightest sun and the happiest events could penetrate the blindfold at the edges.

Perfect couples are the most inauthentic. Their passionate pursuit of idealized notions of happiness leaves no room for real life. Their rigidity precludes individual change and growth. Eventually they stagnate, both individually and as a couple. If they did not sugar-coat their problems, their marriages would fall apart much sooner—or they might have a chance for change and growth. But for the perfect couples, acknowledging that there are problems with the partner does not fit the image of perfection and calls their entire existence together and as individuals into question. In the long run, the need to appear perfect at all times builds a tremendous pressure that ends in combustion. The couple disconnects because they cannot be real with each other.

Frequently the "perfect" wives are poor partners. They are so fixated on the idea of the perfect marriage that they cannot tolerate any evidence to the contrary. Nowhere in the fairy tale is there talk of Cinderella providing for her prince. The prince does not show any weaknesses and Cinderella does not need to support, guide, or help him. Visions of being swept away, being cared for, and living happily ever after do not allow for male weaknesses, indeed, they do not allow a man to be human. Perfect husbands do not get to express their needs, doubts and weaknesses.

The Perfect Stay-At-Home Wife

The majority of the women in perfect couples gave up any educational pursuits and work after marriage, and those who did work at the beginning of the marriage did so with the implicit or explicit understanding that they would stop when children arrived. In fact, getting married seemed to predict the loss of ambition for many women; they wholeheartedly followed the conventional idea of not ever needing to work during marriage. Once married, they slipped into a socially sanctioned oblivion with regard to their economic circumstances.

Nicole Raffaella

My parents got married after dating for three years. My father worked in a small company as an architect, and my mother was a nurse practitioner. Two years into the marriage I was born and my mom decided that she wanted to stay home to take care of me; so she gave up her job. When I was four years old, my sister was born. Around that time my father designed a house for us to live in. A week before Thanksgiving the house was finished and we moved in. I loved having my own room, and I was allowed to decorate it the way I wanted. I colored it all pale pink. I remember being extremely satisfied with my life. I loved my sister to death and, to my knowledge, there were no problems in our family. I can only remember my parents being very happy together. We enjoyed many family activities such as going out on our boat and having picnics on the beach. We also spent a lot of time with my grandparents, aunts, uncles, and cousins who lived close by. My parents enjoyed gardening and entertaining friends and family. I remember my parents hugging, kissing, and dancing together in the kitchen. They also had separate activities they were involved in. My father was board member of our homeowners' association, and my mother started a crafting circle with her friends. My father worked to support the family and my mother took care of the household responsibilities and my sister and me. Then out of the blue my parents divorced. When I asked my mother why, she said that she wanted to be an "at home mom," but Dad wanted her to work. According to mom, this led to conflict, which eventually led to a breakdown of the marriage.

In this story, the apparently perfect marriage failed because the husband did not share the wife's fairy tale version of a "perfect family." She wanted to be a stay-at-home mom and leave the dragon slaying to him; he, however, was looking for a helpmate rather than a traditional princess. In the following story, the mother lived her stay-at-home role to perfection, and her husband did not object—but in the end it was not enough. Their perfect family was only a dream in her mind.

Elisa Petrov

My mom was a saint. She was totally dedicated to being a mother and a wife. She was always cooking, cleaning the house, supervising our homework, or taking us to school. She had my father's suits perfectly laid out for him every morning—together with a matching shirt, matching socks, and the right amount of change in the right pocket! I have a clear image of Mother in front of the ironing board, ironing my dad's suits. Another image of her is curled up with a book. One of Mom's joys was reading. Whenever she got done with her household chores, she would find escape in the imaginary world of romance novels. She was always a dreamer; she liked to think that everything would turn out well in the end, as it did in her novels. My father spent most of his time at work. He would say "There is always something to be done at the office." Most days he would come home late from work. Years later we found out that he wasn't always at work; he was having affairs. Mother knew, or at least suspected, and would confront him about it, but they

kept their arguments hidden from us. Their divorce was
the inevitable consequence to the life of deceit that we
had all been living.

Couples who are locked into the stereotypical breadwinner-
homemaker roles have a particularly rough time keeping
their marriage on course when the needs of one spouse or
the financial circumstances of the marriage change. The
most common reason that the marriages of perfect couples
eventually fall apart is that the wife begins to work. Through
work, women become more self-confident. The appreciation,
praise and acknowledgment they receive from others
boosts their self-esteem and increases their awareness that
something is missing in their home life. The money they earn
makes them realize that they can take care of themselves
and are not as dependent on their husbands as they thought.
Husbands, in turn, notice their wives' newfound confidence
and independence and often feel threatened by it.

Kathy Mandis

My parents' marriage went along great as long as
my dad went to work and my mom kept house. They had
a perfect life, or so they thought. But then my dad was
laid off and they decided that my mom should go back
to work. She had been a teacher before they got married,
and so she applied for a teaching position in our school
district. The next year, she was out of the house every
morning at 7:30 to spend her day with a room full of ten-
year-olds. She loved it! She was back in the world, doing
a job that was important and rewarding. But the strain
of her working and my dad not working was too much
for them. He withdrew from her and then from us and
finally from our home. It was very sad, but there was no
turning back to find our perfect family again.

Happiness for Sale

Many perfect couples rely heavily on material means of obtaining satisfaction. They engage in flurries of activity, many of which involve shopping and acquiring all the right things. They keep buying cars, clothes, cosmetics, furniture, and gadgets as if they are trying to purchase the perfect life.

Suzanne Knowles

Everyone kept saying what a perfect family we were and how happy my parents looked. And indeed, we were the perfect family on the outside. We took family vacations and went to church every Sunday in the matching outfits that my mom had made. My Dad was vice president of a bank and did very well. But beneath the perfection were waves of pain that eroded our family life and eventually destroyed it. I have blocked out a lot of the fights my parents had, but I remember that there were days when it was better not to be seen or heard. My dad always wanted the best of everything even if it meant going into debt. We had all the toys we wanted and we often ate in restaurants. We were the first family on the block to own a video camera, and my dad loved to record our family outings. He also bought a speedboat, and I have fond memories of sitting on his lap and steering it. But even with the money my dad made, we couldn't afford to live in such a big house in an expensive neighborhood, plus take vacations, attend private school, and have all the goodies we had. When my mom tried to talk to him and make him see that we couldn't afford the lifestyle he wanted, he dismissed her concerns and told her she didn't understand finances. He was bringing home the paycheck and he handled the money and my mom's job was to take care of the house and kids. After all, he was in banking and knew how to deal with things. But the money problems grew, and eventually my mom got a part time job. I think that was the turning point. One day, my mom called us into the family room where she had been folding laundry. She sat us down and told us that both she and Dad loved us all very much and always would, but they didn't love each other anymore and couldn't continue to live together.

In the next story, too, the family learned that buying things fills the house but not the heart.

Kathy Lee

In the Korean tradition, marriage is based not upon love but upon a secure future, and that is what my father offered us. So by his standards we were the perfect family. We were always materialistic. Our way of showing concern for each other was with things and money. We had all the material goods money could buy. We had a TV in every room, even in the kitchen and the bathroom. For my sixteenth birthday I got a red BMW, and we owned five cars. We enjoyed a life of abundance and lived in a beautiful home in a rich neighborhood. My father wanted us to live a carefree and comfortable childhood because, like many Koreans, he had lived in great poverty in his youth. But his desire to give to us what he had missed in his youth was a big factor in my parents' divorce. As the years passed, my father became obsessed with making money. His work became his sole focus and he spent less and less time and energy on the family. It was rare to see him around the house. He replaced his presence in our lives with material objects. We were indulged economically but starved emotionally. There was no intimacy in our family to hold us together. My mother also was spoiled. She constantly used my father's money to buy excessive amounts of make-up, clothes and unnecessary furniture. She joined health clubs and beauty clubs to take up her time. She did not spend much time, effort or energy raising us. All of us were pretty much leading our own lives, doing our own things. Outwardly, we looked like a great family who had it all, but in reality we were no family at all.

Let's Play House

Another characteristic of perfect couples is that they want to be "cute." Their children often have names that start with the same letter: "Jessica, Jill, Jonathan, Julie." Their dogs wear the same sweater as the family members in the annual Christmas photo. Their children dress up like dolls in matching outfits. They seem to live their family life like children who are "playing house," spending vast amounts of time and money decorating their houses, buying matching items for everything and everybody.

Jerica Cowie

I just realized that my parents fit the picture of the "perfect couple" perfectly. All children have my dad's name, Rick, included in our names: Erica, Jerica, and Rick. We did send out every year those stupid photos with matching sweaters, and, yes, even the dogs wore them. We always thought it was so important to look perfect... right up until my parents' divorce.

Jennifer Vermont

My mother was very much into how things ought to be. She had this picture in her mind of how her house, her husband, and her kids needed to be so we could be the perfect family. One time, when we were sitting in the kitchen, it struck me how the flowery pattern of her dress matched the cushions of the kitchen chair that she was sitting on and how the fabric of the cushions was identical to the kitchen curtains.

Many parents are preoccupied with playing out rituals that symbolize for them the perfect family life. Some of the rituals are so elaborate that they border on the obsessive in their detailed and rigid carry through.

Kitty Krumboltz

Every evening, my mom and dad would take me and my sister to bed in this major procession. It would start in the kitchen. My mom would say, "Daddy, I see tired girls." This was the signal for us to line up. My sister went first, then me, then Dad, then Mom. On the way to the bedroom my parents would sing the first lullaby. Then we would climb into our beds and they would tuck us in and say, "I love you sweetheart," and we would say, "I love you Mommy," and "I love you Daddy." My mom would check that all our stuffed toys on the shelf above the bed were in order and then each of the stuffed toys was saying good night to us and would "help" Mommy and Daddy sing another lullaby.

Ruth Foxworthy

My parents did this really crazy thing when we got into the car. In order to get us kids to buckle up my father would say "Papa Bear is buckled" then my mother would say "Mama Bear is buckled," then I was supposed to say "Ruthie-bear is buckled" and my sister finally said "Marcy-bear is buckled." Then Dad would say in a deep bear voice "All right, now the family can go for a ride." Maybe we thought this was fun when we were small, but I distinctly remember my dad still doing this when I was fourteen. He did it even when I had friends in the car and he expected them to chime into our refrain! But we weren't really the happy bears' family.

Family traditions can be a good way to strengthen family bonds. However, if the rituals become more important than the family members themselves, something is amiss, and the family eventually disintegrates. In this "bear" family, Mama Bear became an alcoholic, who years later, left one night without word. Papa Bear had affairs during the marriage and thereafter one failed relationship after another. The two Baby Bears are still, fifteen years later, going to counseling, trying to cope with the damage they incurred growing up unprepared for real life.

Lessons to Be Learned

The "perfect couples" are mired in rigid and romanticized roles that suffocate their authenticity and growth. As a consequence, they do not develop, change, and adapt to changing circumstances. Ultimately, the couples' compulsive insistence on roles and appearances strangles their relationships. These couples' misguided attempts at perfection offer the following lessons.

1. Have realistic expectations. The primary lesson is this: Don't romanticize marriage and don't live your marriage and your family life according to clichés you picked up from TV, magazines, and "the Jones's." Think about your goals, values, and needs and whether they will truly be met by living those clichés. Think about your weaknesses and whether they will be truly overcome by being "cute" or by having the perfect house with the white picket fence and lots of gadgets. You are not a character in a TV show, so don't act like one. Don't put appearances above the reality of your feelings, above the needs of each family member, and above change and personal growth. Be sensitive to the needs of each family member, discuss problems, and work on solving them—rather than pretending that they don't exist. Work on discovering your true nature and work on living an authentic life—not life as you think it ought to be to get Brownie points. Learn to accept ambiguity and to be at peace with the imperfect.

2. Be open to change. Marriage, like life, is a journey, not a destination. You need to realize that you must adapt to new realities in your circumstances and your spouse—sometimes disappointing and painful ones—in order to grow and to sustain the relationship. A healthy marriage does not remain static over time but adapts to changing circumstances. Healthy families negotiate goals and renegotiate these goals and keep changing and growing. People in unhealthy relationships, in contrast, view change as a threat and block any deviation from the customary—sometimes violently—until they self-destruct.

3. Realize that marriage is not an end in itself. Often young people are so focused on "getting married" they don't think about "being married." Do you know what are you going to do with the rest of your life after the wedding? Marriage should be an important part of life—but not your whole life. Marriage is the icing on the cake, but you are the cake. You must offer the substance for your own existence. It is good for husbands and wives to have their own lives, their own joys and accomplishments—independent of their spouse's. This enriches family life. Having a life of your own also helps if, despite the best intentions and efforts to communicate, the marriage fails. Your identity will not be shattered if your marriage ends, and you will be able to behave in civilized way.

4. Don't rely on stereotyped roles. Clinging to stereotyped roles undermines couples' respect and trust in each other, because stereotyping ultimately objectifies each partner. Perfect couples unwittingly create a mechanistic, almost robotic, existence for each other, in which their unique feelings or experiences do not matter. Only the "program" matters. "Perfect" spouses do not view each other as real people but see each other in terms of the scripted functions that they associate with their roles. The rigid adherence to stereotyped roles and rituals (e.g., "What a husband or wife should do") stunts individual growth and undermines the relationship, because in the long run people live lives, not roles.

5. Think through economic issues. It is important to talk about money and work in an honest and open way both before and during the marriage. You cannot assume that your spouse feels the same way you do about these issues. You cannot blindly rely on his income or her willingness to stay home or to continue working after children come along. Women should not expect or demand that their husbands support them financially from the day they tie the knot. Although many men derive satisfaction from being the family "provider," the constant pressures of being the sole breadwinner may, in the long run, in today's world, breed stress, resentment, and disrespect. Living in two very different worlds—he at work, she at home—may also lead husband and wife to develop very different perspectives on life. This can create tension if little common ground remains. Even after children are born, women can maintain some contact with the outside world by working part time, taking courses, and keeping up their contacts. If a woman chooses to devote herself exclusively to being a homemaker during the marriage, her chances are higher that she will be left destitute and depressed if the marriage doesn't last. Having a career of her own will not only protect a woman in case of divorce but will also be better for married life; she will have higher self-esteem, she will have more to contribute to the relationship, and there will be greater mutual understanding and respect.

4
Rage and Violence: Family Dysfunction

All of us, at one time or another, manifest behavior that is dysfunctional. There are events and individuals that just drive us "crazy" and make us act in ways we later realize were irrational. In dysfunctional families, however, this human propensity to act irrational is taken a step further. In these families, dysfunction is not limited to rare occasions and extreme crises but spirals out of control over long periods of time. Eventually there is nothing normal or healthy about these families. Human hurt, anger and denial take on stupendous proportions, and chaos, pain and destruction become a way of life. These families are unique for the frequency, severity, and the duration of their fights. They are also surprisingly common. By the time they finally got divorced, about 45 percent of our students' parents were acting in these dysfunctional ways.

Brittany Roberts

The first signs of trouble in my parents' marriage appeared just three months after their wedding. My father was working as an engineer for the city, and he was under a lot of pressure. He worked long hours and wasn't getting paid enough. Soon he began coming home later and later, often drunk. There were times he couldn't even get his key in the lock. My mom was shocked by his behavior and tried to talk to him about it, but he didn't want to talk. He ignored her or stayed away from home for several days after she brought up the issue. One morning my father was too hung over to go to work, and he asked my mom to call in sick for him. She refused. At that moment she saw a side of him that she had never seen before. He began slapping her across the face telling her, "You will do what I tell you." My mom was so surprised he hit her that she pretended it hadn't happened. After that, whenever my mom tried to talk to my father about his drinking problem, he'd either give her a good beating on the face to make her look ugly or throw her down onto the floor and kick her in the stomach until he got tired. He began using extremely foul language and screamed at my mom to make sure she would mind her own business. Then he would tell her that she was worthless without him.

My mom was so stunned at what was happening she made herself believe that he didn't mean to do all these nasty things. She kept telling herself that things would get better. She never told anyone what was happening. No one should know about her husband's problems because his actions were not like him and only temporary. She did not even tell her own parents because she worried that they would be disappointed in her and view her as a failure. On the mornings she woke up with a bruised and swollen face, she'd call into work saying she was sick or that there was some sort of family emergency she had to attend to. My mother was too proud to let anyone find out. And so, over time, denial and lying became her way of life.

When my mom was pregnant with me, my father didn't physically abuse her as much—nor did he ever stay around long enough to lose his temper. My mom was alone most of the time. She kept herself busy by working or talking with friends and family, and whenever anyone asked her about my father, she would say, "he's fine" or "things couldn't be better." She hoped that with a child her husband would once again become the man she had fallen in love with. And for a short time after I was born, things did get better. My father was home more often, although he always had to have a beer or two as soon as he got home. Before I was a year old, however, the abuse became more brutal than ever. At night, when I let out a cry, my father would smack my mom's already tired body and yell at her to do her job and keep the baby quiet.

The years passed, but circumstances didn't change. I don't remember my father being at home much while I was growing up. The only time I'd see him was at my softball games. I knew my father loved me and was proud of me because he came to support me at my games. After the games, when the rest of my teammates went out for ice cream, I went with him to his favorite bar. He would drink and brag about what a great softball player I was, while I entertained myself playing video games. At the time, I thought it was normal, because I was with my daddy. I wouldn't say I enjoyed it, but I never complained because this was really the only time I got to spend with him. My father would tell me to lie to my mom and say that he had taken me out for dessert. My mom was so controlled by my father she didn't question him for fear of what he might do to her.

I remember many nights when my mom came into my bedroom and slipped into my bed next to me, shaking and cold. I remember cuddling next to her and putting my tiny arms around her. I had a feeling of what was happening, but I was too young to really understand that she was being beaten. One night, when I was eleven, my mom took her last beating from my father. He had beaten her so badly that she had to be admitted to the hospital. She had a broken nose, black eyes, and two broken ribs that had punctured her lung. She couldn't keep my father's violence a secret any longer. Both my dad's family and her family were shocked when they saw her. They couldn't believe their eyes. All this time they had thought that their children had a wonderful marriage, but now my mom had nearly died because of what my dad had done to her. It was as if a spell had been broken and she had been released from her duty of inventing excuses and pretending that everything was fine. After that she only wanted her nightmare to end. She filed for divorce.

Like the couple in this story, dysfunctional couples experience frequent and severe disturbances at home. They typically start out their marriage as high-risk or mismatched couples and then deteriorate over time into complete dysfunction, marked by volatility, emotional and physical abuse, alcoholism, and other addictions. These dysfunctional couples have the poorest coping skills, and under stress—which is typically related to men's work, substance abuse, or money problems—their dysfunction escalates into self-destruction. More and more they lose touch with reality. Like Brittany's parents, dysfunctional couples carry on their carnage year after year and stop only after a complete breakdown.

Sitting on a Volcano
Emotional volatility is the common denominator in dysfunctional families. Although their interactions are marked by destructive behaviors, things are not necessarily bad at all times. Some students said that their parents had some wonderful years before the terrible years began. Others, like the following student, saw their parents fluctuate between great highs and desperate lows.

Amanthi Chandra

As in all dysfunctional relationships, our family interactions weren't all bad. They followed a pattern of being really great when things were good and really terrible when things were bad. We especially liked to travel as a family, and our trips were filled with laughter and fun. I remember seeing my parents hug and kiss. There were times when they seemed very happy. But then there were the fights; they would scream and say horrible things to each other. When my parents fought there was no place in the house that felt safe.

The screaming, the insults, the hostility, and the fits of rage become a "normal" part of family life in these dysfunctional families.

Traccy Sanchez

My parents fought most of the time, but, according to my mom, when they got along, it was "wonderful." She felt the fighting was normal, because she came from a very dysfunctional family where fighting was the norm because of her alcoholic, abusive father. I remember my mother tearing up their room and throwing my dad's clothes on the lawn and turning the hose on them during a fight and then, a couple of hours later, she was in the kitchen making dinner.

To trigger a change and finally break away from their cycle of dysfunction often takes a serious crisis that exceeds every prior turmoil. Often, such a crisis is precipitated by escalating violence, alcohol abuse, or infidelity, and sometimes—when parents are deeply entrenched in their dysfunction—one of the children will take it upon himself or herself to set off the crisis. Typically the child will unconsciously act out the family turmoil, thereby becoming the family's "identified patient."

Julia Garcia

We lived a typical middle-class lifestyle—kids in baseball and soccer leagues, summer vacations and holidays with the family. But over time, things changed. My father started to suffer from anxiety attacks, supposedly the result of work stress. On two occasions he had anxiety-induced chest pains so severe that he was rushed to the emergency room. My mom, too, had to be taken to the emergency room with a spastic colon and bladder condition that her doctor attributed to stress. At the same time, my brother started getting into trouble at school. He was cutting school and picking fights with everyone. At first, everyone thought it was just teenage rebellion. But eventually my brother was expelled from school for physically threatening the principal. The fights between my father and brother also increased. My brother was so full of rage that he literally could not control himself; at one point he held a knife to my father's throat. With the escalating violence, my parents decided that we could no longer live under the same roof with my brother. They bought a trailer, and my brother lived in the trailer in our driveway. Eventually his problems at school and at home took us into counseling. The focus was on my brother, but it soon became clear that our family's problems were by no means limited to my brother's behavior, and my parents also became involved in the therapy. The stress with my brother brought their problems to the surface and underscored their miserable communication. For the first time they were able to talk about their "marathon fights," in which they would literally stay up all night yelling and crying, accomplishing nothing, only to start a new day and face the mounting tension and problems.

Unlike "perfect couples," who try to avoid open disagreements, dysfunctional couples have little control over their emotions and often unleash their tantrums in front of the children.

Susan McDevitt

My father is very intimidating and used to getting his own way. We were all scared of him. He has a very bad temper and we knew to stay out of his way when he was in a bad mood. The trouble was we never knew when he would blow up. One moment he would be kind and loving, and the next moment he would fly into a rage, screaming at us so much that he would spit and the veins on his neck would pop out. At dinnertime, I would just keep staring at my plate so I wouldn't set him off. I never knew what would trigger his rage—it happened with the slightest provocation.

Adults Acting Like Kids

Maybe the most shocking realization derived from our student's stories was the extent to which dysfunctional parents get out of control. Characteristics that one attributes to parents, like maturity, self-control, insight, kindness, and consideration, evaporate. Instead these parents throw temper-tantrums like toddlers, acting as egocentric as preschoolers, and rebelling against anything and everything like teenagers. But while children's fits pass as they advance in their development, dysfunctional couples continue their childish behavior, with all its irrationality and absurdity, until the final breakdown. Some couples engage in utterly erratic and bizarre behaviors, and sometimes even criminal behavior.

Scott Mallard

My mother admits that she had an infidelity problem in her marriage. "At first, this guy was just a friend," she said, "but your dad didn't want him around. He was constantly accusing me of sleeping with him. So eventually I did. We would hang out in the afternoons doing drugs." When my father found out about my mom's affair, he told her that he was going to go out and have affairs of his own. She figured that it was what she deserved, but she thought that he would come around if she waited. He didn't, and she panicked. She begged him to come back, but that only pushed him further away. She even took a razor and slashed her wrist, not to kill herself, but as an attempt to get my father to realize that she really needed him. The fight that ended the marriage was when she flushed her two-carat diamond wedding ring down the toilet. After she did that my father was so enraged that she thought he was going to kill her. Instead he grabbed his shotgun and went out and shot the cat. I was on the porch when he came out with the rifle in his hand; he took aim at the cat and just shot her. Our cat had been pregnant and I kept stammering "The babies ... she's having babies ... what about her babies."

Are these parents crazy or just out of control, helpless, unstable adults? One of our students astutely describes the challenges of coping with parenting while being an unhappy person.

Stephanie Conaway
Until we become parents ourselves, we never really grasp how hard it is to be a parent and only then do we begin to understand our own mothers and fathers. As children, it is difficult to see our parents outside of their roles as parents, to see them as individuals with weaknesses and imperfections. As children, we hope that our parents will remain the people we can count on, in spite of any problems they might have. We look to our parents for protection, guidance, and care. Even as teenagers, when we rebel against Mom and Dad, we still want them to be there for us. But sooner or later we realize that our parents are not perfect and that they cannot be all the things we need them to be all of the time. After we grow up, we finally begin to realize how difficult it is to juggle the roles of being a parent and a spouse at the same time—especially when as a person and as a spouse we are desperately unhappy.

This student continues to talk about the toll children pay when their parents just cannot function normally.

My parents were not very happy. In fact, during the twenty-eight years that they were married, I can count on both hands the number of times they were happy. Instead of happiness, our home was filled with resentment, regret, and, at times, pure hatred. My father provided us with food, clothes, and shelter but little love or understanding. At times, he would flat out tell us to leave him alone and that if we had any problems, we should just shut up and deal with them on our own. My mother gave us attention and even tried to compensate for what our father did not give, but she demanded a lot in return, and I ended up fearing her more than my father. She had become a very depressed and angry woman, from all the years of being so unhappy in her marriage. When she was depressed, she would become sick for days; sometimes she would not even get dressed. Then my father would get angry, because she was neglecting the house and the business. His anger would feed her cycle of depression. She became increasingly demanding of my support and help to keep the household running. If I was not fulfilling these tasks to her satisfaction, I would get yelled at and beaten. When she became angry, I was terrified about how far she would go. Although my mind now understands better what caused her behavior, my heart still cannot understand why she treated me the way she did.

Although this student's parents were adults, they behaved more like irresponsible, confused children, which had dramatic consequences for their own and their children's lives. Trapped in their own misery, their commitment to their children takes a back seat. Dysfunctional couples are preoccupied with their own needs and emotions and stumble from one extreme action and one poor decision to another, leaving little energy to attend to their children's needs.

Abusing Alcohol and Drugs

One common symptom of family dysfunction is alcohol and drug abuse—especially among men. In approximately 40 percent of our student's stories substance abuse contributed to the parents' divorce.

Brad Dawson

My parents engaged in activities that many people would see as inappropriate for parents. Smoking marijuana use was one of these activities. Lots of times when we came home from school and tried to talk to them about our day, they were so stoned they couldn't listen.

Alex Peterson

I blame my parents' divorce on my father's drinking. My dad was always having a beer with his buddies, or sitting at home drinking by himself. He had learned from his own father how to escape behind the bottle instead of facing reality. Even after one drink, I could always notice the transformation. Dad was no longer warm and funny. He turned quiet and moody, clutching that damn silver can with the blue bull on the front. He was dejected and hopeless, weak and frail.

Ginny Rook

As my father's alcohol abuse got worse, he became more and more neglectful. A typical night would start with what my mother referred to as the phone game: my father would call from the bar; my mother would ask, "When are you coming home?" and my father would answer, "I'll be home in an hour." But he never came home in an hour; sometimes it was three hours, sometimes six hours, and one time it was 48 hours. My mother was crying one minute and wishing he was dead the next. When he did come home, my father would rarely remember how he got there, where he had been, or who he'd been with.

He would verbally abuse my mother, who would either be cleaning up after him (because he had gotten sick), or serving him dinner. My mother attempted to solve their marital problems through counseling and attending AA meetings. But after many failed attempts to salvage the relationship, she gave up.

The abuse of alcohol threatens every facet of a couple's relationship including their communication, their sexual relations, their mood and behavior, their trust in each other, and daily family life. It exacerbates existing problems and creates new ones.

Traci Jones

Often, my dad's drinking led to terrible outbursts. When he came home drunk, my mom would be upset and angry and he would try to smooth talk his way out of the situation. But the more my mom resisted, the angrier he would get. We were lucky when he just threw up and passed out. When he stayed awake he would show a very ugly side. He would slam doors hard enough to put a hole in the wall. He would throw shoes out windows and ashtrays at the walls. A few times he even got physically violent with my mom. I remember one time when my mom and dad were arguing and my dad was drunk and screaming, he knocked over my fish bowl with a sweep of his hand. I was crying and my mom was telling him to stop and was trying to comfort me, but he just went on screaming. Eventually, my mom learned to pretend to be asleep when he got home so he would not lose his temper.

Kelsi Nogawa

When I think of my childhood, my mind flashes to a time full of madness, as our family crumbled right before my eyes. My father was seldom around, but when he was, he did nothing but flush down his stress with alcohol and yell at my mother. He would call her names and become physically violent. One time, I came into the room when he was hitting Mom. He saw me, and in a flash he was gone. He ran to the local bar and got drunk. On the freeway coming home, he miscalculated the space between the road and the off-ramp, took a detour down a hill and crashed into a brick wall. He survived—but barely.

As people keep caving in to their weaknesses and as frustrations rise on both sides, there is always the potential for additional damage. Automobile accidents are one such "side-effect" of alcohol abuse. Other consequences include deteriorating health, depression, and job loss. One of the most common and probably most tragic outcomes is emotional and physical abuse of the spouse and the children.

Lisa Brock

My mom was twenty-two years old when she married my father. She was studying to become a nurse, and my father had plans to become a veterinarian. He owned a pet shop, where they both worked. Things were going wonderfully for them, until my dad started drinking. Actually, he had always had a drinking problem; he just did a superb job of hiding it. The drinking started out as no big deal. It was just a few drinks at night. But this gradually turned into drinks for breakfast, snack, lunch, dinner, and dessert. Drinking became his most important priority. When my mom got pregnant, she separated from my dad. She was trying to convince herself that she would be better off without him when she had the baby. Just as she was almost convinced, he came knocking at her door, begging her to let him back into her life. Mom was young and scared and uncertain about what would be the best for the baby. She agreed to move back in with him. Things were all right for a few weeks, and then he started drinking again. When I was born, my father wasn't even there. He was in a bar. Soon after my birth, my dad developed a temper when he was drunk. He threw things at my mom. Several times he hit her. She was scared to death, not only for herself, but for me too, her brand new baby girl. Mom stayed away when my dad was drinking and protected me the best way she knew how. My dad's big plans to become a veterinarian became a thing of the past and his life gradually slipped through his fingers. When mom initiated the divorce, my dad became very upset. He gave her a huge guilt trip, asking her how she could walk out on him and take "his" child. Mom told him it was his drinking. He told her that she was the one who "made" him start drinking.

In addition to alcoholism, other addictions, too, can damage a marriage irreparably. Twelve percent of our students reported that their parents struggled with addictions to drugs or gambling. Another, more unusual addiction was thrill-seeking. The need to experience states of high psychological arousal associated with unusual thrills or danger leads some families on the path to destruction. Regardless of the type of addiction, the transgressions that accompany them do not permit healthy spousal relationships and family stability.

Pete Chu

When they were dating, my father treated my mom like a queen. He was a "true gentleman." He listened to her thoughts and laughed at her jokes. He would walk through a thunderstorm just to see her. After they got married, their relationship was still excellent. My father still thought my mom was the queen of his life. Although he would spend many hours at work in his chemistry lab, he would always come home to spend time with her. Having children made their dream complete. But when I was about nine, strange things began to happen. Strange men began to come around our house late at night. They looked like the Mafia, my mom said. My dad assured her that these men were just interested in his experiments.

One night, after attending a dinner reception for my dad's company, my parents were followed by several men. The men stopped them in the restaurant's parking lot and took them to an alley where they beat my father senseless and would have raped my mother had the restaurant's security guards not stopped them. Afterwards, my father reassured my mom again that everything was going to be all right. The following Saturday, my father didn't make it home. He was lying in the emergency room, shot three times. When Dad got better, he finally admitted that he was involved in making cocaine. He owed money to a drug ring. My mother was stunned. Was this the same man she had married? My dad promised he would change. To start afresh, they moved to a new state. My father was home more often and spent time playing with us and having romantic nights with my mom. Then it happened again. Within months of moving, my father was convicted and sentenced to prison for manufacturing cocaine. My mother couldn't believe it. She realized that she could no longer live with my father. He was endangering not only his life but also hers and ours. Today my father still wanders from one relationship to another and from one failed business venture to another. In between, he keeps himself busy with rock climbing and sky diving. He always tells me that he "feeds off the dangers in life." He loves the adrenaline rush, the thunderous pounding of his heart, and the thrill of overcoming his fear.

Maybe one of the most vexing aspects of life is that things are not black and white. People are not only good or bad and few situations are clear-cut. This father was in many ways a good man, devoted to his wife and family, but he was not able to tame his thrill seeking, and despite a full understanding of the dangers of his behavior and his promises to change he continued to endanger himself and his family. How can an intelligent person with many positive qualities at the same time behave so deviously? Discrepancies in human nature have puzzled mankind for eons. There is the potential in all humans to have their dark side emerge and dominate their actions, and indeed, most people have moments in which those forces slip out and take charge. Fortunately, most can rein in their dark forces and manage to regain control of our lives. Dysfunctional couples, however, lose the battle with their dark side more often.

Family Violence

The most common and salient symptom of dysfunctional couples is violence. Frequently it is the consequence of alcohol abuse, but it also occurs without it. There are families who fight violently and constantly—verbally and physically. Psychologists who work with violent families report that violence within the family results from a need to control. Most commonly we see husbands using violence to assert their control over their wives. The following story portrays a typical scenario where violence became the husband's last trump card when he felt otherwise unable to control his wife.

June Kim

When I was in my sophomore year in high school, my mother was given an opportunity to begin a career. A business acquaintance of my father's wanted to start a computer manufacturing company in Korea with my parents' financial backing and the clout my father's name had in the computer industry. My father turned down the proposal, but my mother saw it as her chance to start a career now that her children were in high school. She invested her own money and, when the business took off, my father started to flip out. He screamed at her for using "his money," and "What the hell do you know about computers? You don't even know how to turn one on." The arguing and the fighting continued for months. But my mother finally had a project of her own and it was evident that it was good for her. The years of my father's domination and "keeping her in her place" were giving way to a new Mom. She gained a lot of self-esteem and self-respect. She went on a diet and went from a size 10 to a size 6. I was proud of her because she looked good and felt good. I respected her for overcoming the obstacles my father threw her way. I also came to see my father as the enemy. I realized that he was a misogynist and hypocrite. He would tell me that it was important in this day and age for a woman to have a career and that he believed that women could do just as well as men in almost everything and sometimes even better, yet these beliefs did not extend to his own wife, because it was her job to be his housekeeper.

My mother's company did well; it was even profiled in a major Korean publication. Seeing this, my father agreed to support the company. But as always with my father, there were strings attached. He demanded a consulting fee for any advice, got a percentage of the profits, and required the company to buy computer parts only through him. This had the effect of raising prices higher than what my mom could have gotten in the open market. Although my father fully realized what was happening, he would not release my mother from their contract and even threatened her with a lawsuit. He only got off my mother's case after her company declared bankruptcy. Nobody understood why my father did what he did, because it was detrimental even to him, as "his money" was wrapped up in it. I think he just couldn't stand to see my mom doing well and he felt threatened because she was on his turf. There was only room for one person to be the computer whiz and he was it.

After Mom's business failed, things went down hill. My parents fought all the time and their arguments lasted for days. It was hard to believe they were husband and wife. And then the fateful last fight happened. My father could not stand it that my mother was withdrawing from him more and more, and in yet another argument he threw her against the wall and slapped her until she fell to the ground. Then he kicked her and screamed

that he was going to kill her. He only stopped when my
brother came running into the room and pulled him off
my mom.

Violence erupts when other ways of controlling the spouse
are perceived as insufficient. Even very violent families start
out hopeful and, at least for some period of time, they appear
to live a normal family life.

Samantha Sandman

My father was the youngest "up-and-coming
executive" at Goodyear, and within a year after my parents'
marriage, he was given a big promotion. But with this
new promotion came managerial meetings and lunches
in which the "boys" got together for drinks. Then the
lunches turned into dinners and the beers turned into
bourbon. Three years and several promotions later, my
father was starting to spike his coffee with hard alcohol.
Soon, he did not even hide the alcohol in coffee, but
blatantly drank all the time. Along with the increase in
drinking, my father became physically violent. Ever since
he started drinking, he had been emotionally abusive, but
now he physically abused my mother. During one fight,
she tried to hit him back. In return, he broke her right
hand. After another physical assault, my mother suffered
a miscarriage. It was at this time that my mother and
Goodyear realized that my father needed professional
help, and they sent him to alcohol rehabilitation. My
father completed the program, but this did not stop his
drinking or decrease his acts of violence. Eventually he
was fired from his job, and, much later, he was fired from
his family.

Christy Klein

I lived with my parents and my brothers, Max and
Bobby, in a warm and large home in the suburbs of
Chicago. I remember wading in the backyard swimming

pool, and I remember my father telling us stories of his childhood. Of course we owned a parakeet, "Tweet-Tweet," and a black Labrador dog, "Licorice." Both my parents worked hard and were successful. My father was a Certified Public Accountant, who commuted downtown each day. My mother worked hard to provide us with the ideal home life. She cooked and cleaned like Betty Crocker and entertained us day in and day out. She was my Brownie and Girl Scout leader and a classroom volunteer at my school. Both of my parents participated in setting up block parties that the entire neighborhood attended. I have only pleasant memories of those early years

But by the time I started school, dinner at our house had turned into a battle zone. My parents would disagree about something and this would escalate into a screaming match. At times my father would yell so loud that his veins would distend and his face would become fiery red, and there were times when he would throw and break things. If my brothers or I made the smallest comment about the food or if we started to bicker, it was a sure thing that my father would start beating one of us. The screech that his chair made as he forcefully pushed it back to get at us is vivid in my memory. I cannot say how long the kicking, slapping and hitting would last, but I am sure that it lasted as long as his rage did. The rest of the family would sit in silence until my dad's fury was released. I would just gaze into my bowl and not look at anybody.

Eventually, on any given day of the week, under any circumstances, my parents would argue, and if my brothers or I were around we would inevitably end up getting a beating from my father in the course of his tantrums. Sometimes my mother was the target of my father's fury. Twice, that I know of, he tried to kill her. Both incidents occurred while we were driving in the car. The first time, my dad was on the expressway driving us home late one night, and as usual, a disagreement arose.

My father started screaming at my mother, and I looked the other way and tried to block it out. When I looked up again, I saw my dad's hands on the steering wheel, shaking it so hard I thought it would fall out. I was so scared that we'd have no steering wheel and that we'd crash and my mother would die. I just shut my eyes hard and hoped to get home alive. The second time was a Sunday, our usual family day, as we were driving to K-Mart. As always, my parents started arguing. When we reached the K-Mart parking lot, my dad ordered my mom out of the car. At first, she wouldn't get out, but I think she recognized the seriousness of my father's command and feared the consequences if she disobeyed him. She finally got out of the car and started walking through the parking lot towards the store. My dad was yelling at us about what a terrible person my mother was and that he was going to kill her. I was so frightened. I wanted to close my eyes and make all this go away, but this time I kept my eyes open. My dad accelerated and drove towards my mother. When he got directly behind her, she jumped onto the concrete divider in the road, and my father sped past her. After this, life at our house got progressively worse. I used to wonder why my mother couldn't or wouldn't defend herself. I wondered why she didn't stand up for herself or leave my father.

Violent behavior always has a way of escalating. What started as a slap across the face soon turns into a full-blown beating. Sometimes, as in the previous story, the children were beaten as well as the wife. Sometimes, as in the following story, the abuse shifted to the children only later.

Paul Woo

Managing a motel 24-hours a day, seven days a week, took its toll on my father, and he started abusing my sister and me. My mom often had to endure seeing us beaten. Having been abused herself for many years, she didn't dare speak up. She rationalized that it was just the circumstances and hoped that one day their hard work would pay off and they would have a good life. On the eve of my parents' fifteenth wedding anniversary, my father hit my sister so hard that she was bleeding massively from a head wound. At this point, my mother tried to stop him. But he hit her so hard that she fell down. I remember seeing blood everywhere.

Dysfunctional Personalities

The most common conditions leading to family dysfunction are a high-risk marriage, stressful circumstances, poor coping skills in both parents, and self-centered, controlling, or aggressive personalities. In the family described by following student, the father's selfishness, in combination with a stressful environment, led to dysfunction.

Denise Leblanc

Within a few years after I was born, my father started to find married life boring. He craved excitement. His work as a police officer was very stressful, but it was exciting. He told me, "In that job there was never a dull moment. Gunshots would go off at night that would get your adrenaline pumping. After work you want to wind down with your buddies. It was a real drag to get off work and go home to a house where everyone was sleeping." He began to go to bars and nightclubs after the late shift. "Going to clubs was a chance to have fun. My needs were not being met at home, so I looked to other places for entertainment." He complained that my mother was not supportive of his needs and believed, therefore, that he had a right to go out at night after work. It was fun to be out with friends, and the women at the bars just wanted to have fun like him. He had a series of one-night stands. When my mother demanded a divorce, he protested. In his opinion, they did not have a serious problem. After he got a woman pregnant, my mother filed for divorce. He was outraged. He thought she was having an affair and wanted to beat the guy up. He tapped her phone and followed her when she went out. Although the legal divorce was granted quickly, my father has dragged on his harassment of my mom to this day.

This father's needs for entertainment and stimulation determined his actions within the marriage. When he got bored, he became promiscuous. With his selfish personality, he saw nothing wrong with his actions; to him, they were just a result of his wife's failure to keep him adequately entertained. His singular focus on his own needs and his impulsiveness made him profoundly unresponsive to his wife's feelings and needs. When he wanted gratification, he got it. He continued to cheat regardless of the pain he was inflicting. When his wife finally had had enough, he was furious and harassed her. He could not see how his actions—his years of cheating, betrayal, and unresponsiveness—led to her decision. His only focus was his own needs and a divorce did not fit his needs.

In the next story, too, the father was completely self-centered. But he displayed additional characteristics that we found among the dysfunctional couples.

Roxie Levine

My dad wasn't making enough money, and my parents had a lot of financial difficulties, so, when I was ten, we moved to Israel. My dad bought a Ticketron franchise and made a lot of money. But that didn't solve the family problems. My parents were always fighting. Most people in Israel live in apartments so they are close to their neighbors, and I felt always embarrassed about my father screaming so loud. Many of their fights were about my dad's compulsive gambling. My mom always let him play cards, and when he would win and bring home some money, she would be happy because he was happy. When he lost, though, they would fight. His solution was to play behind her back so she never knew if he won or lost.

After five years of living in Israel my father wanted to return to the States. He hated life in Israel. He didn't care that my mom, my sisters, and I didn't want to leave; but we left. I remember on our way back to the U.S. we stopped in Paris for a few days. As usual, my parents got in to a huge fight. We were all tired, but my father wanted to go out. He ended up screaming and throwing things at my mom. I was terribly worried that someone from the hotel would come and kick us out.

From the minute we arrived in California, we all had a hard time adjusting. My father had sold everything we owned in Israel, so we had to start from scratch. But instead of going out and finding a job, he watched television all day long. The money he made in Israel was running out. We started borrowing money from my mother's parents and friends. My mother couldn't stand it anymore, so she found a job as a receptionist for five dollars an hour. My father kept doing nothing but sleeping and playing cards. He would go out at night and come home very late and sleep on the couch. My parents were both depressed. My father got in a car accident and that made things worse. When Mom and Dad tried to talk about things, it always ended up in a huge fight. My father would scream and lock my mother in their room. We never knew what exactly was going on in that room behind the locked door. We were scared and often wanted to call the police—but we never did.

Today, although they are divorced, my parents still fight. My father won't leave my mom alone. He gets in fights with my sisters and me and blames it on my mother. He thinks that she says bad things behind his back. He lived with a friend for a while, but he got kicked out because he kept picking fights. He dabbled at various jobs, like being a realtor and a car dealer, but he never stays at a job long because he always ends up fighting with the people at work. He thinks that he is treated unfairly; he wants to jump from being a salesperson to a manager within a week. He still gambles.

This father's impulsiveness is reflected in his gambling, his erratic work life, and his volatile reactions to his family members. Like all dysfunctional people he is quick to lose control, quick to get angry, and consistently feeling sorry for himself when things went bad. Typical, too, is the tendency to deflect responsibility for his actions and instead blame somebody else. This father had a life-long habit of blaming others—his wife, his boss, co-workers, and friends—for things that did not go right in his life. The outcome of such egocentrism, impulsiveness, and irresponsibility was a highly stressful and unstable life that eventually led to the demise of his family.

Spouses with sociopathic tendencies present an even more extreme version of personality problems. These individuals take the personality problems we have described a notch higher. The problems resulting from selfishness, irresponsibility, and impulsiveness are amplified by the sociopath's inflated sense of self-worth, complete emotional unresponsiveness, poor judgment, deceitfulness, and callousness. Sociopaths have a genuine lack of feelings of love or loyalty for any person—even their own spouse or child. They do not hesitate to engage in antisocial and even criminal behaviors if they think these might be of advantage to them. Unthinking impulsiveness turns into recklessness that is conscious and calculating. While most dysfunctional parents act irresponsibly in states of crisis, sociopaths act irresponsible and impulsive in cold blood. They have no concern for the harm they do to others. The only thing that matters is gratifying their own needs.

Andrew Fernald

As a hobby, my father collected, restored, and raced classic cars. This hobby provided access to "the upper crust" of society, and my dad was well known among the members of the car clubs. He had charisma, and perhaps that is how he made so many friends. He is also very manipulative and uses his charm to get what he wants. My mother, on the other hand, is quite reserved. She is also more careful with the finances, which my father never considered. If my father liked something, he impulsively bought it and left it up to my mother to figure out a way to cover the check. For a while they lived the good life—a huge home, a Mercedes, a Cadillac, two children, and a live-in housekeeper. It was all a facade. It looked good, but the reality was different. Their problems stemmed from the fact that my father is a compulsive gambler. I am not speaking of a trip to Las Vegas once in a while; I am referring to a habit that cost thousands of dollars each week.

My mom thought that if she became the perfect wife, my father would change. Her constant striving for perfection led to anorexia nervosa. Her weight dropped to 80 pounds. She developed ulcerative colitis and became deathly ill. She begged my father to take her to a doctor. He refused, claiming that she was just fine. After several refused requests for help, she drove herself to the doctor. When she arrived, she collapsed on the floor; she had lost about five pints of blood due to internal hemorrhaging. The doctor phoned in a code blue, then he called my father and told him that my mom was not going to live and that he should make funeral arrangements. Knowing this, my father took steps to cash in my mother's life insurance policy, planning to use this money to pay off his debts. He contacted the insurance company to arrange the pay out. He rushed to the hospital and had her sign several legal documents, which stated that she was involved in his financial dealings.

Luckily, my mother survived and gradually built up her strength—emotionally and physically. She got into therapy to make herself better. My father initially went along, at her urging, but then he quit. He got annoyed with the therapist who had suggested that he take responsibility for his behavior. When my mom asked for a divorce, my father was shocked; divorce had never been in his mind.

The divorce took place, and a year passed. Mom was feeling better. Then her world tumbled down again. Among the legal documents she had signed in the hospital were several business deals that had crashed and now she discovered that she owed a great deal of money. Her creditors filed several court cases against her, and for some time she lived with the constant fear that she would go to jail. She ended up filing for bankruptcy—but not soon enough. Two months later, she was served with an eviction notice by a local sheriff, because my father had failed to pay rent on our house for about five months. These occurrences were extremely stressful, and I was terrified that my mom would get sick again and die. The whole time my father witnessed my mother's misery and did nothing to help her. He kept acting as if he were heartbroken because my mom had torn the family apart and taken his children away from him. He says that we are his pride and joy and that he lives for us. It is so easy to believe his words—everything he says sounds so heartfelt. But then you look at what he has done and nothing makes sense any more.

Life with an erratic spouse or parent is stressful, unpredictable, and unstable. Life with a sociopath can be downright dangerous. Their personality characteristics preclude the development of a healthy marriage and family life. They destroy any sense of security, support, and respect. What is left is complete dysfunction.

Personality flaws usually don't happen in just one spouse; people select mates whose weaknesses complement their own. For example, an aggressive and dominant man finds a passive wife whose personality permits the full manifestation of his hostile traits. In the long-lasting dysfunctional marriages, the obvious offender—typically the husband—is usually paired with a dependent, passive-aggressive spouse—typically the wife. The wife plays an important—albeit unconscious—role in maintaining the cycle of dysfunction. The couples have an interlocking set of pathologies and are quite adept at feeding off each other's weaknesses. In a strange way, these couples, in their dysfunction, depend on each other.

Mike Garcetti

My mother's parents were foster parents, and over the course of twenty years they took in more than 100 children. My mom grew up with four younger, adopted brothers, the oldest of whom was ten years younger than she. Thus my mom became a caregiver at an early age. When she met my dad at a youth group picnic, she knew right away that he had a lot of problems. He drank heavily and didn't have a "moral background." But she was attracted to him because he said he needed her and would change for her. He said he would go to church, stop drinking and settle down—and my mom believed him. She knew that, in the past, he had always acted as if he didn't need anyone. So when he finally broke down and admitted that he needed my mom, it really affected her. She had a strong need to be needed, and his promise to change made her feel as if she had special powers.

For a long time she didn't mind that he became pathologically possessive as soon as they started going out. She didn't mind that after they got married he expected her to sit with him and watch him while he did his homework for his night classes, not allowing her to talk. She didn't mind that he wanted her to go with him to get gas for the car or to get the car fixed. She didn't mind that he needed her even to do things with him that are normally done by oneself, like shaving. She liked the fact that he wanted her just to sit there and talk to him. It made her feel special to know that he needed her every second. She wanted to be there for him, and she thought he would appreciate her, respect her, and focus his life around her.

My father was very demanding. He wanted my mom to have dinner on the table when he walked in the door.

He made the rules, and my mom fell in line trying to make him happy. Of course nothing she did was ever enough. No matter what she made for dinner or how clean the house was he never showed any appreciation. He always found something else to yell about. My mom could tell what kind of mood he was in just by the way he slammed his car door when he got home.

Four years into their marriage my mom got pregnant with me. My dad had a good job, and my mom wanted to quit work so she could stay home with me. After I was born, she did quit her job, and, as a result, she became more dependent on my dad. She had no income, and she had to ask my father for everything. She also had to listen to him yell about every penny she spent—like for a can of hair spray! My mom and I were "costing" him, and he treated us like extra baggage. Every night, when I was young, he made my mom take me out of the living room because he wanted to watch TV without being disturbed. My dad had a negative attitude toward women in general and my mother in particular. He believed that women were not his equal and never could be. During my parents' marriage, all of their possessions were "his"— even though my mom was responsible for half the bills. She had her own checking account and had no access to his checking account, but my dad always made sure that she never had any money in her account. He even charged her $17.00 a month to use her electric blanket! My dad hated my mom's family, and when she wanted to visit them he would simply say that she couldn't go, and that was final. My dad also was jealous of my mom's relationship with me. She played with me, read to me, and took me to the park. We would get together with the neighbors and go places, but my dad always got mad about the "coffee club" as he called it. He made it very clear that he didn't even want to know the neighbors. They were not allowed to come over or call when he was home. My dad completely controlled my mom's activities. On Thursdays, she was allowed to play bingo at the Lodge, but she had to be home by 10:00 P.M. If she was even five minutes late, she got lectured about how unreliable she was and about all her other character flaws. My mom's friends warned her that giving in to my dad's power plays was only fueling the fire and warned her that he could become physically abusive. They didn't know the whole story and Mom didn't tell.

She tried to leave him on numerous occasions, but she couldn't support us financially and so she buckled under his threats. My dad made it very clear that it would be a cold day in hell before he paid any kind of support for either of us. She did file for divorce once, but she couldn't handle the pressure because she was scared. My dad threatened to try to get custody of me by pursuing an "unfit mother" case—which was utterly ridiculous—but she was scared and went back to him. In his few nicer moments he would say that he would try to make things better. But things just got worse. He couldn't control his possessiveness or anger. It was his way or no way. The name-calling was constant, and his language toward her was atrocious. He always called her a "bitch," and his favorite response to her was "f—-you." Over the years, my mom got tired of hearing what a lousy wife and mother she was when she knew that she was doing everything in her power to make him happy. Finally, she did get a divorce. Because of my dad's need to have complete control, he lost his family. He will never understand the joy of loving and caring. But now he does have total control—over his dogs.

This particularly poor match brought out the worst qualities in each person. Although the husband was the more obvious offender, the wife maintained his dysfunctional behaviors in less obvious ways, which played an important part in the ongoing cycle of dysfunction. Being needed and caring for the other person's problems has traditionally been a socially sanctioned way for women to exert control in a relationship.

Like this mother, many women accept an amazing range of problem behaviors in their men. Possessiveness, aggression, drinking, even abuse are tolerated in the belief that the woman will be able to change the man. The essence of this all too common behavior is epitomized in the story of "Beauty and the Beast." The woman gives herself to the beast believing that her love will transform him; and in the fairy tale it does. In real life, though, the beast does not change, and the woman ends up paying a high price for her "caring." Low self-esteem, humiliation, dependence, depression, and sometimes abuse become the price for trying to live the fairy tale.

Rooted in Dysfunction

Often, as for the mother described in the preceding story, one can find the roots of dysfunction in the adult's own family history.

Tracey Sanchez

My mother was a product of her alcoholic, abusive, and dysfunctional family. When she was ten years old, she found her father in bed with another woman. After that, she never trusted men again.

Sandi Rodriguez

I believe that my mother's emotional instability and manipulative behavior were the result of her fear of abandonment. Her father had died when she was ten and her brother died as a young man.

Elena Parker

My father was put into an orphanage right after his birth. During the first five years of his life, he received hardly any warmth and love. He wet his bed until age five because he was so afraid. At the age of five, my dad was adopted into a stable household, with two parents and two older brothers. Over time, he grew close to his family. However, he was forever marked by his early years in the orphanage.

Stephanie Lozano

My father was fighting an invisible enemy. His enemy was the inferiority he felt growing up Mexican-American. I know at one time in his childhood he had to sit in one part of the movie theater, separate from Whites. I think that he grew up thinking that he had to prove that he was somebody.

Past traumatic experiences can make us insecure in later life. People who experienced dysfunction or trauma in their childhoods often report that they are unduly concerned about maintaining control, have exaggerated expectations of themselves and others, are hesitant to become intimate with other people, are hypersensitive, and experience unpredictable mood swings. Outwardly, they may appear strong and confident. But when intimate relationships trigger their insecurities, an internal alarm goes off, and their behavior is less and less under conscious and rational control. For fear of being abandoned, betrayed or hurt again, they engage in behavior that fulfils their worst fears. Rather than asserting their expectations in an open and consistent manner, or leaving the relationship, they are in an alarm mode waiting for the spouse's next transgression—in order to react. Concern turns into accusation, hurt into aggression. Innocuous behaviors are perceived as evidence that the spouse is not loving and not committed. When, in response, the partner distances himself or herself, the initial assumption that relationships are dangerous is confirmed.

Helplessness may be the most powerful trigger that makes people overreact. Their despair makes them spin out of control. The fear of being hurt and of losing control in the relationship powerfully compels them to mobilize their defenses. Defenses turn into offenses. Fear of weakness urges men to assert their control—in dysfunctional ways. Their extreme actions in turn trigger a response from the partner that provides a momentary illusion of control. This sense of control, however, evaporates quickly. The aggressor is left with depression and the urge to find ever more dramatic behaviors to regain a sense of control. There is not much that can stop the person at this point from acting crazy; it is as if an inflammatory disease is eating away the person's sanity. People report that on a cognitive rational level they know that are behaving crazy and that they shouldn't be doing the things they are doing—yet they seem to be incapable to stop themselves. The dysfunction has become an addiction: "I know it is bad but I can't stop it."

Lasting Hell

Why do these dysfunctional marriages so often last for a long time? Our students' stories suggest that after people have made a commitment to a relationship, it becomes increasingly difficult for them to remove themselves. Several things happen. An unspoken social contract is formed between the two spouses. The initial acceptance of a partner's problems establishes a precedent. In new relationships initial missteps are often interpreted lightly because, after all, mistakes can happen to anyone, nobody is perfect, and we just don't want to believe that the behavior or remark is as bad as it appears. If the person accepts and supports the partner's problems the first time, however, it becomes more difficult to change gears thereafter—to change from approval to disapproval. Each further incidence of support and acceptance strengthens this silent contract. Second, the more invested one is in a relationship the more difficult it is to recognize that one's initial reactions were wrong, or that indeed, the whole relationship is wrong. After publicly committing themselves to a relationship, people have a strong need to maintain their stand, and the more invested they are, the more painful it is to accept any evidence that they were wrong. Prior investments or sacrifice would lose all meaning if the person abandoned his or her prior belief in the relationship, and the public commitment that the person made by marrying and having children would look like a failure. People realize that they voluntarily chose marriage and so they resolve their dilemma by thinking that the relationship is especially important and, therefore, worth their commitment and sacrifice. With less personal investment, it might be easier to admit that they were wrong. But given the deep investment in the relationship, it would be a blow to their ego and image to admit they made the wrong choice. So they stay a little longer. Better to be a supportive spouse than a sorry fool. Finally, dysfunctional couples stay together for all the reasons that battered wives stay with their batterers: implicit and explicit threats keep them together and undermine the ability of the weakened victims to leave.

Lessons to Be Learned

The life of dysfunctional couples is marked by frequent and severe disturbances that result from emotional volatility, poor coping skills, emotional and physical abuse, and addictions. These individuals are masters at creating their stresses and crises—money problems, problems at work, infidelity, substance abuse, and violence. They are so completely wrapped up in their self-destruction that they lose touch with reality. What lessons may be learned from their stories?

1. Get help early! There are three strong lessons here. The first is, don't wait; get help early. This chapter describes in painful detail the downward spiral of dysfunctional patterns of behavior into episodes of rage and violence. So be on alert. Don't comfort yourself with the mantra "this, too, will pass" when you or your spouse start behaving in ways that you would consider in others unacceptable. If things are bad today, they will not be better tomorrow. Watch for signs of emotional volatility. Do you or does your partner quickly and unpredictably lash out? Are there threats or verbal abuse? Are addictions affecting the relationship? It does not help if the addict or abuser feels tremendously sorry after an outburst. Without effective intervention, there will be another blow-up and another one after that ...each worse than the one before. So it is important to stop such behaviors at their first sign. At least talk to a trusted friend or family member. Even better see a marriage counselor. If your spouse is not willing to come along, see a counselor on your own. Find a substance abuse program for the addict, an anger management program for the person with the temper.

2. Get more help! The next lesson is that if the downward spiral continues, more help is needed. What seems obvious to an outside observer is often difficult for the insider, in the midst of the turmoil, to see. Being desperately unhappy and depressed, hurt and aggressive, or helpless and uncertain muddles the mind. If you or your spouse is completely losing it, it is time to get more help. Chances that you are going to repair the relationship on your own are extremely slim. You may think that you want to hold on to the relationship, that the violent rampage was an isolated incident and won't happen again, that it was all your fault and you will do better, that your spouse will change ... and that you will get the relationship back on track and be happy and healthy again without getting help. You would be the first! Getting help is nothing to be ashamed of. Losing it completely and hurting yourself, your children, and the relationship is.

3. Keep the children out of it. The third lesson is just as strong: parents must keep their children out of their violent scenes. Children can be scarred for life by witnessing these blow-ups. It is up to the parents to act like adults even when they want to yell and scream like children. Take it outside, guys! It is job of responsible parents to protect children from their marital outbursts. This doesn't mean putting on a happy façade when there are problems in the relationship;

it is important to discuss your differences and express your disagreements. But it's destructive and damaging to expose children to screaming, knockdown, drag-out fights. Just don't do it.

5

I Want You, I Want You Not: Breaking Up Is Hard to Do

Finally, after months or years of misery or discontent, the marriage disintegrates to the point that one or both spouses decide to separate. This is a traumatic and highly stressful experience for all concerned.

Kathy Lee

We were a middle-class family, enjoying the good life. My father owned his own business and several other properties. My mother was a housewife who sometimes helped out in the business. There did not appear to be any serious problems in my family. But I realized that I had been missing a lot when my mother shockingly and secretly left, four years ago.

My father's intentions were good. His main goal was to take care of his family. But, as the years passed, his work became his first priority, and we seldom saw him. Home was just where my brother and I went for dinner and money. All of us in the family were pretty much leading our own lives, doing our own thing, while our busy father poured out the money. My mother often complained about my father's work habits, but she didn't make a big deal of it. She also often asked me to go places with her, but I refused, preferring to spend my time with my friends. So my mother found other entertainment. The "other entertainment" she found was my father's best friend. My father had helped him learn the skills to become a locksmith, and he had gradually become close to our family, joining us for trips and dinners. He started giving my parents dancing lessons and trying to make a good impression on us all. He made my mom feel special and wanted. He took her on trips—using her money of course—giving her the adventure and attention she was not getting from my father. Then, in an effort to persuade my mother to leave my father, he arranged for my father to be seen with another woman.

In my last year of high school, I started to see the signs; my mother was beginning to change. She stopped making dinner for the family. She began going out almost every night looking beautiful. She would not come home for days, often without telling us where she was. Then came the attitude change: she would get angry at us, screaming over little things. She looked tense and stressed. There were fights with my dad, broken dishes, demands to know her whereabouts. But nothing could prepare us for the day when all her belongings disappeared.

It was too much for my father. His wife had left him for another man and the only explanation she would give him was that "he was working too much." My father was terribly depressed. He was not prepared for my mother's departure, let alone for being betrayed by his best friend. He could not understand what he had done wrong and what the other man had that he did not. He went through a period of anger and sadness and confusion. He said how much he hated my mother. He did not believe in divorce and was willing with all his might to work it out with my mother—even resorting to counseling, fortune-tellers, and begging. Many times he just wanted to quit his work, go crazy, or run away.

This student saw changes in her mother's behavior, but she didn't understand them, and she was taken by surprise at her mother's abrupt departure from the family. Her father, too, was shocked when his wife left and he reacted with intense depression, anger, and guilt. It is common for separation to come as a shock to one parent, because, often, the emotional processes leading up to the separation are private and personal rather than being discussed openly and together. It is also common for the parent who is "left" to be totally devastated. Invariably, people find the decision to separate difficult and painful—whether that decision is reached together or independently.

Deciding To Separate

Getting a divorce is not something that happens overnight. It is a long, drawn-out process that may involve ruminating, separating, reconciling, separating again, litigating and, often, relitigating. The first step for some unhappy couples, whether consciously or unconsciously, is to perform a "cost-benefit analysis" of the pros and cons of leaving the marriage. They consider the barriers to the divorce—religious vows, obligations to children, financial costs of divorce, social pressure to stay married, the stigma of being single, and so on—and they weigh the alternative attractions outside the marriage compared to the attractions of the marriage. This may not occur in a calm, rational manner. Only one of our students' stories suggested that her parents had come to a mutual decision, sitting down together, having a rational discussion, and deciding to break up after they had weighed the pros and cons of divorce.

Tiffani Leach

My mom explained that it was not an easy decision to separate, but they had talked it over during their anniversary weekend at a beautiful hotel, and then they waited until what they thought was the right time to tell us all.

More commonly, one spouse alone chooses to conduct a cost-benefit analysis.

Deanna Knowlson

From the beginning, my parents experienced numerous marital conflicts. These mostly revolved around their conflicting personalities and their inability or unwillingness to compromise. My father entertained the notion of divorce even in the first few years of their marriage. My mother never did, despite their disagreements. As the years went by, and the conflicts didn't lessen, my father began more and more to weigh the pros and cons of staying in the marriage. Sometimes he actually sat down with pencil and paper to list things out. Especially when he and my mom were experiencing intense conflict, he felt the desire to be "free." Eventually, he contacted a lawyer, without my mom's knowledge, to see what he needed to do to gain that freedom.

But even as this student's father was considering his options and calculating the costs, he experienced heart-wrenching ambivalence.

...His emotions were fluctuating from moment to moment. At one moment, he felt responsible for his family and guilty for wanting to leave. At other times, he was overwhelmed with unhappiness and feelings of disillusionment because of his tumultuous relationship with my mother.

More often than sitting down with a pencil and paper, people think about the possibility of terminating the marriage in a context of conflict, when things are bad. They then linger in a shaky marriage with divorce in the back of their mind, held together until an alternative attraction, such as a new love, enters the picture. We saw this in Kathy's story and in the following student's story.

Clarissa Cambridge

My mother was working as a flight attendant while my father attended law school and the racetrack full time. At first she was confused when she started receiving notices that her checking account was overdrawn and her checks were returned with a signature that wasn't hers. She finally traced it to my dad. She discovered that, unbeknownst to her, while she was working to earn the money to pay the bills, he was working to spend the money paying his bookies. These deceitful acts, as well as frequent nights when he didn't come home or came home late, made her begin to realize that her costs were outweighing her benefits—both literally and figuratively. With each dishonest act she trusted him less. Yet although my mom had a number of reasons to leave the marriage, it took another man to open up her eyes and get her to leave. He showed her the type of relationship she deserved and wanted. He was older and famous, and he swept her off her feet with gifts and fancy dinners. He showered her with attention and money—the two things that she was not getting from my dad. This new love helped my mom realize how unfair her marriage really was. At this point she knew in her heart that she wanted to get a divorce. She was leaving on a flight to Colorado for three days, and she told my dad that they could use the time apart to reevaluate their relationship. My dad did not show any emotion, and when she returned from Colorado and told him that she wanted a separation, he was shocked. He begged her to stay and give him another chance. But at this point she felt that separation was her only choice. She had been thinking about the pros and cons for months. The alternative attraction of her new "honey" and her dreams of a better, richer life outweighed the external

pressures to stay married. She and my dad had no shared
assets, no strong religious affiliations, and no pressure
from his family or hers to stay married. I was their only
child, and I was not enough to keep these two members
of the "me generation" together.

This is a perfect example of how an increasingly unhappy
and resentful spouse is fertile ground for a new relationship,
which then provides the impetus for a separation. Seldom do
both spouses reach the point of no return together. Usually,
whoever reaches the point first brings the other spouse in line
with the decision to divorce. This student's mother made the
decision and imposed it on her husband, ignoring his pleas.
In the next story, it was the father who wanted to leave, but
he stayed a while until his behavior led his wife to give in and
initiate a separation.

Gale Fisher

My dad was the one who made the decision to
separate. I think he just decided he would rather be single
than tied down with a family. My mom thought that the
marriage had been good, that she had been an excellent
wife and mother, and that they had a great family and
home together. She could not understand why my dad
wanted to leave. When he told her that he wanted to leave
immediately, she suggested that they stay together until
after Christmas, at least, for the sake of the children. By
the time Christmas was over, though, my mother realized
she might as well go along with the separation, because
my dad was never home anymore anyway. At that point,
she asked him to leave.

Usually, the unhappy spouse doesn't really want the
marriage to be over. He or she stays because of external or
internal barriers to divorce, hoping that the marriage will
improve. When it doesn't get better, he or she may, perhaps in
anger, threaten to divorce. This can provide the other spouse

with the escape hatch that she or he has been waiting for. This is what happened to the couple in the following story. The woman struggled to make the marriage work. But then, as a last resort, she threatened divorce—and the marriage blew up in her face.

Elizabeth Harrison

Two weeks after my brother was born, Mom had severe medical complications. The ambulance took her to the hospital. She almost died. When she called home to ask my dad to bring the baby to her, he was nowhere to be found. Later she found out that he was out playing music with his friends. She was deeply hurt. Mom said, "When I was so ill, I desperately needed him to be there for me but he didn't care enough about me to give up his buddies for one evening." As the months went by, Mom continued to have medical problems. It was difficult for her to care for my brother and me by herself because there was always the chance that she would faint at any moment. Her illness and the problems in her marriage made her extremely depressed. She wanted the marriage to work, because of her religious beliefs and because she had children, so she kept hoping and working on the relationship. But after a year of this, she became desperate. She threatened my dad with divorce. She really did not want a divorce, but at this point it seemed to be the only way to get my dad to try harder at the marriage. Her threats made no impression on him. Finally, in a fit of anger, she told him to leave. Then, with incredulity, she watched him calmly pack and leave—never to return to our family.

In this family, the mother was bewildered by her husband's willingness to go along with her suggestion that they separate. She did not know what had been going on inside his head as she struggled to survive in the marriage. As outside observers, we might infer that at the same time as the wife was suffering, her husband was thinking about ending the marriage himself, burdened by his wife's illness, depression, and demands.

Not surprisingly, if even the adults are unaware of the mental processes going on in their spouses' heads, their children find the events leading up to a separation bewildering. They don't see their parents thinking through the decision to separate. They are not privy to their ambivalent ruminations. They don't know what the parents are discussing behind closed doors. To them, the parent's behavior can be mysterious and irritating, as the next student described.

Melissa Shipman
        Months before my parents separated, my mother began acting strange. Several nights a week she would go shopping and not come home until eleven or twelve at night. I felt really weird about her not being in the house and I often got up late at night looking for her. In the morning, I would ask her where she was the night before, and she would tell me that she was out shopping because she needed time to think. Sometimes she said that she had sat in her car thinking for a couple of hours and lost track of time. But she never said what she was thinking about. I remember that this seemed very strange to me at the time. Pretty soon, her disappearing acts moved from the weekdays to the weekends. She would tell us that she was going up to Santa Barbara for the weekend to think. When she came back on Monday morning, she would be late driving me to school. It was not until months later that I found out that she had been struggling with the decision to leave my dad and that she had started seeing another man. Finally, she could not handle coming home and seeing my dad and my sister and me, so she moved out.

Violent Endings
What was not so mysterious to our students was that their parents fought...and fought...and fought...until that fighting

eventually impelled one of the spouses to demand a separation. The children saw their parents battling until finally one or the other parent worked up the courage to separate. They saw the escalation of violence until it reached a breaking point. There were many descriptions of final battles in which the wife eventually left a violent husband and brought down the curtain on a dysfunctional marriage like those described in the previous chapter.

Roxie Levine

The last fight, the one that made my mother decide to leave my father, was an argument that ended when my dad threw a barbecue at her. It hit her on the arm and left a scar. The coals were still hot and they burned her feet. She opened the balcony door so that the neighbors would hear her scream and call the police. She begged my dad to leave. She realized that if he didn't leave the house she would either have a nervous breakdown, kill herself, or be killed by him. She couldn't take it anymore; she wanted an end to this marriage. They fought all night, and in the morning he took his things and left the house.

Samantha Sandman

My mother sought help from her church minister to deal with my father's violence and abuse. Then an incident occurred that changed things for her. One night my father struck her on the head and she literally "saw stars" and passed out. She awakened when my five year old brother was wiping the blood off her face. It was at that moment that she realized she needed to get out of the marriage, not only for herself, but also for the sake of her children.

In these cases, it was not until the physical abuse had clearly become life threatening that the battered wives came to the realization that they had to separate from their husbands.

But not all wives wait for the abuse to escalate. Sometimes all it takes is a single slap and the woman is done with the marriage.

Susan McDevitt

I had watched my father berate my mother for years and years, but what finally precipitated the divorce was physical abuse. There was only one incident, but that was enough. We had all gone out to eat, and we stopped for gas on the way to the restaurant. My brother, who was sixteen, was pumping the gas, but he couldn't get the nozzle to work. When my mom tried to help him, my dad got upset and told the two of them to get in the car and he would do it himself. When they got to the restaurant, my father told my brother to go inside and wait because he wanted to talk to my mom for a minute. When my brother left, he yelled at my mom for trying to help my brother, because he thought she did everything for him. They got out of the car and walked toward the restaurant. My father was criticizing my mom, and when she tried to disagree with what he was saying, he hit her. That was the last straw. My mom was afraid that it would happen again, and that when it did, it would be worse. She took my brother and stayed at a friend's house for a week, and then she met with my dad at our pastor's house. She said that she wanted him to move out and that she wanted a divorce.

Sometimes the child saw that the marriage should end before the mother did.

Cecilia Gutierrez

For as long as I can remember, my father beat my mother. I remember one time when I was six years old. My dad came home drunk again, reeking of alcohol and barely able to walk. He opened the door, and when my mother saw him, she ran as fast as she could to the bedroom, with my brother and me running behind her and crying. My father threw my mother inside the closet and began to hit her. She was screaming and telling him to stop because she was pregnant. My brother and I tried to help her. I ran up to my father and started hitting him and my brother followed me, but my dad grabbed us and threw us to the floor. We sat in the corner hugging and crying. After that, I remember crying myself to sleep every night and praying to God that He would make my father disappear. But God never heard my prayers; in fact, I came to believe that He did not like me much. When my brother was born, he was mentally retarded as a result of my father beating my mother when she was pregnant. Eventually, by the time I was eleven or so, when my father came home drunk and began to hit my mother, I would call the police and report him. I told my mother to leave him, but she wouldn't, because he threatened to kill her if she did.

A Final Fling

The other thing that children see, along with violent conflict, is the "other woman" or "new man" that brings their parents to the brink of a separation. Our students' stories illustrated how one spouse would find out about the other spouse's infidelity and this would precipitate an insurmountable crisis ending in a separation. Often, however, the discovery of infidelity was just a final drop in the bucket. After years of trying to save the marriage, the discovery of infidelity makes it abruptly clear that there is nothing in the relationship worth saving.

Christy Klein

My mother made one last attempt to save their marriage. My father had been on a strict diet called the Cambridge diet, and my mother prepared a birthday celebration for him. She had a cake decorated to resemble the Cambridge canisters. We all waited by the cake until my dad arrived home that evening. The cake looked almost identical to the cans and we were sure my father would love it. Finally, my dad walked in. We wished him Happy Birthday, and he calmly ate cake with us. He seemed to appreciate the effort, because he remained calm that evening. Later that night, though, my mom discovered that he had had sex with another woman just before he came home for his birthday cake. This realization finally gave my mom the incentive she needed to ask my father for a divorce.

Spouses sometimes can forgive a one-time transgression, but not repeated affairs or a "meaningful relationship."

Connie Phillips

We discovered the first sign of my father's infidelity when the four of us were going to the drug store. My mother pulled down the sun visor to put on her lipstick, and there it was—a kiss mark in red lipstick on the mirror with the words "I love you" written next to it. Every one was shocked. We asked our parents what it was about, and my mother angrily replied, "Your daddy's got a girlfriend," to which my sister exclaimed, "Daddy, you can't have a girlfriend. You're married!" My father tried to explain it away. He said that it was just a joke and that he had to take an employee somewhere in his car and she left it there. And with that, the whole incident was dropped.

A few months later though, my mom discovered charges on their credit card bill for a motel near my father's work. That night, she confronted my father. This time my father admitted that he had a lover, his secretary—but he said it was over and it would never happen again. My mother, wanting to believe my father to save her marriage, decided to forgive him.

But it did not stop there. A couple of months later, my father went on a business trip. When he came back, he gave my mother a gift. It was a bottle of perfume and a card that said "I miss you when I'm away." My mother thought it was very sweet, but when he gave it to her it was still in the bag with the receipt. The receipt showed charges for two cards and two bottles of perfume. She knew what that meant. My mother got angry and told my father that at least he could have been a little more original than to give his wife and his lover the same card and the same perfume.

Incidents like these went on for about a year, but finally my mother had enough. My father had been away on a business trip for the weekend and when he came back my mom sent him to the grocery store to get some things for dinner. While he was gone, she went out to the car and looked around. In the back seat she found a bag, and when she opened it, she found sex toys and lingerie, and a bottle of the same perfume my father had given her after the previous business trip. My mother went into the house and packed a bag for my dad. When he got home, my mother told him to go to his lover's house—and he did.

In this story, the wife was unable to tolerate her husband's continued affair. This theme showed up repeatedly in our students' stories. In the following case, as well, the wife could not tolerate a persistent, pervasive affair after she had found out about it and the husband had promised it was "over." But who could forgive the most blatant transgression—catching the spouse in the crime?

Lindsay Schoonhoven
My parents' marriage lasted twelve years. In their twelfth year, my dad had an affair. When Mom filed for divorce, he said he was going to stop seeing Betty and that he wanted his family together again. He wanted to repair the marriage and asked my mom to go to marriage counseling. But secretly he continued to date Betty. Then

one day, my mom walked in on my dad in bed with Betty. That was the end.

In the next case, the coup de gras was that the husband actually moved the "other woman" into the family home and told his wife that his girlfriend was the "boss" now. This would cause trouble even in a harem; in our society, it is intolerable.

Jennifer Weinstein

When my father's long-time secretary retired, he hired a new administrative assistant. He had been having financial problems with his law practice, and this woman was a good influence on him. She got him to start buckling down, working harder, and returning clients' calls. He started working late at night with her. Then one day he moved her in with our family, because "she had such a long drive from her house to the office and was working such long hours." My brothers and I hated her. My mother suspected that she and my father were having an affair, but she couldn't prove it. The last straw came when my dad told my mom that this woman was now the head of our family. Mom said there was no way she was going to agree to that and that the woman should leave our house right away. My dad said that if she left, he was going too, and my mom said that he should leave then. So late that night my dad (and his administrative assistant) left our home forever.

Emotional Breakdown

Sometimes it takes a life-and-death crisis or a mental breakdown to precipitate the decision to separate. Hitting the lowest low brings some people to the realization that they have only a few choices: go crazy, die, or leave.

Emma Wozniak

After years of ignoring the woes in her marriage for the sake of us children, my mother finally contacted a counselor for therapy. She was deeply depressed. The counselor confirmed what she already knew—that she needed either to change her life or to continue to suffer from her miserable marriage. The counselor suggested that my mother go to a psychiatric hospital. She agreed. She saw this as a last resort to try to solve her marriage problems. It took three days of over-medicated, dazed wandering in the hospital for a psychiatrist to test and release my mother on the grounds that she did not belong there. Although three days does not seem like a long period of time, it was enough for my mother to realize that if she did not get out of her marriage she would be right back to the blind and dazed state she was in at the hospital. This gave her the inner strength she needed to leave my father.

In the next story, the wife had been through hell with her husband for several years, but it took a criminal act to shake the scales from her eyes.

Sandra Hayward

When I was fourteen years old, my father became severely depressed. His depression lasted at least a year and involved serious suicidal tendencies. My mother did not know if he would make it through each day. She was not able to discuss her problems or feelings with him because he was always on the edge of suicide. She became emotionally and sexually withdrawn. Then my father took control of their bank account and began taking money out and putting it in an account with only his name on it, leaving my mother with barely any money. My mother hit rock bottom when she found herself stealing a pair of shoes. After that, she realized that it was not worth losing her dignity to save the marriage, and she initiated a separation.

A Push from Outside

Sometimes it takes a push from someone else to enable the adult to come to a decision to separate. Family members, friends, therapists, and even the children themselves can provide the encouragement to initiate a separation. We are all always looking for approval for our behavior, and it is especially important to have approval for a significant and painful decision like deciding to end a marriage. In the following story, it was approval from the wife's family that finally allowed the husband to seek a divorce.

Marlene Tingley

My mother was being treated for manic-depression, but as soon as she started feeling better, she would stop taking her medication and start having manic episodes. With each new episode, the symptoms got worse. She ran up so many bills my dad couldn't pay them. One time, she offered to pay $100 on the department store bill, but when we got to the store, she gave my dad the $100 and asked him to go and pay it. Then, while he was paying the $100, she took us up to the children's department and spent $200 buying us clothes. She began to get violent. She would throw dishes, clothes, and jewelry outside. Finally, it got to the point where my dad had to call the police. I watched her being taken away in handcuffs by the police—for their safety I presumed—after she attacked my father. It was at that point that my dad decided to talk to my mom's sister about seeking a separation, in the interests of his own safety and that of us children. My aunt told him that the only thing to do was to get a divorce. My father took that as her "okay" indicating that he had the support of my mother's family, and he initiated a separation.

Other husbands and wives in our students' families sought the counsel of their own parents before making a decision to separate.

Pete Chu

When my father was sentenced to prison for manufacturing cocaine, my mom consulted with her parents about what she should do. She was very confused. She truly loved my dad and didn't want to divorce him, but she also didn't want to be involved in a life of crime. His deviant activities and his propensity to endanger himself and us terrified her, but, on the other hand, she worried that a divorce would be detrimental to our emotional and psychological well-being. She was especially concerned about me, because I was a boy, and she worried that not having a father figure would damage me. After consulting with her parents, she decided that a divorce would be best for everyone. She went to visit my father in prison and told him of her decision.

It is also helpful to get the objective opinion of a professional—a therapist, a lawyer, or a pastor. This can validate the unhappy spouse's concerns and feelings and affirm the decision to separate. When individuals seek psychotherapy because they are in mismatched or dysfunctional relationships, it is common for them to come out of the therapy with personal strength that allows them to leave their bad life and begin a better one. The professional will push the person to make a decision and move on. This was true for the mother in the following story:

Sean Fitzpatrick

Soon after my father's income jumped from $2000 to $6000 a month, he started drinking, staying out, and criticizing my mother. He criticized her weight, her looks, and everything she did around the house. After six months of this, he moved out. My mother could not believe what was happening. She loved him very much. She wanted their life to return to normal. Three times she convinced him to move back. But then she discovered that he was having an affair. She found receipts for hotels in Palm Springs and canceled checks. They went into counseling, and the counselor advised her to make a decision, for her own good. With the therapist's help, she did; she petitioned for divorce.

It is also important for people contemplating divorce to have the support and approval of their children. This is not always forthcoming. Children rarely advise their parents to get a divorce. They are invested in having their parents stay together, because otherwise, their lives will have to be disrupted. But when the child grows up watching one parent abuse the other, watching the helpless "victim" suffer and not be strong enough to say no or leave, when the child reaches adolescence, he or she may provide the push needed to get the parent to safety or to a better life.

Mike Garcetti

Eventually, after years of emotional abuse from my demanding, controlling, possessive father and years of thinking about leaving him but being unable to do so, my mother got into counseling. She then began to realize that she had been brainwashed into believing that she couldn't make it on her own and that she needed my dad. Building on the counselor's suggestion, I persuaded her that it was time to leave and move on with our lives. On my eighteenth birthday, we moved out in secret.

Lynn Milstein

For years my mother put up with my father's lies, his angry outbursts, and his business failings. She internalized her anger. Her body was covered with rashes and she constantly over ate. She was short-tempered and depressed. She came close to a nervous breakdown. But

she stayed in the marriage because she was afraid—
afraid to hurt my father, afraid of change, afraid of what
it would do to us children if she left him. When I was
fifteen, I told my mother that I had no respect for the way
she was handling her life and that she should divorce my
father. She cried, worried that she had been a bad mother
and that she had set a terrible example for her children.
I reassured her that she was a wonderful mother but told
her that it was time she began living life for herself too.
It gave me a strange feeling in my stomach when she said:
"I want to grow up to be just like you."

Moving Out—Again and Again

Eventually, after one of these crises causes an insurmountable
rift, the couple separates. After an emotional upheaval or a
prolonged negotiation, a violent showdown or a final fling,
perhaps with a push from a new lover or a therapist, a friend
or a member of the family, the husband or wife moves out.
For couples with children, usually it is the father who moves
out while the mother stays with the children in the family
home. The time between making the decision to separate and
actually separating varies. It may be quick, if it follows a big
fight, or it may be slow, if it follows rational deliberation. Most
couples separate without a final decision about whether the
separation is temporary or permanent. After the separation,
they live in a state of continued uncertainty. This may lead them
to re-evaluate their decision to separate and to recalculate
the costs and benefits. The person may reconstruct a memory
of the marriage and the spouse as even worse than they were
in order to live with the decision to separate, or they may
lower their expectations about the single life.

If this attempt to live with the separation doesn't work,
the couple may reconcile. It is estimated that only about two
thirds of separations are permanent and end in divorce.
Some people get so anxious, they try to turn back the clock
and get back together. In fact, many do get back together and
reconcile for a while. The only people who feel little or no

attachment to the spouse at this point are men who initiated the divorce after years of thinking about it while they were in emotionless marriages. Among women, attachment to the spouse and to the role of a wife continues even for those who initiated the divorce. But attempts to reconcile are often doomed to failure, because the problems that led to the separation still exist.

> Deanna Knowlson
>   The first time my dad moved out of the house I was five years old. After that, I remember numerous times of Dad moving in and Dad moving out. I had been told that my parents were separated, but as far as I knew, this was a temporary state, because it was usually followed by Dad's moving back in. After my brother was born, there was a short reconciliation period when my parents lived together and our family was "intact." My father had a renewed sense of responsibility for his family and especially his newborn son, and my mom and grandparents all strongly urged him to keep working at the marriage and not pursue a divorce. My mother found this time to be emotionally draining, and her feelings pivoted between depression and anger. She refused to look at divorce as an option. Then came the day when my dad arrived home to find an upset wife who asked him questions about another woman she had seen him talking to. My father was very defensive, claiming that my mom was insecure, that he was "just talking" to the woman. A fight erupted, and I was sent out into the backyard while Mommy and Daddy settled things. This was the day my dad told me that he and my mom were getting a divorce.

This husband's inability to make a commitment to his marriage led to repeated separations and reconciliations, and ultimately devolved into deception and infidelity. This pattern is common among divorcing couples, as people waffle back and forth, buffeted by competing pressures and attractions, unable to make a clean break, for months or even years. In the next story, we glimpse something of how difficult it is to make a final break and the back and forth this involves.

Susan Nomura

When my father informed my sister and me that he was moving in with his best (male) friend in order to stop the daily confrontations with my mom, it seemed like he was leaving on a business trip. He made it sound like a temporary arrangement to give him time to think. During the next two weeks, he came home every night after work and ate and watched television—until my mother told him that if he wanted a separation he should be separate. Two weeks later he moved back in, just in time for Thanksgiving. It was a tense holiday. My mother initiated the second separation in February. My father again left the house, but this separation lasted only a week; he moved home on Valentine's Day. They started counseling to improve things. Nothing improved. During the next four months I had many talks with both of my parents, in which they both essentially said, "Your mother/father doesn't love me anymore." This seemed tragic to me, because it was so easy to fix; they were both operating under an incorrect assumption. All they had to do was admit that they still loved each other. But as time went on, my father began repeating over and over, "I have nothing left to give." In June he told my sister and me that he needed a thinking vacation—again a temporary situation—and he moved back in with his friend. It took two more separations before the divorce proceedings began.

In this student's family, the parents separated five times before they finally decided to get a divorce—illustrating just how difficult it is to make a final break and terminate a marriage. In the following story, the couple separated even more than five times. When the pressure got too much they fought to let off steam, or they separated. But then, without having resolved their problems, they mindlessly reconciled.

Amanthi Chandra

The first time I became aware of trouble in our house, I was six years old. My dad explained to me, "Mommy and I won't live together anymore so that we won't fight." But after a brief separation, he was back again, and they were fighting with renewed vigor. Fighting and arguing were a way of life in our home, and on several occasions these fights escalated into physical abuse. My father was a pilot and my mother was involved in the theater, which kept her away from home for long hours, and this was the source of great tension. When I was seven, we moved from England to Hong Kong. When I was eight, we moved to Jordan. We stayed there only six months, because my mother was so unhappy. After a series of stormy discussions and one particularly nasty fight, my parents decided to call it quits (again). My mother packed our bags and we came to the United States. A divorce was to be the next step. However, it didn't happen, because, when I was ten, my father quit flying and came to live with us again. This was the beginning of several very chaotic years. My parents split, my mother moved out, my brother and I stayed at home, and then some months later my mother moved back in and for a short time, there was some sort of marital truce. This whole sequence of events repeated itself five more times. Once, during such a separation, my parents filed for divorce. But again, things smoothed over and in a few months my mother was home again. By then my father's business had really taken off and he was making a lot of money. We bought a new home where we lived—not always together—for six years. When I started college, once again, the divorce was on. My father decided to move for good to a vacation home he had bought in Palm Springs. As you can probably guess, he moved back in about a year or so later. But some things had changed. He had stopped drinking and now there were fewer fights than before, maybe once every two or three months. My parents kept busy with spending money on landscaping, furniture, and new cars. Then the recession hit and Dad's business rapidly started losing money. We were heading straight for bankruptcy. At this time the fighting over money and about who was to blame reached an all-time high. My father moved back to Palm Springs and my mother filed for divorce. To our total amazement, the divorce was final by the end of the year.

In this family it took twenty-five years for the couple to finally divorce, after repeated separations and reconciliations. This is an extreme example, but as we noted above, at least a third of marital separations are not permanent and do not lead to divorce. They convincingly demonstrate that breaking up is hard to do.

Babies as "Band-Aids" for Failing Marriages

For centuries, "old wives" tales have claimed that having a baby is a "quick fix" for relationship troubles. Both men and women who are drifting apart cling to the hope that a baby will resurrect their love and reconnect their bond. However, the truth is that children do not repair relationship problems. On the contrary, a pregnancy during this already volatile and uncertain time only raises the stakes. The material and emotional demands on the couple and the level of stress in the relationship increase even more and issues of trust and commitment become heightened. For the same reasons that it is not advisable to have children early in a marriage—because the arrival of children taxes the couple's emotional, physical, and material resources—bringing children into a troubled marriage to fix the relationship is unwise and irresponsible. A volatile, unhappy, or unfulfilled marriage is not likely to withstand the added stress of having and raising a child and puts the child at risk for a childhood full of turmoil.

But strangely enough, pregnancies often occur when a marriage is in trouble, even after a couple has separated. Often it seems that neither spouse has made a conscious choice to have a child at that time. What is going on? When a loss of something important is imminent, it is a natural human reaction to mobilize your resources to prevent that loss. In deteriorating relationships, the person stands to lose many things—the spouse, the children, family life, the house, financial security, the status of being a married person, and, last but not least, one's sense of self-worth. The desperate attempt to avert these losses turns into a chain reaction of maladaptive behaviors. Often both spouses become more controlling, they tend to cling, they cajole, they bluff. Despair has a way of bringing out the worst in people. Spouses inflict pain—by saying hurtful things, by creating jealousy, and sometimes by physical violence. Some threaten to kill the other or themselves. And some get pregnant.

Denise Leblanc
    In their eleventh year of marriage, my father had an affair, and my mother kicked him out of the house. After a few months of living apart, they thought they could make a fresh start, but just before my father moved back in, my mother found out that he had continued the affair with the other woman. My mom petitioned for a divorce. My dad had long talks with my mom to get things settled. On her birthday he brought her a bouquet of roses and stayed for the night. A couple of weeks later my mom found out that she was pregnant. My mom and dad stayed together for two more years but their problems only got worse. When my dad got another woman pregnant, they called it quits.

As we see in this story and other similar ones, although the creation of children can prolong ill-fated marriages, it does not save them.

The Experience of Separating: Shock and Uncertainty

One reason that couples get back together again after dipping their toes into a separation is that that the water is icy! Separating is the most dramatic step in the divorce process and often the most stressful. Even thinking about it ahead of time and rehearsing the steps that will be involved does not prepare a person for the initial shock of separation. Even if the person is leaving an abusive situation, he or she still experiences shock waves. Why? There are many changes for which one cannot be fully prepared. There is the sudden shock of being alone. There is the less-than-expected social whirl. Fewer alternative mates than the person anticipated or hoped for are knocking at the door, and contact with former friends and acquaintances, who don't know how to deal with divorced couples or individuals, is dramatically reduced. The newly separated spouse may encounter isolation and unexpected social disapproval from family, friends, and colleagues. A mother may find that the demands of being a single, custodial parent are more than she expected. A father may find that the amount of contact he has with his children is less than he expected. The shock of separation is particularly severe if the person experiences a substantial financial drop.

Veena Sankar

During the last four years of their marriage, my father was physically, verbally, and sexually abusive to my mother. The abuse had become so frequent and so violent that it was necessary for us to leave; it was a matter of life and death. We left the house in secret. After being in hiding for two months, my mother obtained restraining orders against my father. It was then that she discovered that he had been committing fraud against her for the past ten years. He had taken all their joint property and put it in his name, and my mother was not legally entitled to any of their properties. She was devastated. She couldn't believe that my father would do this behind her back. This loss of property made my mother's life after the separation almost impossible. She had to work long hours just so we could survive. We had gone from being rich to having absolutely nothing. We were used to the good life, but now we had to start from scratch. There were times when we visited the local soup kitchen to get free food. My mother felt that her whole life had suddenly been pulled out from underneath her.

In addition to the devastating effect of a drop in income, when the separation is sudden and unexpected the newly separated spouse suffers intensely. Particularly if the victim has had the separation foist upon him or her without time to prepare, adjustment is difficult.

Lisa Kurdek

After my sister was born, my father, who was a photographer, developed arthritis and became very withdrawn and angry. He told my mom that he wasn't happy with the children and that it wasn't working out. Then he stopped coming home. My mom had a twenty-two-month-old baby and a two-month-old baby and no job. She had no money and nowhere to go—and my dad told her to get out. She lost more than ten pounds in one week. She was forced to take my sister and me and go live with her parents. This was a very difficult move for her because she did not want to become "their child" again. When my mom's father drove her back to get our things, they found that all of her clothes and all of our toys had been thrown out in front of the house. Mom was an emotional wreck. Later that week, a man ran a red light and hit her car, causing extensive damage. She got three thousand dollars in payment for the damage, and that, plus food stamps, is what we lived off for the next few months.

In this story, the suddenness and brutality of the separation led to dire consequences, which included psychological and economic devastation.

Physical and Emotional Symptoms of Separating

Because the actual separation is the most stressful and traumatic event in the divorce process, and the period immediately after it is the most acutely painful, many people experience physical and psychological symptoms after the separation. These include weight loss, upset stomach, body aches, fatigue, appetite loss, headaches, a "nervous breakdown," difficulty getting things done, and problems concentrating at work. Researchers have found that nearly half of the people they have studied report having a number of these symptoms. In the first year after the separation, the effect of the stress is so marked it is evident in blood tests, which reveal a lower level of cells that resist tumors and bacteria and a higher level of cells that indicate susceptibility to virus infections. All these are symptoms of stress. Not surprisingly, on a scale of "Stressful Life Events," which researchers use to predict people's physical and mental health, separation is the second most stressful event, coming right after a spouse's death.

A multitude of symptoms were mentioned in our students' stories.

Deanna Knowlson

After the separation, my mom experienced a significant weight loss, along with fatigue and headaches.

Clarissa Cambridge

The separation took a toll on my mom physically and mentally. She is five feet and eight inches tall, after the separation her weight dropped to under a hundred pounds. She was skin and bones.

Maria Schaefer

The immediate effects of the separation were bad for everyone. My mother developed debilitating migraines. She could not go to work some days, and everyone had to be very quiet because any noise would make her complain and become irritable.

Veena Sankar

After the separation, my mother suffered emotionally and experienced intense back pain.

Lisa Brock

Coping with the separation was really difficult for my mom. Her self-esteem was low. She hated being alone. She tried to bury herself in her work so she wouldn't have time to face her feelings. She started smoking. She was always fatigued and worn out. She was always run down. She lost weight and was constantly sick.

Jennifer Weinstein

After my mom filed for divorce, my dad felt lost. He missed being a family. He was furious that he had to pay my mom support. All the stress took its toll. His health suffered severely. He had heart problems before the divorce, but after the divorce, they got really bad and his blood pressure increased. Twice they took him to the emergency room in the middle of the night, and a year after the divorce, he had heart surgery.

Anger Spilling Out

In addition to these physical symptoms, another consequence that many people suffer during the separation is anger. Most people, over 80 percent, experience high levels of anger in the period after the separation. As many as half of them are intensely angry. This reaction is the result of violated expectations, uncertainty and disappointment. It is especially strong if the person was the unwilling victim of the separation rather than the initiator. These "dumpees" feel abandoned, outraged, and betrayed—by the spouse and society. They are ready to fight—about money, property, children, and anything else. They may go as far as involving the children as a weapon to act out their hostilities and to get even. Many are openly critical to and about the spouse, saying terrible things to anyone who will listen. Our students' stories included vivid descriptions of deep anger and rage experienced by their parents following separation.

Yolanda Sandoval

After my mother had disappeared, my father was packing boxes and getting ready to move, when a man came to the house and served him divorce papers. This was my mom's way of letting my dad know that she had left him and that she was asking for all the furniture and one of the cars. A few days later, my mom came to pick up the furniture. She tried to insist that my dad keep a blanket, a bed, and a chair, but at this point my dad was so mad he did not want to keep any of the things they had owned together. The only thing he felt was a burning anger. He absolutely hated her. She had abandoned him; she had taken his children; she had bad-mouthed him in front of his friends and family by saying things that were not true. He continued to hate her for a long time. When my mother wanted to reconcile, he wouldn't hear of it. He said, "When you have suffered as much as I have, you can never trust that person again. She could die today and it would mean nothing to me."

Sometimes the anger felt by a separated spouse is directed not at the spouse but at another person who has caused the separation. This was true in the situation described by the following student.

Andrea Keller

My mom was a housewife for the sixteen years she was married. She barely knew how to balance the checkbook. When my father left her, she was completely disoriented. She had no job and no money of her own. It is hard to describe how suddenly our world turned upside down. From one day to the next, my mom was forced to handle her kids, her losses, the bad relationship with her ex-husband, her emotions, and her need to financially support herself. She also had to deal with the fact that my dad was seeing her best friend, Pat. This made my mother extremely angry. One night, she paced back and forth, ruminating about my father and Pat, and whether they were together. Impulsively, she decided that she was going to go see if he was at Pat's house. She waited around the corner from the house. Then she saw my dad drop Pat a block from her house and drive away. When he was gone, my mom went up to Pat and started screaming at her. They began to fight and my mom attacked Pat and beat her up.

Anxiety and Depression

Other common emotional consequences of separation that our students described were anxiety and depression. Depression is the emotional reaction people have to loss, and in a separation, one loses a lot... the spouse, the house, a position in society, plans and hopes for life, and sometimes, one's children. Women feel a loss of self-esteem, identity, and status; they feel helpless and physically unattractive. Men feel rootless and without identity. They don't know who they are with no wife, no home, and no children. Both men and women feel they have failed and doubt their ability to maintain a relationship in the future. This feeling of depression is more than simple sadness. It can be an immobilizing feeling of hopelessness and failure. It can lead to the physical symptoms of weight loss, lack of appetite, and insomnia.

Anxiety is a person's response to uncertainty about the

future, and with a separation there is plenty of uncertainty. Newly separated individuals, especially women, are anxious about living alone—sometimes for the first time. They are anxious about taking on new responsibilities as the head of the household. They are anxious about discrimination and disapproval, especially from family and church members. They are anxious even about how they should act: They have no guide for how they should feel, or what they should do. What should I tell people? How should I act with my spouse? They are uncertain about their new roles, new tasks, and new financial arrangements—and there are no acceptable rituals to help them through this period. When people say they are getting married, the acceptable response is "Best wishes!" or "Congratulations!" There is no expected or accepted response when people say they are getting divorced. ("My sympathies?" "Poor you?" "Best wishes?" "Congratulations?" "What took you so long?")

In one clinical study of the consequences of divorce, researchers interviewed parents and children for a number of years, starting at the time of divorce. More than half of the newly separated spouses in the study experienced anxiety, and two thirds reported depression. Depression is particularly likely if the person is the one who has been left and if he or she does not have custody of the children.

Sandi Rodriguez

My mother was very depressed after the separation. I remember she was always crying. I talked with my brother and sister about it. We were concerned about upsetting her too much. We would come in from playing only when it got dark and the streetlights were turned on, because it was terrible to see Mom upset all the time.

Tiffany Maurer

After going to a handful of counseling sessions, my mother told my father for the first time that she wanted a divorce. He was upset and confused as she handed him the divorce papers. He had no idea that it had gotten to that point, and he said he would do anything to make the relationship work. My mom, who had always told me that if Dad wanted to change they would work it out, decided that she wanted the Porsche instead. My father moved out of the house into a dumpy apartment with poor lighting and ventilation. He felt like the entire world had collapsed around him, and he went into a deep depression. He started seeing a psychiatrist, who put him on Prozac. He stayed on Prozac for six months, and during that time he acted as if he were a zombie.

Cindy Chow

After my mom left, all that my dad wanted was to get his family back. He suffered terribly because he had lost his daughters and he felt like we were the most important things in his life. It was a blow that hurt him severely. He developed a clinical depression and had to go through a year of therapy and drugs. He felt empty inside; he felt he had no future.

A Sea of Irrationality

As many as 20 percent of the people going through a separation have an emotional reaction of anger, depression, or anxiety that is so severe and disorganizing that they need psychiatric help or hospitalization. The shock of rejection and feelings of helplessness cause emotional disequilibrium for days, weeks, or months. About one quarter of people have less severe symptoms of irrationality. These heretofore respectable members of the community find themselves spying on their spouse, breaking down his or her door, making obscene phone calls to his girlfriend, threatening her boyfriend, or vandalizing the spouse's car. Sometimes they have fantasies of murdering their spouse. Feelings of intense anger dangerously add to people's stress level, and often, impair their judgment. At the same time, during this period, even if they have agreed to the separation, even if they have initiated the separation, as many as one third of separated individuals continue to feel an emotional attachment to their spouse. They think about the spouse with longing in bed at night; they think about the spouse during the day and try to find out what he or she is doing. They feel jealous of the spouse's new lover. They feel the urge to call the spouse, to meet, and even to get back together. They swim in a sea of conflicting and irrational emotions. The following story by one of our students describes the irrationality that accompanied the separation of her parents.

Lauren Gordon

Three weeks after we moved to England, my dad decided to leave my mother and move in with his girlfriend. He gave my mom a lot of excuses about why he had become involved with someone else, the main one being that my mom had "left" him emotionally with all her "bitching," and therefore, it was her fault that he was leaving her for another woman. Now all he wanted was to be "free." He left us sitting in the house full of boxes that hadn't even been unpacked. My mom was devastated. She threw all of my dad's things out in the alley. She called his girlfriend every name in the book and then telephoned her and reminded her that my dad hadn't been faithful to her either. For months, she called my dad incessantly; if he wasn't at home she would let the phone ring for hours until he picked up. My mom was like a walking zombie. She felt like nothing would make her feel better. She lost twenty pounds, suffered incessant insomnia, and experienced a persistent vague nausea. My dad often came down to our house for home-cooked meals and to do his laundry (while living with his new girlfriend). One day when he came over for our Saturday outing, we all had lunch together. Things were tense but civil until my dad abruptly got up from the table and said, "Let's go, Lauren" while my mom was still eating. My mom snapped. She said, "Where are you going?" and when my dad didn't say anything; she hurled her plate, still full of spaghetti, at the tile kitchen wall, barely missing me and my dad. She started screaming at the top of her lungs. I just started quietly crying while trying to pick up the spaghetti from the floor. My dad didn't say anything. After the mess was cleaned up, we left and before we had even gotten to the bottom of the driveway, my mom came out of the front door and was yelling at my dad, screaming obscenities.

The painful experience of the separation and the continued exploitive contact with her spouse exacerbated this mother's volatility. Not all people who are divorcing act uncontrolled, obsessive, hostile, aggressive, and inconsistent to the extent that she did. The full range of her maladaptive actions likely reflected an underlying hypersensitivity that led her to overreact in dramatic ways to any perceived infraction. Her moods swung from one extreme to another. One moment she had lunch with her estranged husband and daughter, the next moment she exploded into a mad rage, throwing spaghetti and screaming obscenities. She was so engulfed in her rage that she had no consideration for her daughter. She was so preoccupied with her own needs and feelings that she was unconcerned about whether the child was afraid of these outbursts, or whether she might hit and hurt her with the objects she threw. The only thing that mattered to her was her feelings and her hurt.

Positive Reactions—Relief
But not all reactions to separation are negative. A small minority of people going through the separation (one tenth of the people in one study—all of them initiators of the separations) felt only positive emotions after the separation. More commonly, people had periodic or occasional mood uplifts when they felt competent and free and good about themselves or when they felt relief or hope about a fresh start, a new beginning, and a new chance. Almost half the people

in one study experienced some relief. For these people, the separation reflected the end of a difficult marriage, the culmination of a difficult decision. They now experienced, along with the pain, the relief of knowing they no longer had to worry about whether the spouse would be drunk or violent, critical, or crazy. The following students described their parents' reactions to the separation as generally positive.

Staci Chen

After my mom walked out on my dad, she behaved perfectly reasonably. She even seemed happy. I think her grief for the loss of their relationship had happened long before the separation. She expressed no anger, maybe because she had already reduced her emotional investment in the marriage. The immediate effect of the separation was that she felt like a great burden had been lifted from her shoulders. She felt relieved.

Martina Nunez

My mom parted from her marriage with a feeling of relief. She was finally out of a marriage that was going nowhere. She was free now to make her own choices and to lead her own life. She was happy because she could make her own decisions about where her life was going. She regained herself—someone she had lost during her marriage—and she was ready to begin a new life away from my father.

Of course, the feeling of relief, like the feelings of anger, anxiety, depression, is not usually long lived. There are obstacles aplenty ahead and emotional peaks and valleys to follow, as the following student described.

Naoko Russell

Immediately after the separation, my mom experienced a brief period of relief because the tension was over. It was like the opposite of the honeymoon stage, and there was some relief that the decision had been made. After that, there was only the shock of reality, and the tensions and burdens to follow.

Mixed Emotions

Even in the process of separating and in the early stages after the separation, what many of our students' parents experienced was a mix of emotions. Feelings of relief and peace were interspersed with negative feelings, often leading to severe mood swings. Moods swung from euphoria to exhaustion, elation to depression.

Ginny Rook

For the first few months after the separation, my mother felt a paradox of emotions: euphoria, empowerment, and exhaustion. Her life was an emotional roller coaster. She felt euphoric because she was an attractive, single woman who had never lived on her own; for the first time she could freely date whomever she wanted, on her own terms. She felt powerful because she had made a wise decision—and had stuck by it. But the physical exhaustion, a result of both emotional stress and a three-job workload, manifested itself in newly acquired ulcers.

Jennifer Weinstein

My mother's emotions after the separation were mixed. She was angry, depressed, anxious about money, and in shock. I remember she used to cry a lot and she easily lost her temper with Stephen and me. In addition, because my father's new woman was always jumping out at her to serve her papers, she was jittery. On the other hand, she felt relieved that a bad situation was over with, and she had a better view of herself because she had finally stood on her own two feet. She was happy because there was less tension in the house. The three of us were

able to share some really good times without my dad—
but we could never predict when they would happen.

Even when the person feels positive about the separation,
this positive reaction can be tinged with guilt. The guilt
comes from various sources—guilt about breaking up the
family, guilt about having a new honey, guilt about looking
forward to a better life.

Rachel Hall

After my mother left my dad she felt a lot of guilt,
because she was the one to initiate the separation. But,
on the other hand, she also felt a sense of relief. She
could breathe again.

Clarissa Cambridge

My mom's emotional responses to the separation
included both highs and lows. She felt relieved because
she had left behind the lies and mistrust she had
experienced with my dad. She didn't have to worry about
checks bouncing or whether or not he would be coming
home at night. She felt hopeful because she had a new
relationship in her life, which she believed would be her
road to a better life, emotionally and economically. But,
on the down side, the lies that she was telling to cover up
her new love made her feel very guilty.

In brief, the period preceding and following the separation
is fraught with emotion. It is a struggle to come to the point of
separating, and it is a struggle to survive after the separation.
Making a decision to live apart is just the beginning of the
process.

Lessons to Be Learned

The time of separation is marked by volatility and
emotional and practical dilemmas that need to be resolved.

Heeding the lessons derived from the real-life stories in this chapter can make life easier during this tumultuous time.

1. Know that this will pass. It helps in getting through this difficult period to know that it won't last forever. It will not be easy, but this difficult phase will pass. Once you have made the decision to separate, stay focused on the reasons you wanted a divorce. If you did not choose the divorce, this is the time to develop a plan for your life, independent of your spouse. Remember that it only takes one person to get a divorce and opposing it will probably create more problems down the road. It is important to remind yourself that you can make it on your own and then make a determined effort to focus on your future. This is an opportunity to change course if you have been dissatisfied with your life or yourself. It is time to reflect. It can be a time to discuss your problems, your failures, and your hopes for the future with a trusted and competent friend or a counselor. But beware of "bitch sessions;" they will drain you. Being stuck in the past, ranting and raving, does not empower you; it will derail your ability to focus on the things you need to do to make your life better. Tell yourself every day that things will get better and concentrate your energy on moving forward constructively.

2. Do not get pregnant to fix the relationship. Whatever you do, do not conceive a child during this time of turmoil in the silent hope of saving your marriage. This child will not repair your relationship. Having a child under these circumstances will only amplify all that is wrong in the marriage. It will increase your insecurity in the relationship, your sense of dependency, your inner turmoil and distrust, and all tangible problems. If, during this period, you think you might become sexually intimate with your spouse, be sure to have birth control handy. If you truly want more children, wait until this time has passed and you are again in a healthy, happy, and stable relationship.

3. Regain and maintain your physical and mental health.
During this time of turmoil, it is essential that people do
what they can to keep their lives on a positive course. You will
feel lonely and longing, angry and obsessing, and alternately
elated and despondent. With your emotions in upheaval, it
is all the more important to maintain stability and pursue
healthful activities in other domains of life. Do not throw
yourself into another relationship right away. You are not
ready for it. There are healthier ways to be distracted. You
can spend more time with your children, family, and friends.
You can use your free time to exercise, develop your social
network, and treat yourself to special and positive experiences.
Start a new hobby. Take a class. Learn a new skill. Read up on
relationship issues, divorce, parenting, and communication
and negotiation skills. Consider joining a support group, a
club, a team. Try to learn from your experiences. Start a diary
and write in it regularly. Writing down your thoughts will clear
your mind and help you think and reflect more effectively.
Feeling better about yourself will benefit you at the moment
and in the long run. Steer clear of escapist fixes: alcohol, wild
partying, pill popping, shopping sprees, endless whining
about your misery and all the unfairness you are suffering.
Avoid picking fights with your separated spouse.

4. Take care of your children. Children need their
parents at their best during this time, and thinking about
your children's needs may help you become less mired in your
own. This is a time to conserve your mental and emotional
energy and to focus on your next steps and all that you can do
to create a positive life for you and your children.

6

Dividing It All: The Legal Business of Divorce

Allison Rodgers

My parents married the day after Mom graduated from high school. She immediately went to work at a fast food store, and Dad worked part time and went to college and then on to law school. By the time he graduated from law school, they had two children, my mom had quit working full time, and they had bought their first home with help from Mom's parents. They had been married seven years.

I guess that's when my dad got the seven-year itch. He had his first affair. During the affair, he took the bar exam and failed. The night before the exam he told Mom he was studying, but in fact he was wining and dining his honey all night long. Taking the bar with a hangover is a recipe for failure. After the affair ended, he took the exam again and passed.

The next year my parents had another child, a boy. Mom thought that now my dad had a son, he'd grow up and be a father. Wrong! He was rarely home at night, always claiming that he was working. Mom tried to compensate for his absence with us kids: she was room mother, soccer mom, PTA board member, manager of Bobby Sox, and involved with Little League. When Dad was around, he tried to be a good dad, but I don't think he knew how.

When my brother started school, Mom went back to work part time as a receptionist. She had no education and no significant job history because all she had worked were odd jobs to get Dad through school. After two years, she quit the receptionist job because Dad wanted her to have more time to take care of him, the house and us kids.

Over the next ten years, Dad continued to have affairs and Mom always found out. In their twentieth year of marriage, after hundreds of dinners that Dad missed and constant reminders of his cheating—weird credit card charges, lipstick on his collar, two-week "conferences" in the Bahamas and Hawaii from which he would return with female clothing in his suitcase—Mom had had it! She told him to move out. He did. At that time he was a partner in a big Orange County law firm and was having an affair with his twenty-four-year-old receptionist. The two of them immediately moved into a home in an upscale community, and a month later they went on a cruise to the Greek Islands.

So here was Mom after twenty years of marriage, with three kids, no education and no worthwhile job experience, and Dad was in the Greek Islands with money and a mistress. What a mess Mom was. Although she didn't want to continue to live with my father's lies, she felt terribly lonely and rejected. She had never dated anybody other than my Dad, and she felt completely unlovable while Dad was romancing his receptionist. She lost thirty pounds, went to divorce recovery groups, started counseling, and took Prozac. We kids were pretty much out of control.

It took three years for the divorce to become final. In that time, Mom went through three attorneys and about $80,000. Eventually they settled out of court. She got the house and the mortgage payments, custody of the kids, $500 a month in child support until we were eighteen, $2500 per month in alimony, and attorneys' fees. Dad got his practice and the Mercedes. But Dad, being an attorney, knew every trick in the book and only paid when and what he wanted. Mom quickly had to sell the house and go to work doing odd jobs. Before the divorce, she was a "corporate wife" and used to living the good life. Now she is struggling on $5.25 an hour. She can't get a credit card or a car loan, but Dad lives in a villa on the beach. He started a new firm with three offices in the Orange County area, but he says he can't pay for my college or our medical bills.

My dad says that when they separated he was just going through his "mid life crisis." He was unfaithful because they had grown apart over the years and did not share the same goals. Although she was a great mother and a loyal partner, what they wanted from life was different. For example, he always wanted to go to Europe, but Mom would rather go to Las Vegas. After the divorce, he says, he grew up; he became less selfish and more responsible for others, including his children. At times, he claims, it was difficult for him to pay the support payments that were ordered by the court. As he puts it, being a lawyer is not always the "gravy train." He claims that ever since the divorce he has been struggling to make ends meet.

I think my father is a jerk. He is wealthy but he treats us like dirt. One minute he's bragging about all his money, the next minute he tries to make us believe that he is financially struggling. He has a beautiful house, two Mercedes, and a Harley Davidson—but somehow he just can't manage to pay Mom or pay for our college. He owns three law firms, but has nothing for us. I drive a beat-up Honda; his girlfriend drives a Porsche. He still doesn't remember where I work, but he feels sorry for himself because he is so disconnected from his children.

This student describes some of the most salient issues that a couple needs to resolve when they go through the legal processes of separation and divorce. First, they must decide whether to end the marriage permanently. Then, they must resolve how to divide any property and debt that were accumulated during the marriage. Third, a decision must be reached about whether spousal support is to be paid and, if so, how much. Fourth, if there are minor children involved, the parents need to know who will get primary custody, what the visitation schedule will be, and how much child support will be paid.

This story also illustrates the factors that led to the "community property" and "no fault" divorce laws that were instituted in this country after 1970. While the husband moved up in his career and accumulated wealth, the wife supported him through school and dutifully kept house and tended the children. Before "no fault" divorce, she would have needed to prove to the court that her husband was at fault and that, therefore, she deserved alimony and various other settlements. She would not have been automatically entitled to half of their assets; these were presumed to be the husband's property because he bought them with the money he earned. The wife would have been dependent on finding a competent lawyer and a sympathetic judge to prove that her spouse was at "fault" and that she deserved compensation. Even then, wives often did not do so well. Based on the presumption that everything belonged to the husband, any award—even the most minimal—was often considered a "liberal allowance to the wife." This made being a homemaker a risky occupation. Family histories like this one convinced the courts that the treatment of homemakers in the case of divorce was behind the times. In the 1970s things changed so that husband and wife were considered true partners sharing equal rights and obligations in the marriage and divorce and that their property was communal, not belonging exclusively to the person whose money was used to acquire it.

This student's story also addresses an issue common in many of our students' experiences: in spite of the efforts of the law to equalize the positions of husband and wife, the overwhelming complexity of the issues in each case and the flaws in human nature make true equality an ideal that is rarely achieved.

Basic Decisions Involved in the Divorce Process

Today, if one spouse wants a divorce, there will be a divorce. Under no fault divorce law, anyone who wants a divorce can get one. There is no decision about whether to go along with the spouse's desire for a divorce and no point in dragging your feet and opposing or contesting the divorce. It won't help. Once one spouse has decided and takes the necessary steps, the divorce is going to happen.

There is also no decision about the grounds for the divorce. With "no fault" law requiring only evidence of irreconcilable differences, anyone can get a divorce without proving the spouse's bad behavior. There are no decisions to be made about who is going to claim adultery or other problems in order to get the divorce. The objective of the no fault law was to eliminate the issues of guilt or innocence, vindication and revenge, retribution and punishment. It eliminates bargaining—"I'll give you the house if you give me a divorce." It eliminates compensation for being wronged—"You're the one who's been running around, so I want the house." It eliminates the double standard for men and women. Men no longer are expected to pay alimony to their ex-wives for the rest of their lives. The law attempts to be democratic and treat men and women as equals. However, because of the inequality between men and women in this society, "no fault" may also eliminate justice and fairness—as we saw in the preceding story. Mothers who devote themselves exclusively to the role of homemaker may be penalized when divorce strikes. The homemaker ends up with no career, is dependent on a good attorney and a good judge to be awarded half of the marital assets and spousal support, and further depends on her ex-husband to actually fulfill the court-stipulated obligations. Rarely is divorce as simple as in the following story.

Cynthia Fiennes

My mother remembers the divorce proceeding as distant and businesslike—once they were in court. She and my dad sat at opposite ends of the table with no eye contact whatsoever. Their attorneys did all the talking. No outside observer would ever have guessed that they used to be a couple. The actual court hearing was "easy." Custodial and property issues were not real concerns and were worked through quickly. My mom received the house and the children; child support was stipulated to be $160 per month. Mom was amazed at how simple it all was.

More commonly things get far more complicated, especially if the couple has accumulated considerable assets.

Division of Property

In the past, marital property laws were biased in favor of the husband, who usually held title to the couple's assets. Under English common law, wives were unable to hold and dispose of property until about 1850, when various statutes were passed to protect the rights of married women. At present, the concept of "community property" is used to determine the division of possessions when a marriage ends in separation or divorce. Contractual agreements may also be made by the couple before (pre nuptial) or during (post nuptial) the marriage to allow them to maintain individual property.

Community property designates the possessions held jointly by a married couple. All property acquired by the husband or wife during the marriage is usually considered community property. In case of a divorce, assets and debts are divided according to what is his, hers, and theirs. "His" and "hers" are what each person owned before the marriage or was given during the marriage. That is, property owned prior to the marriage and any income from such property remains separate and apart. Inheritances or gifts specifically made to one spouse during the marriage or personal injury awards are treated as separate property. "Theirs" is property acquired by the couple during the marriage. This includes wages, money in the bank, retirement pensions and other employment compensation, insurance, real estate, household furnishings, royalties, gains from investments, stock options, business assets (if both contributed), business good will, tax refunds, art collections, copyrights and inventions, automobiles, and other types of consumer goods that people have accumulated together. Community property also includes all debts incurred during marriage.

The concept of community property is recognized under the laws of nine states in the United States (Arizona, California, Idaho, Louisiana, Nevada, New Mexico, Texas, Washington, and Wisconsin). These states consider all income and property accumulated during a marriage to be owned equally. But in only a few of those states (notably California) is there a mandatory fifty-fifty split. The rest of the states are equitable distribution states, in which courts attempt to divide property fairly, taking into consideration such factors as length of marriage and the contributions of both spouses. Despite the good intent of the community property concept to provide fair and equitable treatment for both parties, it is often not easy to find a fair solution for both individuals. Couples may not agree on what constitutes community property. The husband may claim, contrary to the wife's contentions, that he owned the boat and the art collection before the marriage or that he purchased them with separate funds. If there is disagreement, the process of discovering "who owns what" can itself become costly and time consuming and may not always end equitably.

Most difficult to divide is the home. If the couple has children, the judge may say that the custodial parent should stay there, and the couple should not sell the house. If they don't sell the house, the custodial parent (usually the wife) then has to pay the noncustodial parent (usually the husband) his equity share in the house and to keep up with the mortgage payments, or (she) has to pay the "out-spouse" half of the difference between the mortgage and the fair rental value of the house. Many women cannot afford this. On the other hand, if the couple does sell the house and doesn't buy another, they will have to pay capital gains tax, and then they may still have to pay as much in rent on their two places. A third possibility is that the husband is granted all the property and is permitted to pay off the wife's interest over time. Unfortunately, for the wife this means that the installment payments she will get will be in future dollars, which are worth less because of inflation, and she will likely be forced to spend these property pay-off dollars for daily living because of her low income level and inadequate spousal support. Thus, she will not end up with either the original property or an equivalent lump sum with which to make a down payment on a new property. The high cost of housing puts enormous pressure on couples over the division of property and perhaps just as much animosity as there was in the old days before no-fault divorce.

A further inequity can arise from the way the court treats advanced degrees, career development, and earning capacity—even if they were acquired through joint efforts. There is great variation among states as to whether these constitute community property or whether they are too personal to be part of marital property. In California, the law permits spouses who can show that they supported their mate through school to be reimbursed for the costs contributed to his or her education. This would apply to the mother in the first story, who gave up her own education and career possibilities to support her husband. However, even with the possibility of reimbursement, it is questionable whether an equitable outcome can be achieved. Measuring and valuing what twenty years of support are worth is one obstacle the courts face. Another is the conflicting claims of the ex-spouses. There have been court cases where the husband argued that the wife was not entitled to any compensation because a hired housekeeper could have provided the services she rendered during the course of their long-term marriage. To overcome some of the ambiguities inherent in these cases, most community property states give the court the discretion to divide the property equitably, if dividing the property equally would result in unfairness to one party.

In the following story, the student's parents experienced the "classic division" of property between ex-spouses—she got the house and he got the money—which turned out to be neither equitable nor satisfactory.

> Cristina Bernal
>   My parents divided their assets so that my dad took the business, the trucks, and the boat, and my mom had the house, the Volvo, and the kids. She paid the mortgage, and he visited my brother and me every other weekend. He was ordered to pay $100 a week in child support, but in order to avoid conflict, my mom requested no spousal support. She wanted to keep the house, because she felt this was the only thing she had left to hang on to. But this turned out to be a mistake—which she discovered after she was stuck with having to make major payments for the mortgage, the taxes, and the upkeep.

In the property settlement of a divorce, women typically want to have the children and the house. Their reasons include the difficulty of finding a new more affordable place, sentimental memories about good times in the house, and the desire to maintain stability for the children. But what sounds good at first sometimes turns out to be a disaster. The mother's "deal" has a catch. Both the house and the children mean a considerable financial burden and no possibility for financial gain. Meanwhile, the father's "deal" leaves him largely free of obligations and permits him to produce money.

Sometimes, as in the following story, mothers whose foremost concern is to get the children without any hassle from the husband naively agree to forego all financial benefits: the house, spousal support, and child support.

Masayasu Lawrence

My mother did not deal with the official divorce until three years after they separated, which was great for my father because it meant he was under no obligation to pay child support. Then he started pushing my mother toward an official divorce because he wanted her name removed from the house in San Francisco. My mother could not afford an attorney for the divorce, and as a result my father got the house. She said she didn't care about that, all she wanted was custody.

As one would expect, the decision to give up her financial rights to gain the children put this mother on an arduous path into poverty. The more property a couple has the more complex the division becomes. The following story comes from a student whose parents are currently going through the divorce process.

Tiffani Leach

My parents are dividing everything equally, including my father's pension plan. They are getting one lawyer to take care of everything, because they found out it would be cheaper. My mother knows that it takes a lot of trust to use just one lawyer, but they want to avoid as much hassle as they can. Although they have sorted out most of the furniture and jewelry, the rest of the money gets very complicated. My mother is educated and could get a job to support herself, but she put her career on hold while she was raising children. Now, rather than making the $80,000 a year that people in her career typically make, she will make much less, because she is starting without any experience after twenty years absence from the work force. This difference in income comes from choices my parents made together in the marriage, and I think that this should be a consideration in their divorce settlement. My mother does not want spousal support unless she really needs it. At present, the only money she gets is from the rent of their house in Chicago. After the divorce, she will have to pay for the expenses on the house in Hawaii, including taxes. My parents feel they cannot sell the house because my grandmother is living in it and they don't want to kick her out. Another complicated issue is the inheritance money from my paternal grandfather. He left a lot of property, which my mother is not legally entitled to. Even though my grandfather would probably have wanted her to have some of it, she has no legal right to it, and my father has made it clear that it isn't hers. Her inheritance, which she received from her family, was $20,000; it went to pay the college tuition for my sister and me. My mother thinks that if my father is going to keep all his inheritance, which is valued at over $4,000,000, then she should get her $20,000 back. In the meantime, she is scared that she will end up spending her money on us while my father spends his on his girlfriend and her children.

Although this couple seems to be on an amiable course toward a divorce settlement, there are a number of issues that may turn out disappointing for the wife. The mother is at a disadvantage because of their earlier decision for her not to work during the marriage. Even if she starts working now, her income will be only a fraction of his (or what hers could have been). Asking for spousal support would be a way to equalize their unequal incomes after divorce. However, if she indeed foregoes spousal support she will be disadvantaged from the beginning. At present, she believes she can make do with the income from their rental property in Chicago. She does not realize that this money may not be sufficient when she shares all costs such as mortgage payments, maintenance costs, and taxes on the property.

The inheritances each spouse received are, under the law, their separate properties. The mother has no right to the father's inheritance, regardless of what she thinks the grandfather might have wanted. The fact that she spent her inheritance on the children's tuition poses a further problem. Mixing separate and marital property is called commingling. If the separate property was spent on buying something that later can be divided, then, upon divorce, they would have to split the value of the asset. For example, if the couple bought a car with the wife's inheritance, then they would need to split the value of the car. This would ensure her of at least half of her money. However, the effects of commingling are especially problematic if the separate property was used to pay off the couple's debt or other obligations, as is the case here. Here the mother spent her inheritance money on the children's tuition. Now that the money is gone, there is nothing left to be divided. Although the mother feels that it is unfair that she spent her money while he still has his, she has little recourse.

A further problem arises from the fact that the couple shares the same attorney. It is very difficult for one attorney to ensure that both sides get what they are entitled to. Being each party's best attorney is a little like playing chess against oneself: a no-win situation. The mother's attempt to avoid the cost and "hassle" of having lawyers is especially misguided, given the fact that there are complex financial issues. She may not fully appreciate the cost and hassle she is likely to encounter in the long run by not having her own attorney.

Complex property issues get further complicated when one of the spouses hides the assets.

Denise Leblanc

After she had made the decision to divorce my father, my mother adjusted pretty quickly—emotionally. The legal process and the economic fall-out, however, turned out to be far more difficult. She was not working, and she had no money saved up. After she filed the divorce papers, my father removed all the money from their checking and savings accounts and cashed in all the stocks they owned. There was no way of tracing the money. She was left with an overdrawn account and virtually no money for a lawyer. Child support was based on my father's income, which, at the time of their trial, he somehow managed to show as zero.

In cases in which one spouse is hiding marital assets, the other spouse can initiate a formal procedure called "discovery." Discovery helps the spouse get information he or she is seeking to obtain from the other party. Several devices, which are strictly regulated by the law, can be used in the discovery process. For example, the wife in the story above could have asked for the husband to make a deposition regarding the whereabouts of the money. In a deposition, he would be interrogated by her attorney and would need to respond under oath. She could also have asked that he turn over certain documents, like his bank statements and pay stubs. Going through this process involves, again, the use of a skilled attorney and, naturally, more money.

Spousal Support

These days, the majority of divorcees get little spousal support. If they get support at all—and five out of six divorcing individuals do not—it is limited in amount and duration. The median amount of spousal support is about $400 per month and the median length of support is two years. Most support is only for the short term—just long enough until the spouse can supposedly support himself or herself. No-fault divorce basically eliminated support for middle- and upper class women; certainly it eliminated a level of support that would allow them to live in the style to which they were accustomed. One important rule regarding spousal support is that if it is not granted at the time of divorce, a spouse cannot get support later. If any spousal support is granted at the time of divorce, even the most minuscule award, it can be modified later. Lawyers often advise spouses who do not want to ask for spousal support at the time of divorce to ask at least for $1. Experienced judges sometimes award $1 to retain in the future jurisdiction. This token award makes it possible to increase spousal support at a later time, if it is needed.

If and how much spousal support is awarded depends on a number of factors, all of which get entered into a computer program that returns the figure that the court will award. These factors are based on the earning capacity of each spouse, and include the following: the diminishment of earning capacity by domestic duties, the needs of each spouse (for example, the need to complete college), the obligations of each in regard to the children, the duration of the marriage, the ability of the supported spouse to work without adverse effect on children, the time required for the supported spouse to become self supporting, and the couple's marital standard of living. Spousal support is usually given to the custodial parent of preschool children. If a couple was married for less than five years and has no children, there is little chance spousal support will be awarded.

One guideline in making an award is to attempt to maintain the supported spouse's prior living standard. However, proving the prior standard of living in court can be very time consuming and costly—especially if one of the spouses does not play by the rules, as in the following story.

Susan McDevitt

At my parents' divorce trial, the main issues before the court were spousal and child support. The judge awarded spousal support to my mother in the amount of

$150 a month and set child support at $600 a month. He ruled that the spousal support would be for only one year. This is how long, the judge reasoned, it would take my mother to establish herself in her business and become self-sufficient. My mother felt that the ruling was unfair because she had been married for twenty-five years and was accustomed to an upper middle-class lifestyle. There was no way that $150 a month was going to maintain her former lifestyle. She also felt that the short duration of the spousal support would put her under the gun, and she worried tremendously about what would happen to her if her business did not succeed. As it turned out, the worst was yet to come. In spite of the court order, my father didn't give my mother any money—not for spousal support, not for child support, and not even when his own lawyer advised him to follow the court order. My mother did not make enough money to pay the bills, and this was detrimental to her credit rating. She borrowed money from friends to survive. My father completely ignored my mother's letters and phone calls. My mother's attorney advised her that she would need to go back to court to enforce the court order, but she felt she could not afford the costs of another trial because she was already struggling. As of now, my father owes my mother approximately $25,000 and the figure is rising every month. My mother wonders how she will survive.

As in this story, it is quite common for the needy spouse—typically the wife—not to go back to court, because she does not have the funds to do so. This is one way that delinquent spouses get away with irresponsible behavior.

Division of Children

The third decision in the legal process of divorce involves the children. The decisions concerning child custody and visitation can be enormously complicated. Although it is difficult to divide the assets—because both parties want all of them—it is at least not psychologically complex. Dividing the children, however, is much more difficult. There are trade-offs that may be impossible for a divorcing couple to balance. Both parents presumably want to remain involved with their children, but neither one necessarily wants to bear the entire burden and responsibility of being the sole parent; everyone needs some time for themselves. Both parents want to have some control over their children's lives and want to be free of the other parent's interfering, but each would probably also like some encouragement from the other parent for their efforts. Working out this delicate balance between cooperation and control is tricky. If parents can come to a decision about custody, the court will respect it. If they cannot, the judge has to step in and make a decision based on what he or she considers "in the best interests of the child." (How the judge makes the decision is complicated, as we discuss in detail in the next chapter.)

With the help of a judge or on their own, the couple must decide about the child's physical custody arrangement—that is, who the child is going to live with; about the child's legal custody arrangement—that is, who will have legal responsibility for the child; and about the child's visitation schedule—that is, how much and what kind of access to the child the both parents will have.

What it is really like to go through the process of deciding child custody depends on whether the couple can work out these decisions calmly, agreeably, in the privacy of own home or a neighborhood coffee shop, or go to battle over custody in court. If they combine strong disagreement and hostility with high stakes—money, property, family home—and they disagree about the children's custody and support, or they use custody, support and visiting rights as weapons to get at their spouse, the process can be long and painful. In a courtroom battle, each person is likely to reveal everything bad about their spouse to the judge and lawyers. Everything about the spouse's past—the drugs he tried as a teenager, her eating disorder twenty years earlier, his depression after losing his first job, the abortion she had in a relationship prior to marriage—indeed, any and especially the person's most private characteristics, habits, weaknesses, hang-ups, past mistakes, and sexual preferences are dragged into the open. Virtually every aspect of the person's life from early childhood to future living arrangements is open to attack. This process can be degrading, demeaning, and embarrassing and adds to the depression and stress of the divorce itself.

Emma Wozniak

After my parents separated, my father often did not take his visitation time with my sister and me, and when he did take us for his weekend, he would usually return us early on Saturday because "something else had come up." But then my parents got into a huge fight over custody. During the custody battle, Dad constantly complained that he did not see us enough, and just before we went to court for the final divorce proceeding, my father served my eight-year-old sister with a subpoena to force her to testify in court. He came as usual to the door to pick us up for a weekend, and when he turned to leave, his new wife popped out from behind a bush and served the subpoena to my mother. For my mother, this was the most frightening part of the divorce—going to court fearing that her children would be taken away from her. She was battling for her children against a man who, she thought, had the financial capability to take us away. During the custody dispute, my father portrayed my mother as mentally unfit because of the bout of depression she had had during the marriage. For my father and his lawyer this was the perfect weapon to use to get custody. The lawyer tried to make my mom believe that she wouldn't have a chance in court because of her "mental illness." Fortunately, my dad's nastiness backfired. When he and the lawyer requested that my mom's mental condition be evaluated, they opened the

door for an evaluation on both sides. The outcome was
that the court awarded them both joint legal custody, but
physical custody remained with my mom.

As this story shows, the struggle for custody rarely brings
out the best in parents. Sometimes the conflict is made worse
by the involvement of attorneys who try to win "their" case
but have little regard for what is fair, decent, or best for the
children. Unfortunately, some parents use child custody bids
only as a way to accomplish another—typically financial—
goal, as was the case for the following student.

Masayasu Lawrence

After my parents' divorce, my father never paid a
dime of child support and had no contact with me and
my sister. He never called, never wrote. He made it clear
that he wanted nothing to do with his former family.
Twelve years later my father phoned saying he wanted to
use us children as tax write-offs. My mother hit the roof.
She told him, "NO WAY!" My father then threatened my
mother, saying he would sue for custody. My mother, not
taking him seriously, went to court the next day to start
proceedings to obtain the child support that my father
had never paid. There was a new law in California that
allowed you to start proceedings without an attorney.
My father responded by getting a fancy attorney to fight
the child support petition and charged my mother with
being an unfit mother. Now my mother was forced to get
an attorney.

My father's attorney claimed that the reason that
my father never paid child support was that my mother
had taken the kids and hidden them from him. This was
completely untrue; my father knew where my mother was
living the whole time. Because a case had been brought
against my mother as an unfit mother, though, it was
required that we children meet in the judge's chambers
with a social worker to decide if there should be a change

of custody. I was fourteen and my sister was twelve the day we went to court and saw our father for the first time in twelve years. We each said, "Hi" and then went directly to chambers. After we spoke with the social worker, the court decided to leave us with our mother. Even though my father was ordered again to pay child support, he never did. That day was the last time I ever saw him.

Child Support

All states require that parents support their children financially until they reach the age of majority (eighteen years), and in some instances even longer, for example, if the child is disabled or in college. After divorce, the noncustodial parent is typically required to make child support payments. If parents share physical custody, child support is based on the percentage of time the child lives with each parent and on each parent's income in relation to their combined income. Like the calculation of spousal support, the amount of child support is determined by feeding information into the computer about each parent's income, the percentage of time the child lives with each parent, child care and health care expenses, the needs of the child, and the parent's standard of living. The court also determines child support payments based on the parents' ability to pay.

Judd Michaelson

When they were in court, the judge let my dad off easy. He was not ordered to pay for anything except the mobile home my mom's parents had bought him—and this was only because there was already a written contract stating that he was going to pay them back for that. At the time my father was a student and wasn't making much money. About three years after my dad started his own veterinary practice, my mom took him back to court asking for more child support because he was making so much money. The judge awarded my mom $300 a month until I turned twenty-one. Things went along very well

until my eighteenth birthday, when my dad decided he
wasn't going to send support anymore. Because it was in
the court order that he had to pay until I was twenty-one,
my mom took him back to court again. When the judge
reviewed the case, she ordered my dad to pay $500 a
month until I graduate from college or until I am twenty-
two years old, whichever comes first.

Frequently, mothers who are trying to be "nice" when they
are going through the legal process of divorce do not ask for
adequate child support. To prevent the problems that arise
if the custodial parent has insufficient resources, state law
now mandates the courts to review whether the set amount is
appropriate—even if parents have agreed to a certain amount
of child support by themselves. In cases in which the court
determines that the initial award may not be sufficient, and
in cases in which the needs of the child increase, parents end
up going back to court.

Jenny Messerman

My mother was awarded sole legal and physical
custody of both my brother and me, and my father got
"reasonable visitation." My mother asked for only $25 per
month per child in child support and no spousal support,
because my father had been laid off and my mother
wanted to be nice and not cause bad feelings. When the
judge awarded the amount my mom had asked for, he
stated that it was temporary and would increase when my
father got a job. When my father did get a job, however,
he refused to pay more child support. Two years after
the divorce, therefore, my mother took my father back
to court to petition for increased child support. Still, my
father wasn't making much money and she didn't want
to ask for too much. She asked for and was awarded $150
per month per child. Her lawyer even made her sign a
statement showing that her small settlement was of her
own choice and not because of any negligence on his

part. My father had to pay all the attorneys' fees because the judge thought this never should have come to court in the first place. The next year, my parents had another court battle. This time my father took my mother to court claiming that he did not get to see us enough because my mother was keeping us from him. He made up many lies saying things like he had only seen my brother and me at one of the past eight Christmases, when, in reality, it had alternated every year. This made my mother angry, and she decided she was not going to try to play "nice" anymore. She was going to pursue the child support that the law said she should be receiving. She also asked the court to order my father to pay half our medical costs. Until then, my father had never assumed any responsibility for our medical costs, and he contended that his child support payments covered everything he owed. The outcome of all of this was that the court ordered my father to increase his child support to $350 per month per child and to pay his half of the remaining medical bills. If my mother could change anything about the past, she now says that would ask for the child support payments that the law determined to be appropriate in the beginning, instead of trying to foster good feelings. No matter what amount my father paid—$25, $150, or $350—he always thought he was paying too much. He never appreciated the way my mother was struggling financially to make ends meet for us.

It is common for noncustodial parents, like the father in this story, to resent paying child support. They see it as a legalized mechanism for the ex-spouse to rip them off, not as a way of fulfilling their financial duty to their children. If the obligated parent is short of funds or is angry at the custodial parent, the temptation to skip the payment is great. Many parents refuse outright to pay the child support that the court has ordered. This phenomenon was described repeatedly in our students' stories.

Elizabeth Harrison
About one year after the divorce, my dad stopped paying child support. He told my mom, "Do you realize how much I'll have to pay until she's eighteen years old?" In a gush of anger she told him to stay away if he didn't want to pay, and that is exactly what he did.

Non-payment of child support is common in this country. This situation is disheartening because studies indicate that most noncustodial parents have enough income to provide adequate support to their children. The Census Bureau indicates that among the custodial fathers who are ordered to pay child support, only about 70 percent actually do. However, fathers tend to have an optimistic bias toward their payment record. When asked, most of them think or say that they do pay and they overestimate the amounts they pay. Nonpaying noncustodial fathers argue that they would pay if they had more money, more access to the child, and more control over how the money was spent. Some also cite as reason for non-payment their belief that they are not the child's father. But the evidence to support their argument is not convincing. Although child support payments are indeed related to fathers' ability to pay, non-payers are generally not so poor that they could not afford to pay at least some support. And even if it were true, withholding financial support—for whatever reason—does hurt the children. Fathers' noncompliance has also been related to psychopathic deviance and alcohol use, vengefulness, egocentrism, and irresponsibility.

So what can parents do to get the child support they are owed? Although there are variations in the different states, there are a number of basic steps parents seeking child support can take. First, they need to file a motion with the court to request child support and they need to serve the noncustodial parent with the legal papers. Because of crowded court dockets, it often will take some time to get a court hearing. While waiting for the court date, the parent seeking support should undertake discovery to determine what the other parent's finances are. This involves collecting information about his or her income, assets, and debts. If the noncustodial parent is uncooperative, this may require depositions and subpoenas. Finally, both parents must appear at the hearing, and the court will enter the order for payment. Depending on the state, the money ordered goes to the court, a government registry, a state agency, or directly to the custodial parent. If payment is then made as ordered, no further steps are required. When payment is not made, however, the noncustodial parent must be notified of default. Then he or she is served and brought back into court and another hearing is scheduled.

Most states have tried to enact tough legislation to deal with delinquent parents. They have developed tracing and monitoring systems for parents who are not paying child support. Both, custodial and non-custodial parents can turn to their local child support enforcement (CSE) office. The telephone numbers for state CSE Agencies can be found in telephone directories, usually under the state/county social services agency. CSE agencies help with locating non-custodial parents, establishing paternity, establishing support orders, and collecting support. Many new enforcement mechanisms exist to compel so called "dead-beat parents" to pay child support. Enforcement may include seizure of real property and tax refunds, credit bureau reporting, suspension of driver's, professional, and recreational licenses, withholding of passports, seizure of bank accounts, freezing of assets, and imprisonment, fines, or both. The most widely used (60%) and effective enforcement tool is wage withholding by employers.

But what if the parent is not employed? A parent's unemployment used to be a commonly cited and accepted reason for nonpayment of child support and many parents abused the states' consideration of their circumstances, as in the following story.

Cristina Bernal
    Despite my mom's efforts to appease my dad and
not be a financial burden to him, he rarely made a whole
year of payments. Two years after the divorce, he declared
bankruptcy and his child support payments were lowered.
After that, he would quit jobs he did not like and, declare
that he was unable to pay support at all.

In California, since the beginning of 1998, a Supreme
Court decision obliges parents to work to pay child support.
Calling the financial support of one's children a "fundamental
obligation," the court decided that deadbeat parents can be
jailed for failing to get employment that enables them to make
child support payments. Before this ruling, only parents who
had an income but refused to pay could be jailed. Other states
may also pass such legislation.

Going to Court
For many people, going to court turns out to be a very
different kind of experience from what they expected. They
believe that what is just and fair in their situation is obvious and
that any person in their right mind—certainly an experienced
judge—will see what is going on, take their side, and make
an order that will settle the hassles with the other parent
once and for all. Not so. The court is not exactly a consumer-
friendly environment. It is a whole different world from the
one in which we live; a world with its own authoritarian rules;
a world with its own language (Latin) that most of us don't
understand and don't speak. The foundation of our courts is
the "adversarial model"—a concept derived from English law.
The adversarial model presumes that it is best if the parties to
a dispute openly present their different views to an impartial
third party—the judge—who listens and eventually decides
what should happen. The presentation of evidence is typically
done by the parties to the dispute or by their attorneys. It
is presumed that fairness will result when both parties are

allowed to examine the meaning and accuracy of each other's claims. So far, so good. The first difficulty arises because the presentation of evidence demands very detailed and strict rules that each side has to follow. Typically, attorneys know how to handle this; the client, however, is likely to get lost in the rules and the language within the first minute. The second difficulty arises from certain advantages one side might have over the other. What if one parent has an attorney and the other parent does not? What if one side has a more skilled attorney than the other? What if one side has stronger witnesses or simply lies better? Mistakes can have severe, costly, and often long-lasting consequences.

The adversarial model has been sharply criticized as a forum for family disputes. It developed in medieval times when disputes were solved in combat. Whoever won the battle was deemed right—justice had been served. For all practical purposes, not much has changed. The adversarial process rewards the best "fighter"; it encourages parents to engage in competitive and self-centered strategies that focus on building a convincing case against each other rather than finding solutions to protect the integrity of each family member.

Filing for Divorce
Regardless of whether the courts are the appropriate forum for resolving family disputes, at this point in time, couples seeking a divorce must find their way through the court system. The first issue, then, becomes where and what to file? To resolve this issue requires finding out which court has jurisdiction. Jurisdiction of the court refers to the court's authority to make a decision in a case. There are different types of court that have jurisdiction over particular kinds of dispute. The family law court, for example, decides family cases but does not hear traffic or criminal cases.

In order for a court to have jurisdiction over a family law matter, at least one spouse must have lived in the county for a certain period of time. For example, in California, a person must have lived at least six months in the state and at least three months in the particular county in which the person intends to file. In order for a court to have the jurisdiction to decide child custody or child support, spousal support or property issues, the defendant or respondent in the case must have been personally served with the court papers and must have some contact with the state in which the court is located. For example, if a couple lives in Texas and the mother moves with the children to California, for a California court to have jurisdiction over the father, he must have had some regular contact with the State of California (for example, spending time there to visit his children).

The original divorce petition can be filed in a number of different ways. Many people hire a lawyer or a paralegal service to write up the petition and file it for them with the court. It is also possible to file the petition oneself in court. There are many books on the market that describe "how to do your own divorce." Often they even provide the documents needed. Documents can also be obtained in court. The type of forms one needs to file depends on the type of legal action one desires. Filing the petition involves a fee, which is paid to the court.

Petitioner or Respondent?

To initiate a divorce, either the husband or the wife files a petition for dissolution. This person is called the "petitioner." The other spouse has to respond to the petition and is therefore, called the "respondent." The original filing status, either petitioner or respondent, is retained in any subsequent court case the couple may have in the future. For example, if the wife initiates the divorce and becomes thereby the petitioner, she will still be the petitioner even if her ex-husband files several years later for a modification of child custody—although she did not file for this new court case. The husband will always remain the respondent in court papers even if he initiates every subsequent case.

Different Filing Conditions

There are different filing conditions that determine what forms and procedures are necessary. In California, if the couple has been married for less than six years and they have no children, no real property, no expectation of spousal support, and less than $10,000 in community property, which they can agree how to divide, they can get a "summary dissolution." They don't have to go to court; they just fill out two forms and wait six months. If the couple has been married for less than six years and they have no children but they do have property, or if one spouse refuses to participate, the couple can arrange a court hearing and make a "request for default" or "uncontested declaration." This is scheduled within weeks and takes only a brief appearance in court. Only the petitioner needs to appear and the Court makes a judgment of divorce. Six months after papers are served the dissolution becomes final.

If there are children involved, or if one spouse needs spousal support, the procedure is more complicated. The couple may need to go to court to get temporary orders to cover the immediate arrangements for custody of the children and support of one of the spouses. The couple then must fill out a marital settlement agreement. If both parties can agree on the settlement, they can then schedule a hearing to go before the judge, who would typically grant what the couple asks for. The following student described this situation.

Clarissa Cambridge

Two years of marriage was not enough time for my parents to have acquired any significant property. My dad's father owned the house we lived in, so that was not an issue. Their marriage was shorter than six years, so spousal support was not up for discussion either; the only type of support that my mother would receive would be child support. They decided this would be $100 a month and the judge went along with their decision.

If there are children or spousal support issues and the couple cannot agree how to resolve them—which occurs in about 10 percent of divorce cases—there may be mandatory court mediation. The couple tries to work out a settlement with a mediator, and then they go to the judge with the agreement and the judge grants the divorce. If the couple still cannot agree, even after mediation, the judge then makes the decisions and orders the custody arrangement, the visitation schedule, the amount of spousal and child support, and the property settlement. The couple must abide by these orders.

How much time and money are involved in the legal process of divorce depends on the complexity of the circumstances and the level of cooperation between the spouses. From the time of filing to the time the divorce is granted can take from six months to two years—or even longer in complicated cases. It can cost less than $200—if you do the divorce yourself and agree on everything—or more than $100,000—if the couple hires lawyers and agrees on little or nothing.

The Day in Court

The day in court may be anticipated with eagerness. Some naive divorcers, convinced that their case is clear-cut and will be decided in their favor, can't wait to play their final trump card. Most people, though, await the day with considerable trepidation. Either way, people going through a divorce are likely to find the process quite stressful once they are in court. They are uncertain about what is going on. Attorneys dash in and out of the courtroom, telling them to wait, and that waiting can take a long time. Not surprisingly, under the enormous pressure of awaiting one's fate and with a good push from the attorneys, most people end up settling in a hallway or conference room at the courthouse. This is called "bargaining in the shadow of the law"; with the law so close, the impossible—a compromise—suddenly becomes possible.

Naoko Russell

When asked what she remembered as the "worst" part of the divorce, my mom said without hesitation that it was the day in court. It was stressful having the attorneys run back and forth between her and my dad in the hallways of the court. It was a particularly painful experience because my dad insisted on being stubborn over petty details, such as who would be the beneficiary on his small life insurance policy. She felt that these "fights" were unnecessary, and the experience would have been less painful with some cooperation and some consideration.

Unexpected Problems

Long, drawn-out costly fights are one of the most common problems encountered in going through the legal divorce process. One or the other spouse—or both of them—lose all perspective and wage an all-out war against the other parent. This was a common occurrence in our students' experiences.

Juan Hernandez

While they were working out the details of their divorce, my father fought my mother for everything. They did not speak to each other and had to go to court to settle all of their disputes. It got so bad that my dad wouldn't let my mom have the clothes she had left at the house until the courts specifically made him give them to her. His lawyer relayed messages to my mom because my dad refused to talk to her. He didn't think about the lawyer's bills he was running up because he was too stubborn to talk.

Christy Klein

The ordeal regarding child support was only the beginning of the courtroom drama for my parents. They spent a full six years in and out of court attempting to finalize their divorce. Many days were spent dividing up the community property and formulating further legal procedures. There was a period in which my parents went to court twice a week, every week for months. My mother was struggling to pay her expenses including the outrageous legal fees she was incurring. These demands took a major toll on her career and her sanity. She had become physically and emotionally drained, but she refused to give up without receiving the restitution she believed that she and we children deserved.

In hindsight, some parents said that it would have been better to cut their losses early on—that is, not to fight for everything they felt entitled to. But in the midst of the process, they could only see how unfair their lot was, and they succumbed to the urge to fight for every dime. They became blind to the real issues—that they had children to care for and that they could begin a new life of their own, free of past business. But they just couldn't let go. The obsession with their perceived injustices or their need to punish the other parent took ridiculous turns, such as that described by the following student.

Elizabeth Harrison

In court, my father claimed that Mom was unfit because she still had me in diapers at age one. He also fought for the refrigerator. Mom was upset because she needed the refrigerator and could not afford to buy another one. It later turned out that he did not need the refrigerator after all. The judge charged my father $250 for wasting the court's time. Then he started looking at every other aspect of the case, and, in the end, my father was required to pay $120 per month in child support and the fees for both lawyers.

Frivolous suits like this one are very much disliked in court and often backfire on the spouse who brought them to court.

Problems can also arise when circumstances change between the time the divorce is granted and the time the financial and custody arrangements are worked out. The court can divide the two issues—the divorce itself and the custody and financial issues. This is called bifurcation. This strategy also can lead to problems, as the next student described.

Emma Wozniak

Because of the urgency with which my mother wanted the divorce, the court bifurcated the two issues of child custody and the actual divorce. The bifurcation proved to be a big mistake. While they were getting the divorce, my mother had proposed a deal to my father: he would give her his half of the house so we children could stay in the neighborhood we grew up in, and, in exchange, she would not ask for child support. He initially agreed. But by the time of the trial, he had changed his mind. He demanded his share of the house and, in addition, claimed that he couldn't pay child support. The delay between the divorce and the settlement trial had allowed him to remarry, and he came to court as a married man with a wife and six other children to prove that his resources were limited. The judge awarded my mother no alimony or spousal support and limited child support ($175 per child per month) and told her she had to sell the house.

Do People Really Need a Lawyer?

Many of our students' parents commented that their experience with the court system was exhausting, costly, incomprehensible, unpredictable, and most of all frustrating, and at the heart of their frustration was their lawyer.

Kristin Sanders

According to my father, the legal system in this country is screwed up. The fact that it took three years to legally conclude my parents' divorce completely drained him. Although he was no longer in love with my mother when they separated and was secure in his choice to sever the relationship, he still found himself mired in legal machinations. In his opinion, the legal process of divorce should be made easier. There should be less involvement of attorneys, more creativity in settlements, and the court should encourage simpler and faster resolutions. He believes that the role of attorneys should be diminished so that they are prevented from postponing court cases and thereby prolonging the anger and hostility between the two parties. My father says that divorce attorneys capitalize on people's emotions for their own financial benefit. He thinks that attorneys should not be involved in the divorce process; there should be some sort of court clerk that takes care of the paperwork and ensures that the needs of children are considered.

Actually, lawyers are not necessary for getting a divorce. In theory, every couple could buy a "do-it-yourself-divorce" book and save a bundle. But usually lawyers are involved because spouses can't talk to each other, because the issues they are dealing with are complex, and because divorce is a legal proceeding, involving legal forms and rules. There are lots of details, decisions, forms, and deadlines to take care of, and it's easier to let the lawyer do it. Most people also feel the need for help and support and can only think of one way to get it—by hiring a lawyer. They are angry and hurt; they want money or revenge; they are afraid that their children will be taken away; they have fears induced by threats from the spouse. For all these reasons, most people feel a strong need for legal counsel and strong authoritative support—not just someone sympathetic to talk to. The fact that we live in a litigious society probably contributes to people's dependence on lawyers as well. The following student describes her parents' experience with lawyers.

Rachel Hall
When the decision was made to finalize the divorce, my parents both hired attorneys, because they knew nothing about the court system or the legal papers they would be dealing with. The attorneys they hired happened to have a bad history with each other. My parents' divorce was a battleground for the attorneys. They acted more as roadblocks than facilitators. My parents then decided to sit down themselves and figure out what was best for them and instructed the attorneys as to what they should draw up.

Unfortunately, the lawyer's role in divorce is ambiguous and his or her training may be inappropriate for expediting the divorce. Only a small number of lawyers are family law specialists, and even those who are trained in family law are programmed to argue for their client's position, right or wrong. It is not their job to be conciliatory, to negotiate, or to decide what is right or best. Their role is to win the case. This adversarial style can magnify ill will and increase hostility between husband and wife.

Cynthia Crandall
My parents wanted to save money, so they decided they were going to have a "friendly" divorce and use only one lawyer. But my mother realized quickly that she was not getting what she deserved and so she got her own lawyer. He was cheap and, as it turned out, incompetent, but he was all she could afford.

People assume that lawyers know what they're doing and how to handle divorce best. Still, many lawyers are incompetent. According to one study, people doing their own divorces fared better than those using lawyers. Lawyers are sloppy at filling out forms and following procedures. They may leave some issues unresolved—like care of children, education of children, and life insurance to cover children.

And they may strike bargains with the opposing attorney or the judge that are convenient for them but turn out not to be good for their clients.

Sarah Beller

In the nasty two-year court battle that followed my parents' divorce the only winners were the lawyers. My mother's lawyer took advantage of her and she ended up spending over $15,000 on a lawyer who was always away on vacation and was negligent in defending her. It turned out that my mother's lawyer and my father's lawyer were best buddies; everything was prearranged. Worst of all, her lawyer refused to go after the assets my father had been hiding and that they had found out about in the discovery process.

Of course, not all lawyers are incompetent. A few of our students' parents were pleased with the attorneys they selected.

Stephanie Conaway

When it came to getting a divorce, my mother did a good job in hiring a lawyer. She interviewed a few and decided to go with a referral. The attorney she chose was very bright and on top of things. He did not waste time; he asked the right questions. She told him she did not want someone who would go behind closed doors and sell her up the river, and he didn't. Actually, he did a great job. He told my mom to get copies of all their records, which she did. Then, when my father tried to say he could not afford to pay spousal support, the attorney and Mom proved him wrong. The court ordered my father to buy her out of both the house and her share of the business, because she could not afford to buy him out. The only mistake she didn't catch was that the house was appraised for more money than was written on the escrow papers. She did not have her attorney with her at the time she looked at the escrow papers, and she was so nervous that she did not think to insist on seeing the appraisal. She felt cheated on this one issue, but she let it go so the whole thing could finally be over.

As in this case, even when the lawyer performed well and generally represented the client's interests adequately, there was still one problem that he missed. In one study of women who dealt with lawyers during their divorces, 53 out of 56 had strong complaints about them. The most common complaints were that the lawyers had not informed them about the legal process; they had made oversights that cost the women money, time, and grief; and, most telling, these women claimed, the lawyers were not interested in their problems.

Do People Really Need a Counselor?

It is not surprising that clients complain that their lawyers are not interested in their problems. Even if lawyers are compassionate individuals, they are not psychological counselors, and ethical codes prevent them from referring their clients to mental health professionals. Yet this is what many people going through a divorce are looking for. An alternative to using a lawyer is to use a mediator. Mental health professionals, such as marriage and family counselors, often do mediation and the process emphasizes negotiation and cooperation rather than adversarial procedures. The foremost goal in mediation is not to win or lose, but to make a deal. If handled appropriately, mediation sets the stage for creative solutions that fit the couple's circumstances. Importantly, it gives husband and wife more control over the outcome—which proves to be more satisfying than feeling like pawns of the court system. Mediation is good for people who are basically open minded and cooperative. It can be detrimental in cases where one spouse is a better, more convincing communicator and smooth-talks the mediator, ending up with the better deal. Another contraindication for mediation is cases where there is a physically or emotionally abusive spouse who so intimidates the other spouse that there is no chance for a fair resolution.

Long-term Legal Wrangling

In brief, then, the actual legal process of getting a divorce is complicated; it involves big decisions and lots of them. It is time consuming, involving repeated visits to lawyers or mediators and waiting for court dates. It is unexpectedly expensive, costing thousands of dollars for lawyers, moving, fixing up property to sell, and so on. And it is often painful—not just because of the dissolution of the bond that the person expected to last forever and sustain him or her emotionally, but also because it plunges the individual into an abyss of uncertainty by way of insult, assault, and loss of stability, security, and sleep. Finally, the legal wrangling can continue for many years, as this last student describes.

Marcy Graham

My mom took my dad to court many times, filing false Orders to Show Cause. She claimed that he wasn't paying child support (he was); she wanted a restraining order because he was threatening her (he wasn't), and he was making more money than he was reporting (he wasn't). This went on for eight years. My dad was always overwhelmed by these court actions. It was my mother who, in fact, was behaving illegally. By keeping my sisters from seeing my dad, she was not complying with the visitation order; she was accepting money under the table for her house-cleaning services; the church gave her money and food that was undeclared; and she purposely didn't cash several child support checks just so it would look like my dad wasn't paying. My dad would try to prove these things in court, but he would just make the judge angry by appearing without a lawyer. My mom had a real shark for an attorney, who ended up hating my dad so much that he did a lot of stuff above and beyond what he was getting paid for just to "get him." My dad lost his car and about $10,000, after finally paying an attorney to end this once and for all after eight years in court.

Lessons to Be Learned

The decision has been made. You are definitely divorcing, and now you have to deal with the practical and emotional issues of dividing everything and dealing with the legal system. Reflecting on the stories and the issues raised in this chapter should make clear that there are a number of things people can do to minimize further crises and stress and maximize their own and their children's well being.

1. Educate yourself. One thing that can help is to read all the books you can find about divorce and its legal and financial consequences. Gather information about child custody and support, going to trial, getting and working with a lawyer, alternative dispute resolution procedures, legal terms and legal documents that need to be filed. Know your rights; for example, that a divorce settlement can include job training or education. Read books on negotiation and conflict resolution strategies. Armed with this information, aim for a win-win settlement. The more informed and prepared you are, the calmer you will feel, and the more effective you will be in your negotiations. That way you are increasing your chances that you will be satisfied with the outcome in the long run.

2. Settle out of court. If possible, use a mediator rather than an attorney to help you through the shoals of divorce. This will help you behave civilly toward your spouse. The goal of a mediator is negotiation, not winning a battle—and their fees are lower than lawyers'. Mediators are trained to ask the hard questions (so you don't have to do it), defuse conflicts, and close the deal. Divorce mediation gives control to the couple, not their lawyers, and increases their cooperation and satisfaction.

3. If going to court is unavoidable—prepare! Get the best lawyer you can find—the best one is not the one with the reputation of being a gun for hire. Interview this lawyer (books contain checklists of things to ask). Be sure you can work with this person and she or he can work with you. Go to family court and sit in on other peoples' divorce and custody proceedings—they are open to the public—before you have to go through your own. This will help you prepare your own case. Learn the legal terms the lawyers and judges are using and the different steps of the courtroom process. Check that you understand the motions your lawyer has filed and that you still agree with them. Prepare your argument and your evidence. Nothing does more harm than appearing in court unprepared and either paralyzed with fear or naively overconfident. In the worst case scenario, you will not be able to understand or control any aspect of the court proceedings and then at the end you will be handed a court order that gives you nothing that you wanted and you have to live with it for years to come.

4. Be reasonable and realistic. It is essential in going through the divisions of divorce that people have realistic expectations and make reasonable demands. You should assess your own needs and those of your children and decide how these can be served by decisions about child custody, property, spousal and child support. Individuals have a right to protect all their needs—not all their wants. So don't ask for the moon. You will lose things in the short run—like the china set and precious time with the children. But in the long run the china set won't matter and you can maintain your relationship with your children even if you are not with them every single day. If your starting point for the division of children and property is 95 percent for you and 5 percent for your spouse, you are bound to have a drawn-out legal and emotional battle on your hands. Your starting point should be fifty-fifty on everything. Deviation from this point of equality can come about through evaluation of the specific needs, abilities, and resources of everyone involved. For one thing, it may not be in the children's or even the parents' interest to split the children's time in half. For example, it is not sensible for either parent to ask for time with the children that they cannot realistically spend with them because they are working all the time. Being reasonable and fair will preserve your energy, your sanity, and your finances. And last, but not least, it will leave open a pathway for civil relations and cooperation with your (ex) spouse.

7

These Are My Kids! Deciding Child Custody

The decision of how to divide the children between their parents after a divorce often requires, quite literally, the Wisdom of Solomon. Yet it falls to judges, without the wisdom of Solomon and with very limited information about the child and the family, or to parents, who are often too embroiled in their divorce to be thinking rationally, to make these decisions. How child custody decisions are made is complex, challenging, and often painful, and our students' stories reflect this difficult process.

Clarissa Cambridge

Deciding who I would live with was the most difficult part of the divorce process for my parents, because neither my mother nor my father wanted to give me up. But in the end, my mom got what most mothers want. She got me living with her and she had my dad as an encouraging and supportive presence in the background. This arrangement worked out well, and both my parents were always there for me. But although the ultimate custody arrangement was successful, the path to that custody arrangement was painful. This is our story.

My mother was unhappy almost from the beginning of their marriage because she discovered that my father was a compulsive gambler who was spending their money as fast as she could earn it. So when she met a new man who showed her the kind of relationship she longed for, she told my dad she wanted to separate. Although he begged her to stay and give him another chance, she felt that divorce was her only alternative. At the time, I was being taken care of by a lady named Lucia, who lived in our house. My mom could not care for me without Lucia's help, because she was often out of town for her job. When my parents separated, my mom could not afford to keep Lucia, and she asked my dad to keep me until she got back on her feet. What she meant was that she needed a week or two to find an apartment. Later, in the custody battle, this act of "leaving her baby" was used against her.

After a few weeks, my mom had found an apartment, and I began spending equal time with each of my parents. My mom's job continued to take her out of town often, and she needed my dad to take care of me while she was gone. As it happened, though, my mom's new apartment soon became just a cover-up, because in reality we were spending most of our time at my mom's new boyfriend's house. During the time that my mom and dad were both getting equal time with me and the separation was still in a so-called "trial period," my parents continued to be cordial with one another. It was when my mom could no longer cover up her relationship with Pete that my dad realized that divorce was the next step and my mom would definitely be taking it.

After my dad and his family found out that my mom had "their" child living with an older black man, they determined to take my mom to court to get custody. It became a heated battle. My grandfather was the lawyer for my dad. Friends and family were subpoenaed to testify against my mom. They used her relationship with

Pete to try to portray her as a selfish and unfit mother. My dad's sister accused my mother of not wanting custody of her little girl. "If you really wanted custody of her, you would have taken her from the start," my Aunt Corene screamed in the courtroom. My dad and the judge stopped my aunt's irrelevant accusations, but it hurt my mom to see the bitterness coming from the family she had been part of.

The trial tore my parents' families apart, but miraculously, in the end, my mom was awarded custody of me. My dad was granted weekend and holiday visitation. Throughout the trial, my mom and my dad did not speak to each other. My mom believes that they could have worked out the divorce in a civil manner on their own if it had not been for the tension and anger from both their families. "It was more of a power-trip than anything else," she says. My dad's family used my grandfather as their lawyer to make the case more emotional. My mom felt that they were just taking advantage of their position of power and the fact that they had the law, or should I say a family of lawyers, on their side. She believes that the judge was aware of what she was up against and that this actually worked in her favor. At the end of the trial, the judge told my grandfather never to put him in that position again.

In making his decision about custody, the judge looked beyond each lawyer's case and into who was the more appropriate parent under the circumstances. My mom's extra-marital relationship easily made her look like the bad guy. Most people were not aware of the problems my dad's gambling had caused, because so much of the focus was on my mom's wrongdoing. Fortunately the judge was able to see past all these things and make what I have always thought of as the best judgment possible.

After the judge's decision had been made, my mom and dad were able to put the battle behind them, proving even more how his family had instigated the whole battle. My parents both got what they wanted and were able to work out visitations easily. They really did not need a judge to set down visitation times and holiday schedules, and they worked it out on their own from that day forward.

As this story clearly illustrates, deciding what to do with the children is one of the most difficult parts of going through the divorce. The couple must decide who the child is going to live with—mother, father, or both parents alternately. They must decide if one parent will have sole legal responsibility for the child or if this responsibility will be shared. They must work out how often each parent will see the child, for how long, and on what schedule. As this student suggests, the ideal custody arrangement for a mother might be to have the child live with her and to have the father as a confidant and collaborator, someone with whom she can chat over problems she is having with the child, someone who is understanding, supportive, helpful, encouraging—and still lets her make the important decisions. Unfortunately, the real world is seldom like this. Divorcing spouses can't always work out anything so cooperative—or they wouldn't be getting divorced in the first place. And even in this student's case, it was only after extreme duress that her parents arrived at such an arrangement.

This story illustrates many of the issues that litter the custody arena. One issue is the difficulty that occurs when both parents want the child, which in this case was exacerbated by the desires of the two spouses' families and the complications of having a new man on the scene. A second issue is the likelihood that the legal venue will serve as a battleground for custody fighting. In this story, as in many of our students' stories, the judge had to make the custody decision for the parents. Fortunately, his judgment was wise; not all of our students were so fortunate. It is not surprising that many judgments are faulty; judges face a challenge, making custody determinations based on incomplete and often biased information. As this student suggests, it would have been better if her parents could have agreed on custody and worked it out on their own rather than taking the decision to court. This student's story also describes the most common custody outcome of divorce in this society: the mother gets custody and the dad gets visitation.

The Changing History of Child Custody

Until the 19th century, children, like their mothers and servants and livestock, belonged to their fathers. The father's right to custody was absolute. Fathers were given custody, even of nursing infants, and the welfare of the child was not an issue. During the 19th century, the place of women in society began to rise, and this was reflected in their being given some rights to custody. Concern about children's welfare and rights also grew. In 1881, for the first time, a judge emphasized the "best interests of the child" in a custody ruling. It was generally suggested that for children of tender years (under age seven), mothers were more appropriate custodial parents than fathers, because this was in the child's best interests. Children would then go to the father when they reached a "proper age." In 1925, the notion of the "best interests of the child" was formally articulated and the court suggested that in custody cases the judge acts as parens patriae (prudent parent) to do what is best for the interests of the child. After this, the father's advantage in custody cases gradually eroded, and within a couple of decades the mother's right to custody became far greater than the father's. The argument was made that women were better suited for caring for children than were men. A "cult of motherhood" emerged under the influence of such important figures as the psychoanalyst Sigmund Freud. Motherhood and mother love were raised to lyrical heights. As one legal writer in 1938 wrote, "There is but a twilight zone between a mother's love and the atmosphere of Heaven, and all things being equal, no child should be deprived of that maternal influence." The presumption that mothers were best for children took hold and continued for several decades. In the 1970s and 1980s, significant changes occurred. Courts moved away from the presumption that mothers are always the best parents and developed a more flexible standard, which favored neither parent. They discarded the "tender years" presumption that mothers should always be awarded custody of young children, because it was based on an outdated social stereotype that mothers are more nurturing, devoted, and competent than fathers and more likely to be at home as full-time caregivers. The tender years doctrine was also ruled unconstitutional because it was solely based on a person's gender. Today, custody is awarded according to the best interests of child, not according to the sex of parent or who was more to blame in the divorce. What is considered to be in the best interests of the child depends on state law and on how the judge weighs a number of different factors. Although the sex of a parent is no longer supposed to be considered when courts are awarding custody, maternal preference may still be used as a tie breaker when all other factors are equal, and occasionally it may be a factor in the best interest equation. But the court must then give a specific reason that an award to the mother is in the child's best interests.

So who do courts today favor, if not the mother? In a provocative and influential book written in 1979, Beyond the Best Interests of the Child, Joseph Goldstein, Anna Freud, and Albert Solnit suggested that custody should be given to the child's "psychological parent"—that parent to whom the child is "bonded," with whom he or she has the strongest "affectional ties," the caregiver who has provided for the child's psychological and physical needs through day-to-day interactions. This parent should be given custody immediately, exclusively, and irrevocably. More recently, it has been recommended that young children be placed with the parent who has been more involved in the child's daily care, that is, the "primary caregiver." The basis for this recommendation is that this parent has been taking care of the child and knows how to do it, and it is less disruptive for the child as well, because this is the person to whom the child goes when stressed. Most often, judges try to take into account the child's age and emotional ties with each parent when making a custody determination. Because younger children have a greater need for being with the psychological or primary parent than older children, this factor is particularly important for them. Typically, then, young children are placed in primary custody of their primary caregiver. The fact is, in our society, though, it is still most often the mother who has been the child's primary caregiver and thus maternal custody is still the most common outcome.

The Parents' Wishes as a Determinant of Custody

The major factor considered by the judge in awarding custody is the parents' wishes. About 90 percent of all custody rulings are settled this way. As long as parents can agree, their preference determines what will happen. When parents agree, the court does not look into details of the arrangement. Judges do not know or care or evaluate whether this is good for the child and in the child's best interests. Only if there is a disagreement between the parents about the custody arrangement will the court try to evaluate the best interests of the child. A typical case in which the parents made the decisions about custody themselves is illustrated by this student's story.

Elena Parker
   When my parents got divorced, my sister, Lisa, was three and I was five. Both our parents believed that it would be in our best interests to live with our mother. The result was joint legal custody and sole physical custody with my mom. My dad moved to an apartment about twenty minutes away, and my sister and I spent every other weekend with him. My mother continued to live in our family home, and this arrangement worked out pretty well. There was no animosity between my parents—no court battle, no major disputes after the divorce. My

father paid child support in the amount of $225 per child per month. Although he was making a comfortable living as an attorney and could have afforded to pay more, my mom never got up the courage to take him to court to fight for more. Now, my dad regrets that he didn't fight for joint physical custody. He says that he has missed out on his children's experiences growing up. He is sad that he wasn't able to communicate his feelings to my sister and me, during the little time that we spent together. My mother regrets that she didn't fight for more money. My sister and I are glad that we did not need to experience any battling—for us or for money.

In this case, the couple decided amicably and in compliance with contemporary convention that the mother would have custody and the father would pay child support. It is noteworthy, though, that although the arrangement worked out well, both parents had lingering regrets about what they missed by adopting this arrangement. They did, however, stick with their original custody decision. Other students reported that their custody arrangements changed over the years. The parents found that, over time, their own situation and their children's needs changed, and that the original terms of the agreement were of little importance several years down the road.

Diana Denman

My parents easily agreed about custody. We were to live with my mom, and my dad could see us whenever he wanted. He was supposed to take us to dinner at least once a week and to have us for one weekend every month. He was good about it in the beginning, but as time went by, his visits dwindled. By the time I was in high school, our visits had almost stopped, and after I went away to college, almost all communications ended. He pays tuition and housing for me now, but he never calls or writes.

This pattern is common: the parents work out the custody arrangement between themselves so that the mother gets custody and the father visits, and then those visits with dad gradually diminish.

Connie Phillips

My parents' divorce was neat and clean. There was no fighting. My father wanted to be fair, and my mother wanted my sister and me to have a good relationship with our father. They split their assets 50-50: my dad got the Porsche and my mom got the Mazda; my mom stayed in the house; my dad paid all the bills. There was no argument about custody either. My dad did not want to take us away from our mom. They left the visitation open so my dad could see us whenever he wanted, as long as he let my mother know ahead of time. My father moved to an apartment near where we lived so that he could still see us. I remember visiting there a couple of times with my sister. Other than that, we mostly went out to dinner together or somewhere fun like the movies, the zoo, the mountains, or Palm Springs. Not too long after my father moved into the apartment, he moved again and went to live with his girlfriend. The divorce took one year to be finalized. The next day, my father married his girlfriend. Shortly after, his employer relocated him to Illinois. This was the end of our close relationship. Sure we would talk on the phone, write letters, and visit during the summer, but things were never again the same.

This is the way it usually happens. In one national study, over half of the children in divorced families said that they had not seen their fathers in the last year, and less than one fifth had seen them as often as once a week. A large study in Minnesota revealed a similar situation: there, only one fifth of the children said they had regular visits with their fathers.

One may wonder why fathers who have visitation rights voluntarily decrease their contact with their children. Is it that they are just unstable, unreliable, and unloving people? Although these descriptions may fit some individuals, it seems that on a larger scale a different motive contributes. Many men are caught in an approach-avoidance bind. They want to play a significant role in their children's lives, but at the same time they want to protect themselves from the painful feelings that arise from limited and unsatisfactory contact with their children. They are afraid of losing their significance as fathers in their children's lives and dissatisfied with their status as second-class parents. They dread their children's rejection and their ex-spouse's antagonism. They feel guilty about having disrupted their children's lives. They feel angry and resentful toward their ex-wife. To avoid these dismal experiences, they stay away. A number of our students described how their fathers withdrew from their lives because it was too difficult for them to stay involved:

Amanthi Chandra

After the divorce, my father missed my brother and me tremendously and felt completely cut off from our lives. It was easier for him not to see us than to make contact with us, because he knew he had let us down.

Elizabeth Harrison

My dad had a lot of difficulty adjusting to the divorce. He felt a great sense of loss, because he had lost his wife and his daughter. When I asked him, "Why didn't you visit me then?" he answered that it was because he felt so much resentment toward Mom because she was seeing other men and because he was not able to take me places on his own terms. He could not stand having to get permission from my mom before taking me anywhere. He thought to himself if mom can be "that way" so could he. He would "show her and not come around any more."

Some fortunate children do not lose the noncustodial parent. For them, both parents manage to stay involved in the child's daily life. In the following case, it happened because the two parents lived in close proximity.

Martina Nunez

After the divorce, my mom received sole custody of me, and my dad was given liberal visitation rights. My mom used to let him take me for overnight stays at his house. I remember going over to his new apartment every other weekend or so. The only reason I didn't like going over there was that my dad did not cook the foods I liked, the way my mom did. He was not from the United States—he was born and raised in Jamaica and Honduras—and I never did like the foods he ate. I used to eat them once in a while, but more often I would make him take me to McDonald's. The overnight trips stopped after two or three years because we moved closer to my dad. For several years we lived right across the street from him. He started taking me to school and picking me up every day. In fact, he took me to school every day until I graduated from high school. He gave me my allowance every week. He bought my clothes, toys and anything else I needed or wanted. There was never a point in my life that my dad was not there or I could not find him.

It is not always possible to live in such close physical proximity to the noncustodial father, but another way for both parents to stay involved with the children is for them to work out a joint custody arrangement. In joint legal custody, both parents retain legal responsibility for the child and have the right to make basic decisions for the child about medical treatment, education, and religious training. In joint physical custody, the child spends about half the time living with each parent, and both parents are equally charged with the child's daily care and control. But the problem with joint custody is that it means that parents have to share custody and decision-making with someone from whom they are getting a divorce. In the throes of divorce, a parent's first impulse is often to have as little to do with the other parent as possible. They may doubt the competence or the morals or the lifestyle of the other parent, and they don't want that person having an influence on their child, or spoiling their child, or taking out their anger on their child. Consequently, not all parents are able to agree to a joint custody plan. When parents are able to work out a joint custody, they can both remain involved in the children's daily lives and activities:

Rachel Hall

After our parents separated, my brother Jeff and I moved back and forth from my dad's house to the place my mom was living, every other week. My parents wanted the best for us, and they worked out an informal joint custody arrangement. They felt that this was the best arrangement for all of us, because this way we did not have to make a choice between our parents, and they could both remain involved in our lives. They were able to remain civil toward each other during the entire time. They never used us as pawns, nor did they speak badly of each other.

When the divorce was legalized, physical custody was split 50-50. Jeff and I lived with our dad from Sunday morning until Thursday morning, and the rest of the week, we spent with Mom. We did this for the next nine years.

Because of this joint custody arrangement, my parents had frequent contact with each other. Jeff and I would go to my dad's house after school and wait for my mom to pick us up on the days she had us. Although at first it was difficult for my mom to go back to the house and see my father, it got easier with time. Their conversations also got easier. After the divorce was final, they were able to remain friends, and they have, to this day.

This is probably as good as it gets. The parents wanted joint custody; their lives permitted it; and they were generous and civilized toward each other in working it out. At the other extreme, the custody arrangement occurs by default. One parent just moves out and moves on, and the parent who is left becomes the custodial parent.

Staci Chen

After my mother moved out, my dad tried to reconcile with her many times, but she wouldn't have it. She wanted nothing more to do with him. She wanted to start a new life without him, and, for the most part, without us. My dad took over custody and my mom saw us on the weekends. She paid child support and bought us things. She was sort of like a "Disneyland mom." About four months after she left, she told us that she was pregnant. Two months later she had a baby boy and a couple of months after that, my mom's and my dad's divorce was final and she married the baby's father. My father slipped into a severe depression. He was drinking every day. He was a mess. He couldn't take care of himself, so how was he going to take care of his children?

This custody arrangement may not have been in the child's "best interests," with the custodial parent hitting the bottle—but it was the only custody arrangement available. The mother wasn't interested in having custody—she had moved on to a new family—and the court couldn't force her to take custody if she was unwilling. In such cases, the only available parent becomes the custodial parent.

In some cases it only seems as if parents have decided between them amicably what the custody arrangement will be. In the following story, one of the worst fears of divorced parents was realized—the other parent kidnapped the child. In this student's case, the mother was assisted by clever advice from her attorney and managed to retrieve the child. Not all parents are so lucky. Kidnapping is one of the worst outcomes of an unresolved custody battle.

Judd Michaelson

Although my parents weren't formally divorced yet, my mom knew it wasn't going to work out to get back together. Her theory was proven correct when she decided to let my dad take me to Montana for a week to visit my grandparents. We stayed in Montana for the week, and then my dad took me and left. Nobody knew where we had gone. My own dad had kidnapped me. My mom says this was the worst time of her life. When my dad did finally call, he told my mom that he had filed for divorce and she was never going to see me again. My mom immediately called her attorney. He told her to call my dad back and say that she wanted to get back together with him again. Then, the attorney told her, when she did get together with my dad, she should act like everything was fine. When she had him believing everything was okay, she should seize the first opportunity and get on an airplane and fly back to Colorado taking me with her. My mom went along with the attorney's plan, and when she finally had my dad believing that everything was fine, she got me and took me back to her parents' house. My father thought that she was just going to visit my grandparents for the day, but when we got there, my grandfather took us to the airport and we flew to Colorado. When we got there, my mom immediately filed for divorce. When the divorce proceedings took place, my dad basically got all their assets. He threatened my mom, by telling her that if he had to pay, he would fight for sole custody and tell the court that she had abandoned me. My mom caved because she was scared that she might lose me again.

The Court Awards Custody to Ensure Stability for the Child

When the parents cannot come to a decision about custody, and the court determines the arrangement, one important principle the judge follows is to try to promote continuity and stability for the child. For this reason, the judge may order a custody arrangement in which the child stays with his or her brothers and sisters in the same house and community where they grew up. Preference is given to the parent who plans to stay in the house and not leave town. Sometimes the court orders that the custodial parent cannot leave the state. It is usually the children's preference, too, to stay put.

Ensuring continuity and stability also means that the judge takes into account the child's current care situation. Just as "possession is nine tenths of the law," preference for custody goes to the parent with whom the child is living at the time of the divorce. The court will not change a custody arrangement already in place unless there is an important reason for doing so. The current custody arrangement is like a de facto parental agreement.

The court also tries to promote continuity by ensuring that the child will have continued frequent contact with the noncustodial parent. One way to accomplish this is through joint physical custody. Another way is through liberal visitation. Thus, if one parent says, "No way I'm gonna let that jerk/bitch see my child," the court may award custody to the jerk/bitch if he/she says he or she is willing to allow liberal visitation. In the following student's story, the mother tried to ensure continuity for the children...but it backfired, to the children's detriment.

Brad Dawson

My mom did not fight for custody because she did not want to put us through more trouble than necessary, and she believed that, if we stayed with our father, she would have unrestricted visitation. She also wanted to keep us in a familiar school and home. She wanted to maintain as normal a life for us as possible. In the divorce, my dad was awarded sole custody, and my mom went on believing that she would have no trouble seeing us whenever she wanted. She should have worried, though, when, during the finalization of the divorce agreement, my dad's lawyer tried to get her to give up her parental rights. As soon as the divorce became final, my dad began to increase his control over my mom's visitation. He told her she could visit only every Wednesday night and every other weekend. He began to say terrible things to us about Mom, and he got mad if we wanted to spend time with her. After each weekend we spent with her, he grilled us. Then he decided that it was time to move and start a new life in a new area. So, the day before Christmas, we moved to the suburbs. Now, not only did we have to deal with the divorce and all the resulting pain and anger, but we also had to deal with losing the friends we had gone to school with since kindergarten, with new faces, a new school, and even more fighting between our parents. I had an incredibly hard time adjusting.

It is terribly difficult for children when all aspects of their lives are disrupted by the divorce. Therefore, the principle followed by the court of maximizing continuity is a sound and sensible one. This mother's attempt to maintain stability for her children was a good one. However, she should have realized that her husband was not as well-intentioned as she and that his grudges, in combination with the lack of an adequate custody arrangement, would seriously disrupt her relationship with her children and interfere with the children's sense of continuity and stability. Not having any written agreement with regard to custody and visitation is almost always foolhardy. Even if parents have an amiable divorce and generally co-parent well, it is better to have a written agreement to fall back on should a disagreement arise.

The Court Determines Who Is a "Fit" Parent for Custody

A second factor that the court considers in making a custody determination is the "fitness" of the parent. This means that the parent is capable of bringing up a child. For one thing, the parent must be physically "fit" to take care of a child. This does not mean that he has to have abs of steel or that she can run a marathon. But there is a concern about physical limitations that reduce a parent's ability to care for a child. However, even parents with epilepsy, paralysis, and missing limbs have been given custody, if they can prove they are physically able care for the child.

Whether a parent has to be "fit" morally to be awarded custody is an open question, and the answer varies from region to region and court to court. In general, a parent does not have to be a regular churchgoer to be a "fit" parent. He can read pornographic literature and still be considered "fit"—as long as he doesn't read it to the kids. What if a parent is guilty of adultery? Does this mean that he or she can't get custody? With the institution of no-fault grounds for divorce, the courts made adultery irrelevant to custody decisions, unless it could be shown that the adultering parent was unfit on other grounds. Nevertheless, in practice, moral values are often taken into account even if they have no direct link to child rearing. In California, testimony relating to misconduct of the parent is not admissible in granting the divorce, but it is admissible in a custody hearing.

The parent's sexual behavior also can be considered in a custody hearing; the parent's relationship with his or her lover (heterosexual or homosexual), his or her cohabitation with a lover, and the number of lovers he or she has—can all be taken into account, even though they are not supposed to be important unless they bear on the issue of parent's fitness as a parent. As society is becoming more permissive, courts are becoming more broad-minded, and the current trend is toward a more neutral position regarding the significance of the parent's moral conduct. It is now possible, for example, for a lesbian mother to get custody of her children, especially if she is not living with her lover, although this was unlikely or impossible just a few years ago. But it is still an uphill battle for a parent with obvious moral "flaws" to be granted custody.

Finally, to receive custody, a parent must be "fit" psychologically. Parents with emotional problems, like those with physical limitations, can be awarded custody, if they can prove that their problems will not interfere with their parenting. The difficulty is in proving this. Evidence of suicide attempts, depression, and repeated hospitalizations are used to demonstrate a parent's psychological instability and have provided grounds for denial of custody. Either side can require that the spouse be given a psychiatric examination in order to establish suitability as a custodial parent. Some judges require periodic psychological examinations of the parents or they may depend on expert testimony to inform them as to the likely effect of a parent's mental health on the children. An abusive or alcoholic parent is usually not considered fit for custody but may be granted visitation. Sometimes even this is a mistake, as the next story shows.

Judie Myers

My father was verbally and physically abusive to my mother throughout their marriage. One time, he even tried to kill her. The day my mother left him marked the beginning of a long and bitter divorce. They were in court once a month for the first year following their separation. The judge awarded sole legal custody to my mother based on my father's history of abuse. She received a $10,000 settlement and a small monthly child support payment. She got no furniture or personal belongings. These things did not matter to my mother. She was just happy to escape from the abuse and get on with her life. My father, however, was intensely angry. He hated my mother for "taking us away from him." He continued to take her to court in an effort to reduce child support and drain her of any money she had received from the divorce. When the divorce was finalized, the judge ordered visitation for my father—every other weekend and one night a week. My mother was very concerned about this decision. She felt uneasy about letting us visit my father because he had been so abusive, but she had to follow court orders. Soon after visitation was established, my sister Tracy found passports in my father's drawer while she was playing. She brought them home to my mother. What she had discovered were false passports. My father had been planning to kidnap us.

My mother went back to court and presented this to the judge. She requested that a hold be placed on the passports so that neither parent could take us out of the country unless they both agreed. (The judge concurred.) But we still had to continue to visit my father as ordered by the court. We never liked to go with him. We felt we did not know him. He tried to keep us entertained by going to amusement parks and buying us toys. I don't think we ever felt comfortable with him. He never got over the divorce and always talked about how terrible my mother was because she had left him. He tried to make us hate her by telling us she was a bad person. This only made us dislike him more. Our relationship continued to decline. The verbal abuse continued. Every time we visited our father he tormented us. He lived in Los Angeles and we dreaded the hour-long car ride to his house, because he screamed and yelled at us about the divorce all the way. We also began to fear his outbursts and often he would spank us or slap us when we protested or contradicted his derogatory remarks about our mother. I remember begging my mother not to make us see him. But she did not have a choice. She was afraid that the court would hold her in contempt if she did not send us to our father and that she might lose custody as a consequence.

As the years passed, our father's temper got even worse. One Sunday evening we pulled up to our grandparents' house after visiting him for the weekend. He had been screaming at us in the car that he would kill our mother and we would never see her again. We were terrified. My grandfather came out to greet us, and my father started yelling at him too. He hit my grandfather and knocked him down. I ran inside the house, terrified. My grandmother called 911, and I heard the police sirens and ambulance coming to help us.

When the police arrived my father denied everything that had happened. My mother kept insisting that we go in the other room while she told her side of the story to the police. We were so scared to be without her we stayed and listened to everything the police said about my father. We knew what we had seen, and we knew that he lied.

Finally, my father left and a report was filed with the police. I remember going home from my grandparents' house that night. The car was silent as we pulled up to our driveway. We were afraid my father would be there waiting for us. We were unsure at this point what he might do. A court order had been established shortly after the divorce, stating that my father could not come within 500 feet of our house. This was no comfort to us at all. I was afraid that he would appear and attack one of us at any time.

Our visits with our father, which had to continue per court order, were extremely stressful. I remember having a bad argument with my father and afterward sneaking out of his house and going to a store to call my grandparents for help. My dad found out I had left and followed me in his car up and down the streets in his neighborhood, alternately begging and threatening me to come back with him. I refused. He finally went back home when my grandparents and mother arrived. I was crying. I was terrified. I begged my mother to let me stay home and never see him again. She insisted I had to follow the court-ordered visitation rules until I was eighteen years old.

Shortly after I had turned eighteen, my father and I had another huge argument. We were having lunch at Carl's Junior. My father was angry because I defended my younger sister. She had been using his credit card without asking him. He became enraged. I just wanted him to stop yelling and making a scene in the restaurant. He continued and I got up to leave. He followed me out to the parking lot and yelled at me. He told me if I walked away he would no longer pay for college. I was tired of the ultimatums, the fighting, the verbal and physical abuse and his attempts to undermine my relationship with my mother. I walked away. I haven't seen my father since.

In this case, the court's arbitrary custody determination, which mandated visitation with an abusive father, did not protect the children's best interests. The children's bad relationship with their father continued after the divorce and they suffered years of abuse. The court's decision exposed them to risk, fear, and stress. In retrospect, the mother should have demanded that the court-ordered visitation with the abusive father be terminated. But like many mothers, she may have been afraid to go back to court and risk a change in custody in her disfavor. The moment one parent returns to court to modify an existing custody arrangement, "custody is up for grabs" as one lawyer put it. And because judges have a hard time sifting through the contradictory allegations that parents make—"He is abusive to the children"; "She is trying to take away my time with the kids and alienate them from me"—they sometimes make mistakes. Judges also seek to maintain continued contact between children and both their parents, so they are reluctant to withhold visitation from either parent. In the future, we may evolve to the point that abuse is not tolerated in visiting parents any more than it is tolerated in custodial parents.

The Court Uses Demographic Factors in Determining Custody

Another set of factors considered by the court in making custody adjudications are demographic—the parents' income, education, occupation, race, and religion. Courts do not disqualify a parent based on his or her religious beliefs, but they do consider these beliefs in determining the best interests of the child. A parent might be disqualified as a custodial parent if he or she holds a religious belief that is detrimental to the child's physical health. For example, being a Jehovah's Witness would be detrimental for a child who is a hemophiliac, because Jehovah's Witnesses do not permit blood transfusions. Or belonging to the Plymouth Brethren church might be considered a risk for a child's mental health, because members of this religion are isolated from people of other religions.

The parents' race is not supposed to be considered in determining custody, but if the parents are of two different races, it is assumed that the child's best interests are to be served by living with the parent whom he or she resembles most physically.

The parent's education and occupation may also enter into the custody equation. In a landmark decision in October of 1975, the court first awarded custody to one parent over another on this basis, on the grounds that that parent had a more "intellectually exciting" lifestyle and greater psychological expertise. The parent awarded custody in this case was the child psychologist and author, Lee Salk; his ex-wife was—merely—a full-time mother and homemaker who had reared the children from birth. This legal precedent can penalize mothers for having devoted themselves full time to raising their children, instead of furthering their education and career.

Another demographic characteristic that figures into custody determinations is the marital status of the parents. If one of the parents is remarried or is about to be remarried, he or she can argue that this will provide the child with a better environment than living in a single-parent home. In practice, this argument seems to be most effective for fathers and stepmothers, in which case the father provides the income and the stepmother provides child care, as was the case for the following student.

> Linda Ford
> After my father remarried, my parents had another custody battle. Dad had a pleasant home and a good income, by then, and he was able to provide a stable environment for us, so the judge awarded him full custody.

In contested cases in which both parents want custody, the parent's availability may be another factor the court considers in making a custody determination. In some states, the court favors the parent who is more available, that is, the parent who has more time to be with the child. In a highly controversial case in Michigan in 1994, a judge awarded custody of a three-year-old child to the father and paternal grandmother because the child's mother was a student and had placed the child in day care.

Income also matters. In making custody rulings, the court takes into account the ability of the parent to provide the child with food, clothing, and medical care. Parents, too, include these criteria in their decision-making about who takes the children, as the following students indicated.

> Brad Dawson
> My dad had a better job than my mom, and she felt that he was better able to provide for us financially. Many of her friends encouraged her to fight for custody and get support payments from my dad, but she thought that we would have more financial stability if we lived with Dad.

John Klinger
There was no custody battle between my parents, because my father was working only part time and could barely support himself, let alone his children.

The Lawyer's Skill and the Judge's Values Affect Custody

These factors are considered, implicitly or explicitly, when the court makes a custody determination. But the evidence that is presented in the courtroom is limited. The judge listens to the different versions of each parent's story and must extrapolate from each parent's past conduct to their future conduct—a chancy undertaking. (The movie "Kramer versus Kramer" illustrated just how much a parent's behavior can change over time.) One law school professor has suggested that if courts would award custody by the flip of a coin, the outcome would likely be just as good. In most cases, however, the judge listens to evidence from both sides and tries to figure out how the best interests of the child would be served, or which parent will harm the child the least. In doing this, there are two more factors that influence the decision—the lawyer's skill and the judge's own values.

Just as attorneys pursue their client's interests vigorously and aggressively in trying to get them the best financial settlement, they pursue their interests aggressively in attempting to obtain custody. Not all attorneys adhere to the American Bar Association's ethical mandate to "treat with consideration all persons involved in the legal process and avoid the infliction of needless harm." Consequently, the skill of the attorney to make a compelling (if biased) case for their client enters into the custody equation. In their effort to win their case, lawyers can also create animosity. Recall the story with which we opened the chapter, in which the grandfather served as lawyer for his son and brought great anger and bitterness to the courtroom battle over custody.

It is clear that the current system leaves the judge a

substantial degree of discretion and a whole lot of power to make decisions. Whereas it is easy to agree about what is bad for children—abuse, mistreatment, neglect—it is much harder to decide what custody arrangement would be best for a child or which parent would be the lesser of two evils. Determining custody often turns out to be choosing the least detrimental alternative. Inevitably, therefore, the judge's personal values about what is good for children—be it religion, literature, nutrition, or money—enter into decision. Judges take all the aforementioned factors into account, but they weigh them according to their own subjective values and views. Little wonder that joint custody often seems like an ideal compromise, because then the judge doesn't have to choose between the parents.

Courtroom Helpers for Deciding Custody

In many states, judges may call on two kinds of professionals to assist them in making decisions about custody arrangements. A child custody evaluator makes a recommendation about which of the two parents would make the better custodian in a given case. Unlike a judge, who is limited to evidence presented in the courtroom, custody evaluators actually go out into the real world and assess parents' mental health, parenting skills, and ability to look after their children in terms of available time, emotional support, and money. They may assess parents' attitudes toward the child and children's attitudes toward their parents. They may observe the current caretaking arrangement and solicit information about the parents' past involvement with the child. They try to identify the child's "psychological parent" or "primary caregiver." They probe into the parents' past and present lifestyles. Having this kind of background information about the parents from an objective, trained professional can be very helpful for the judge. Of course, the information is only as good as the custody evaluator's investigation. It is difficult to obtain the necessary evidence in the relatively limited time and with the relatively limited resources available—primarily interviews and psychological tests administered to the parents and children. It is difficult to evaluate the information and to predict the long-term effects for the child of being with either parent. It is difficult to map out a permanent solution to custody; the arrangement may need to change when the child is older. Most problematic of all, it is difficult to choose between two parents if neither is outstanding or both are inadequate. It is difficult to weigh a mother's and a father's relative strengths and weaknesses. What if one parent has more time for the child but doesn't have the emotional availability of the other parent? What if one parent has enough money but doesn't have competent parenting skills? Choosing between two poisons or choosing between two angels is nearly impossible. Nevertheless, it is the job of the child custody evaluator to make a win-lose recommendation about custody, not to assist the couple in working out an optimal arrangement.

Because a custody evaluator has more psychological training and has spent more time interviewing and observing the family than the judge, these evaluations are viewed as an important component of the decision-making process for determining child custody. There is no clear evidence, however, that custody evaluations improve the final outcome for children or that parents are more satisfied. Critics of child custody evaluations point out that evaluators may not have adequate training to assess the quality of parent-child relationships, may not investigate thoroughly enough, may be influenced by their personal biases—just like judges—or may be biased in favor of a certain parent—the parent who talks more smoothly or convincingly, the parent who pays, or the parent who has an attorney who provides the evaluator with many clients.

Another kind of professional who can assist the court in making child custody decisions is a guardian ad litem This is a person who represents the interests of the child specifically. Some people think this person should be an advocate for the child's wishes; others see the guardian ad litem as protecting the child's welfare. Guardians ad litem may be attorneys, mental health professionals, or even trained laypersons. Like child custody evaluators, these individuals perform a thorough and objective investigation of the case. They solicit and advocate the child's views, and they may also interview neighbors, teachers, and friends of the family in their effort to obtain an objective and comprehensive picture. They may serve as a mediator for the parents and counsel the parents to avoid litigation. Guardians who are attorneys also present and cross-examine witnesses in court. Having a guardian can serve to reduce the distortion that may result from the motivated introduction of evidence by the two parents or their respective attorneys.

The Child's Wishes as a Determinant of Custody

A final factor that is considered by courts and parents in making custody decisions is what the children want. This was a major factor discussed by our students in their accounts of their own experiences going through divorce. Over the past two decades there has been a growing emphasis on children's preferences when making custody arrangements. This is part of a general trend in society toward recognizing children's interests in decisions that are crucial to their own welfare and part of a growing acknowledgment that children are capable of making sensible decisions about their own lives.

The weight given to this factor in custody decisions usually depends on the child's age. There is no law that specifies a minimum age at which children can choose the parent they want to live with. Children under thirteen years may be asked for their opinions, but their wishes are not usually given much weight by parents or courts. With children who are thirteen years or older, the weight given to the child's wishes in the legal system varies from state to state. In Georgia, for example, children over thirteen years of age may choose which parent they want to live with and are placed in custody of that parent unless the court deems the parent unfit. In California, less weight is given to the child's preference, even after age thirteen, because of a concern that children may not know what is in their own best interest, that they may pick a custodial parent just because he has more money or she is more permissive. There is also a concern that letting a child choose between the parents places too much responsibility on the young person and will make him or her feel guilty, because choosing one parent implies rejection of the other. The general consensus in most states is that the judge should listen to the child's opinion and take it into consideration but not let it be the sole basis for his or her decision. The child should know that it is the judge and not the child who is going to make the custody decision, based on what he or she thinks will be best for the child.

In the following stories, a twelve-year-old and a thirteen-year-old decided about their custody. Their stories reflect a trend in our students' stories: when the child expressed a preference for custody, it was most often to live with the father. This does not necessarily mean that all children would prefer paternal custody. It probably reflects the fact that the most common custody arrangement is to be with mother, so children do not need to express their preference for maternal custody as often.

Kristin Sanders

The most painful experience of my life was when my father dropped me off from our first visit after my mom and dad separated. I was eleven years old, and I felt as if he was abandoning me. I just stood there screaming and crying as he drove away. I will never forget that day. For the next year, visits with my father were awkward. The novelty of going to his house wore off quickly, because none of my friends lived near him and it was such a different world from what I was used to. It annoyed my dad that I didn't want to spend more time at his place; he could not understand why I did not want to live in

Malibu. But he was dating furiously and had little time for me. About a year after the separation, he reduced his dating and became less of a "Disneyland dad." We did more normal parent-child things when we were together. When it came time for the court to make a decision about custody, therefore, I asked to live with my dad. He was awarded custody and moved back into our family home. I moved in with him, and life became happier and more stable than it had been living with my mother.

Connie Phillips

At the end of the first summer that my sister and I went to visit our dad in Illinois, my sister decided to stay behind and live with him. She was thirteen years old. She said that there were many reasons for making this decision. One of them was guilt. My dad kept saying that he should have one of us, that it was only fair. My sister was able to see his point of view and, because she felt that I was too young to move and leave our mother (I was only nine), she decided that she would be the one to stay with Dad. Another reason she came to this decision was that it was hard on our mother to have to support all of us—especially because the child support payments had stopped coming.

Seeking stability, searching for fairness, appeasing one parent, and reducing the burden for the other parent are some of the complex reasons that children choose to live with their fathers. Our students were not just choosing a parent for superficial and self-serving reasons like more money and less supervision. Their choices quite mature. Sometimes, it seemed, the children acted more mature than the adults. In the following story, the parents themselves could not come to an amicable and stable custody arrangement, and the children strove for a compromise. They tried to make both their parents happy by going back and forth between them rather than choosing one over the other. As a result, they were painfully caught in the middle of their parents' battles.

Scott Mallard

After the divorce, the custody battles began. My mother always was awarded custody, but that wasn't enough. She and her new husband wanted to move to Idaho, and the court would not let her move out of the state with her children. Therefore, after years of court battles, we children made a deal with our father. We said that if he would let our mother move out of state, we would live with him every other year. My father's only condition was that we live with him for the first year. I was nine years old at the time. Some decision for a nine-year-old to make, isn't it? But I just kind of went along with my brothers and sisters. At nine years old, I could never have imagined how difficult it would be to live up to this agreement.

Living with my father that year was very difficult for many reasons. I changed houses. I changed schools. The rules changed. Even my clothes changed. But most critical, I changed parents. I didn't have my mother and my stepfather, anymore.

The next year, we moved to Idaho to live with my mother and stepfather. This was also a difficult year, for many different reasons. I changed states. I changed houses. I changed clothes again. I had to go to a school without any of my brothers or sisters for the first time, because they all went to private school and I went to public school. And, of course, I changed parents again. In addition, I had to fly back to visit my dad in Kansas every other weekend, which made it difficult to establish friendships.

At the end of that year, we told our father that we would not return to Kansas. We wanted to stay in Idaho. Again I was just going along with my older brothers and sisters. Needless to say my father was very upset with us because we were not keeping our end of the deal. (I don't think he would have been upset at all if the tables had been turned and we wanted to live in Kansas with him and not live with our mother in Idaho, though.) I remember he came up to Idaho to tell us how upset he was. He said that he was going to disown us. I didn't understand what that meant. I loved my father, but I did not want to leave my brothers and sisters.

The next year in Idaho was still difficult. I missed my father, and at the end of the summer I decided I wanted to move back to Kansas with one of my sisters and live with our father. This was a difficult decision. My sister had gone to visit our father over the summer, and after she left, I decided that I would go visit too. When I got there, she told me that she was staying. I think that part of the reason I stayed with her was so that I did not want to have to say good-bye to her. By this time, I was eleven years old, and it was very difficult to tell my mother, my stepfather, and my other brothers and sister that I wasn't coming back. It tore me apart inside. This was another decision that had very rough consequences. By that time, I had already betrayed both of my parents in an attempt to make each of them happy.

This story shows just how painful it can be for a child to make a decision about which parent to live with. This boy was too young and immature to be making a choice about his own custody. He, not surprisingly, followed the path of least resistance—doing what his father or his siblings wanted. Although it is important to take children's wishes and preferences into consideration in making custody arrangements, there are psychological dangers in giving the children responsibility for deciding their own fates when their parents can't act maturely and cooperatively. The children in this family were like pawns in a game played by their parents, pushed and pulled across the country as if it were a chessboard. Custody arrangements chosen by the children are often unstable. As in this story, arrangements keep changing from one parent to the other as children continue to feel the pull from both sides and cannot settle in—neither with Dad nor with Mom.

Custody Changes

A custody determination must be made at the time of the divorce, but, as the preceding story shows, custody questions do not end there. Until the children are independent adults, shifts in custody, and renegotiations and relitigations of custody are common. Parents—and children—can never close the book on custody. Even after months and years of a stable custodial arrangement, significant changes can occur. These changes may be the result of changes in the parents' status—unemployment, remarriage, another divorce. They may be responses to children's changing needs and desires. They can be the result of a continuing tug-of-war between competing and conflicted parents. They can result from the discovery that the custodial parent isn't fit after all. Most often it is the children's desire to change custody that leads to a change.

Sandi Rodriguez

I was nine years old when my parents' divorce was final. In the divorce settlement, my mother got the house, the car, and full custody of the three children, ample alimony and child support. My father got the truck, his fishing rods, the lawyer's fees, and reasonable visitation, which was stipulated to be every Wednesday evening for two and a half hours, every other weekend, alternate holidays, and the month of August each summer. From the beginning, my mother never cooperated with the visitation schedule. With friends, in our presence, she often discussed moving to another state to limit our contact with our father. Every time Dad came to pick us up was a hassle. She would often keep us someplace late on purpose so that he would have to wait in the car outside the house. One time, she sent all of us to our rooms for getting gum on the carpet and told us our punishment was that we were to stay home for the weekend. So we went to our rooms, but we could hear our father arguing at the front door. He eventually left and returned with the court visitation order, his calendar, and a Newport Beach police officer—at which time we were scolded for not being packed on time and sent with Dad for the weekend.

The year after the divorce, Dad got remarried. Mom wouldn't let us attend the wedding, saying that it would be terrible for children to see their father marry someone else. We were allowed to attend the wedding only after my father had gotten a court order specifying that we be allowed to attend. We had to go home before they served the cake.

After a while, my dad had a long talk with us about how we would feel about living with him and his new wife, Mary. He also asked if we felt Mom would be hurt, and if we were worried about that. After a number of these talks, several attorneys who refused the case, and lots of frustration, my father joined United Fathers, found an attorney who would take his case, filed for custody, and got a court date (five years after the divorce). This infuriated my mother, who constantly asked us who we wanted to live with and told numerous stories about how terrible my father was for leaving "the family"—mixed with Biblical accounts of what a family should be. This was supposed to be proof that my father had not only left her, but us too. This only made us mad. She also became more overprotective and more intrusive at a time in our lives (early adolescence) when we were least willing to accept this.

Eventually, we were ordered to see a court-appointed psychologist and underwent extensive testing. It seemed that everyone, including the court-appointed psychologist, assumed that if fathers want custody, something must be wrong with them. Or if children want to live with their fathers, it must be because they think that living with father means a permanent vacation or there is something wrong with them too. And if mothers do not have custody, there is no question that something is seriously wrong with them. In our case, our father was certainly the stricter disciplinarian, but we still wanted to live with him. And the court-appointed psychologist could find nothing wrong with any of us, except that in the pictures we drew of our "family" each of us kids drew two pictures: one with my mother and the kids, and one with our dad and the kids, and all of us drew ourselves closer to our father.

As the court date approached, our mother grew even more intrusive—buying diaries for my sister and me and then reading them—and less consistent in her parenting—sending us to our rooms for time-out and then coming in crying and apologizing. At every soccer game, she would tell anyone who would listen about her terrible ex-husband and how he had left "the family," which probably seemed strange when these people would see my dad there hugging us after each goal we scored while she kept ruminating upon her tales of woe.

The summer before the court date, Mom sent us to summer camp at Yosemite. She did this every year (always over one of my dad's weekends), but this year it was for three weeks—the three weeks that began with Father's Day and ended after my father's birthday. Then, rather than letting us take the bus home with the rest of the campers as planned, she showed up and took us on a road trip to Washington for three more weeks. The weekend we got back, I just couldn't take it anymore. The next morning we went to church. We were supposed to meet my mom after the service at the fountain. But after I had been dropped off at my Sunday school class, I walked out of my class and headed straight for my father's house, about three miles away. After church, my mom couldn't find me, so she had my brother call my dad to ask if I'd called him. Dad told him that I was there and that, if it got too bad at home, my brother could always come there too. At that point my mom managed to get the phone away from my brother and heard my dad, so my brother took off running and he, too, showed up at Dad's house.

As a result of this incident, we got an immediate mediation date for the next Thursday. The mediator interviewed each of us separately then called all of us together and said that children should not be rewarded for running away. She ordered us all returned to my mother's house until our final court date. The next few months were horrible. Mom was so depressed and so angry with us that at a subsequent court-ordered mediation date, we were finally allowed to go live with our father. He was granted temporary custody until the final court date scheduled three months later.

My mother constantly called us early in the morning and showed up at our house "to drop off things that we might need." One evening, when no one was home, she dropped off my brother's dog and my sister's cat on our front porch, along with a bag of old clothes. At that point, my father filed for a restraining order and she was not allowed to call us or visit. Finally, the court date arrived. The judge informed us that our input would be taken into consideration and that we should be prepared to tell the court, up on the stand in front of both of our parents, who we wanted to live with and why. He asked if we were prepared to answer his questions. Then we all waited for my mom to arrive. She never came. My father received full custody with no specified visitation rights granted to my mother and a restraining order against her initiation of phone calls or visits at home or school.

Eventually we each called and saw our mother, but our visits were rare. I spent quite a lot of time with her the summer before I left for college, because she had been diagnosed with leukemia. My brother and sister also each tried short stays with her to help her after her health became unstable, but they had to move out because of her manipulative and intrusive behavior. She intercepted their mail, listened to their phone calls, and called and talked to my sister's boss while she was at work. She lied to my sister's boyfriend. Recently, she forged all of our signatures and refinanced all of our cars without our permission. I believe that we had to leave my mother; no child should be raised by a parent who was so emotionally unstable.

This is a particularly vivid and poignant story, but it is typical of our students' reports of custody changes, in that the requested change was from mother custody to father custody. It is also typical in that it reflects the difficulty of making a custody change. Unless the new arrangement is by mutual agreement, any change must be justified, argued, supported, and defended in court, just as vehemently and just as bitterly as custody was determined in the first place. In this case, the change required extensive psychological evaluation of the parents and children, a clear preference expressed by the children, a father who was remarried and could provide an adequate and stable home, and a lawyer willing to fight for a father's rights. Deciding custody—and living with it—is often painfully difficult.

Lessons to Be Learned

The basic lesson to be learned from the real-life stories in this chapter is the following: The issues of child custody and child support are complex, but they do not need to be combustive. When parents cannot agree on custody or support issues they may take their dispute to court where a judge will decide the arrangements. The problem with this route is that such a third-party decision is less likely to address the needs and interests of all involved. The people most knowledgeable about the family's specific needs and circumstances are the parents, not the judge. They, therefore, are in the best position to make a good decision regarding child custody and support—provided they do indeed consider everyone's needs and circumstances, are willing to negotiate fairly, and act in the most enlightened and empathic manner of which they are capable. The following lessons contain concrete suggestions to make this process successful.

1. Children need both parents. It is important to keep one basic fact in mind as a fundamental premise during the process of negotiating custody and child support settlements: children have two parents and they value both of them. Parenthood is a lifelong responsibility for mothers and fathers, and children benefit from the involvement of each. Custody should be shared, if possible, and if that is not possible, the arrangement should allow for children's continued contact with both parents.

2. Children need money. Joint custody is one arrangement that encourages both parents to contribute financially to the child's welfare. In sole custody arrangements, though, the nonresidential parent often fails to contribute financially to the household where the child resides. When this happens, steps should be taken. If you are a residential parent and you are owed child support, go after it—your children deserve it. Although it may be easier at the moment not to "rock the boat" thereby avoiding conflict with an ex-spouse who is unwilling to pay child support, it will not serve you or your children in the long run (unless you are wealthy and have no financial needs). Growing up poor is a burden for you and your children and is associated with many adverse outcomes. Children often come to resent the custodial parent who let them grow up poor and later drift toward the parent who is financially better off.

3. It helps to be flexible, fair, and cooperative. It is a challenge to divide a child and to rear that child in two separate households. Most parents feel gypped in some way by the custody arrangement that is worked out. Even if they get sole custody—which is often what the custody battle was about—they miss the support of a co-parent, somebody who can take over when they need a break. A custody arrangement is always a compromise. There will be differences and dissatisfactions. Realize that you do not control how the other parent raises the children. Unless the other parent verifiably abuses your children, you should do your best to get along, uphold the other parent in your children's esteem, and be fair, flexible, and accommodating. Treat the other parent the way you would like to be treated. Be open to change. Custody arrangements made at the time of the divorce may not last; over time, as children get older and circumstances in the family change, the original agreement may need to be changed too. It is possible to work out an arrangement that accommodates these changes without going back to court.

4. It's important to be organized and businesslike. Leave personal feelings out of it. Keep discussions about child custody separate from discussions about property and money. Mixing discussions about money and time with the children is not a good idea. Draw up a parenting agreement that spells out the details of the arrangement. Leaving details to good will, good luck, or a gentleman's handshake is likely to backfire. After you have an agreement, stick to it as if it were a business contract. If a change is necessary, discuss a revised agreement and put that in writing too. Keep up your end of the bargain. If a temporary exception is needed, discuss it with the other parent. Don't just take the child on weekend vacation or out of school expecting the other parent to understand that "something came up." This kind of behavior will undermine trust in the co-parenting relationship.

5. Take a long view. Divorced parents have to deal with each other until they (or their children) die. Their association does not end when the children enter high school; it does not end when the children turn eighteen. Even when children are grown up, there are graduations, family emergencies, birthdays, weddings, births, grandchildren—all of these important milestones and events will be affected by the quality of the parents' relationship. Therefore, taking this long view, it is obvious that parents should do all they can to maintain and promote civility.

8
Running On Empty: Parents Adjust to Divorce

After the legal wrangling is over and the divorce is final...
after the initial pain and chaos and shock of the separation have
dissipated...what happens next? What is life like for divorced
adults? What happens to them emotionally, financially, and
socially? How quickly and easily do they adjust to the divorce
and to their new single life? In this chapter we discuss the
problems parents suffer and the factors that either help or
hinder their adjustment.

Samantha Sandman

With the help of counseling from her minister,
my mom had finally decided to separate from my dad.
Before she left, she prepared herself by training for a
job. She got a typewriter from the library and, through
diligent practice, learned to type 110 words a minute.
She sharpened up her calculating skills. Then she told
my dad that she wanted a separation. He did not protest.
Nor did he protest when she asked for the house and sole
custody of the children. He did not even demand any
legal visitation rights. She could have asked for spousal

support, but she did not, because she knew that my dad was financially unstable and might resent it. All this time, things went smoothly and according to my mother's plan.

But, then, the proverbial shit hit the fan. After the divorce was final, my mom discovered that her efforts to prepare herself for an independent life had been totally inadequate. Unbelievable turmoil, frustration, and depression marked the next few years. The most devastating blow was financial. Her monthly income dropped drastically—to one fourth what it had been before the divorce. The $150 per month in child support my father was ordered to pay was not nearly enough to support us. We lived on noodles-in-a-cup. My father's income should have increased, but it did not, because of his drinking. When he remarried, soon after the divorce, his child support payments to us were made thanks to the efforts of his new wife. Even so, my mother had to take out a second mortgage on our house to help pay back the money she owed from the divorce settlement. One of the ways my mom tried to compensate for our limited income was to take in boarders. Even so, we did not have enough to live on. We had to go on welfare.

My mother hated to be on welfare, but it was necessary, because although she had worked hard to build up her typing skills, she did not have a college education, and finding work was a challenge. She walked from door to door looking for employment, as well as going to an employment agency. Eventually, she was able to find two jobs, and after some months we were able to get off welfare. Sometimes we made it to the end of the month with enough money left over for all three of us to go to the corner store and get ice-cream cones as a treat.

My mother suffered emotionally, too. She suffered from deep depression and often thought of suicide. She felt like a failure, because she had been raised a devoted Catholic and was taught that divorce was a sin, and now she was a sinner. She felt stigmatized, because, among the people she knew, there was a lot of social pressure to stay married. Her acquaintances did not consider divorce to be acceptable. She felt lonely, because the friends she had made during the marriage through my dad's work never called or offered her any support after the divorce. Luckily, my mom had one close and intimate friend, who was extremely supportive and helped her through the divorce.

My mom's relationship with my father did not improve over time. My father often harassed her, and on a few occasions it turned physical. I remember one time when he criticized her for something she was doing with us kids. When she stood her ground, he hit her. This happened one year after the divorce. The only reason she made it through these years, she says, was that she wanted to make sure that her children would have a better life.

This story highlights many of the effects divorce has on adults. After divorce, most women suffer economically, are depressed, and feel lonely. They are stressed by work or the difficulty of finding work. In this case, the mother's situation was particularly bad because the violence and abuse that led to the termination of the marriage continued after it. Research documents the fact that divorce creates economic hardship and emotional turmoil, social isolation and physical symptoms, tattered relationships and role confusion, stress and anger, illness and anxiety. Compared to married couples, according to one study, divorced people are seven times more likely to be hospitalized for depression or psychosis, six times as likely to be treated for psychiatric problems, twice as likely to abuse alcohol, three times as likely to be involved in a car accident, twice as likely to commit suicide, and six times as likely to murder or be murdered. To some extent, these problems are the result of the stressful relations and circumstances that lead up to a divorce and the stress of going through the separation and divorce itself. But beyond this, there are also stressful circumstances in the divorce "afterlife" that contribute to these psychological and physical problems.

Disintegration of the Social Network

One reason that the aftermath of divorce is stressful and leads to psychological and physical problems is that divorce usually causes dramatic changes in the person's social life. It's not just that divorced people lose a spouse. Typically the divorced person's entire social network and support system changes, too. As in the story above, friends and family often vanish along with the spouse. The couple's shared friends don't want to take sides, and they stop calling either husband or wife. Many of our students described these problems afflicting their parents.

Rachel Hall

After my mom got divorced, the "friends" she had before the divorce did not want to have anything to do with her or with us. Families, who had been our friends for as long as I could think, and whose kids had been our playmates from toddlerhood on, stopped inviting us to their house and didn't let their kids come to our house anymore.

Gale Fisher

My mom felt that she lost her identity when she and my dad got divorced. Her life previously had revolved around my dad; her social life had centered on my dad's clients and their married friends. She lost all contact with these people. They did not invite her to parties anymore because she was single. Part of the reason that she felt so alienated was that she felt humiliated. She believed that everyone knew that dad had been "running around" except for her. This was one of the most difficult things for her to cope with.

As this last story suggests, it's not just that other people drop the divorcee. Sometimes the divorced person initiates the social isolation. If he or she is embarrassed because of the ex-spouse's behavior or reputation, it is difficult to put on a happy face and socialize with the old gang as if nothing has happened. It is also difficult to socialize if seeing the old gang brings up painful memories of the way it used to be when he or she was part of a couple. In the following case, the divorcee deliberately dropped out of sight after the divorce to avoid these memories.

Connie Phillips

After the divorce, my mom's social activities and friends changed. She stopped doing things with her old friends and neighbors because they were all married and had always socialized as couples before the divorce. She stopped going to the church we had always gone to because it brought back too many memories and made her feel uncomfortable. Instead, she watched religious shows on television and we rented videos on Friday nights. Television became her new best friend.

This student's mother may not just have been avoiding memories of the past; she may also have been avoiding perceived pressure and criticism from friends and family. That pressure may be cultural, as the following students described.

Veena Sankar

In the aftermath of the divorce, a large part of my mother's social support system disappeared. In the Iranian culture, divorce is considered a taboo; those women who ask for divorces are looked down upon, no matter what the circumstances surrounding the divorce are. After the divorce, my mother felt shamed and guilty and isolated.

Kathy Lee
My mother wanted to return to Korea after the divorce, because she was so lonely here, but she could not, because her family in Korea kept giving her a hard time when she did not go back with my father. She was seen as a "bad girl."

Pressure and isolation from friends and family also came from criticism directly aimed at the offending spouse.

Kathy Lee
After the divorce, my parents' friends sided with my father because my mom was the one who had left the family. In fact, her friends pressured her so much that she had to move to a different city.

A Network of Friends Helps
People adjust to the divorce better if they don't suffer this fate of social pressure and isolation. If they retain their social networks and are able to continue their social activities, they suffer less loneliness and boredom and, therefore, adjust better to the divorce. When their friends approve of the divorce and offer help and support, adults feel better about themselves and their decision and adjust to the divorce more easily.

Allison Rodgers
Thank god my mom had great friends who supported her after the divorce. They were a great comfort, taking her to movies, plays, and dinners. They understood her problems and told her she was a great person, which helped her to build up her self-esteem.

Sometimes it is not old friends, but a new social network that helps parents through the adjustment to their unmarried state.

Rachel Hall

The people who helped support my mom were friends she made through my brother's elementary school. They paid special attention to my brother and me and tried to help us when we needed it. They were there for my mom, too, and listened to her problems and often helped her out. The support network my mom developed during this time helped her to adjust to her overwhelming feelings of depression and guilt.

Parents also did better when they participated in social groups and organizations like Parents without Partners.

Jenny Messerman

Life was very hard for my mom after the divorce. She was devastated. She suddenly realized what a huge responsibility she had. She had to make all decisions and do everything herself. Working, taking care of the kids and the home, taking care of the car, refinancing the house, and doing the taxes were now all her responsibility. She also had the added pressure of doing well at work in order to provide more money for her family. She joined 'Parents without Partners' about a month after the divorce, and this helped. There, she met other single parents who were going through the same experiences and who were understanding and supportive.

Generally, participating in groups in which people share common characteristics and interests—going through a divorce, being a single parent, looking for adequate child care—is beneficial. Realizing that others share similar—or worse—experiences helps people put their own problems into perspective and helps them overcome the sense of being social outcasts. The groups can also offer tangible assistance by providing members with useful information and opportunities for trading child care.

A Supportive Family

Like a social network, support from family members is helpful in combating loneliness and isolation. After divorce, it is common for people to have increased contact with their family—often they even move back home—and this makes them feel less lonely. The extended family can offer social support that eases the transition through divorce. But, as our students noted, family contact can also be stressful. The divorced person is likely to get not only support but also criticism from family members. And if the family opposed the divorce, the divorced person might not even get any support. People who have no family available or who have family members who disapprove of the divorce have more trouble adjusting to the divorce.

> Naoko Russell
>
> My mother received no social support from her family. Even her own mother, although she lived nearby, was never available to help in times of need or crisis, such as when a babysitter was fired. One time, when a neighbor called my mom at work to tell her that our babysitter was staggering home from the local bar with my baby brother in a stroller, my grandmother refused to go get my brother, simply because she "didn't want to have a confrontation with the babysitter." This lack of support significantly contributed to my mother's feelings of loneliness, helplessness, and abandonment.

Conversely, the people who receive help and support from their family members are able to deal with the divorce afterlife much more easily. One helpful kind of support is emotional reassurance.

> Brittany Roberts
>
> How did my mother survive the divorce? For starters, she had plenty of family support. Her family didn't look

at her as a failure; they saw her as a victim who needed all the love and support in the world to help her recover and become strong and confident again.

When family members also offer practical support, this, too, eases the divorced person's adjustment.

Jenny Messerman
My mom's parents offered her endless hours of babysitting, innumerable dinners, and help cleaning and repairing the house. They supervised my brother and me with our homework every night. They also gave her money. When we moved to San Diego, they gave her $10,000 for a down payment on a house. Without their practical support, we would have been in dire straits.

Support from a Best Friend
Divorced people who have a best friend, a confidant, someone who offers them social intimacy, also feel less depressed and anxious and adjust better to the divorce. Like the mother in the opening story of this chapter, whose close friend offered her support, divorced people benefit from the companionship, the advice, and the help a good friend can provide.

Melissa Shipman
My mom confided in a friend from work—to pour her heart out and to get somebody else's perspective on things. These talks helped her come to terms with her new life.

The most supportive friend is a capable counselor, who may have developed experience in the trenches himself or herself.

Staci Chen
After the divorce my dad was seriously depressed.
He felt empty inside and thought he had no future.
Having a best friend really helped a lot—especially since
his best friend had already gone through a divorce of his
own.

As long as friends do not form a coalition with the "victim"
against the "ex," and as long as all the talking isn't moaning
and groaning about the person's horrible fate, experienced
friends can be a great blessing. Sharing experiences may
make the "victim" feel understood, and offering insights may
help him or her to regain perspective.

A Flurry of Dating or a Significant Other
After the divorce, the best thing to fill in for the old social
network may be a new social activity—dating—or a new social
relationship—a "significant other." Nearly half of the people
who get divorced are involved with a new "honey" within the
first two months after separation. Half of these relationships
start even before the separation. But does this really help the
person adjust to being divorced? Research suggests that casual
(sexual) encounters and activities are not related to better or
easier adjustment. This research finding was confirmed by
the following student's experience.

Kristin Sanders
After the separation, my father was preoccupied with
living his life as a single man. He rented an apartment
right on the beach. Then he bought a new black sports
car and started dating a lot. My mother increased her
drinking and started an affair with a man that she met at
a bar. Both of them were just pathetic.

On the other hand, research shows that being "meaningfully
involved" with a new partner is related to better adjustment
after the divorce. In one study, for example, among divorced

individuals who were casually dating, 45 percent had adjustment problems, whereas among those in serious new relationships only 7 percent had problems.

Melissa Shipman

When my mom met her present husband, he helped her tremendously. She felt that he met all her emotional needs and allowed her to express and receive love. With him, she felt hope for the future and was able to put her failed marriage behind her.

Self-Improvement and Outside Help

After a divorce, many people go through a flurry of self-evaluation, self-improvement, and help-seeking. They go on a diet, grow a beard, get their hair dyed, get implants, buy a sports car, start a new hobby, and seek new friends.

Andrea Keller

My dad was very lonely right after the divorce, but he overcame it through deliberate self-improvement. He constantly searched for books and tapes on spiritual development and attended workshops and retreats. After 36 years of living, he claimed, he finally got to know himself. This helped his relationships with other people. He now says he never knew how repressed he was, being married to my mom.

Tiffany Maurer

After the divorce, my father spent a lot of time with us. He began to open up to new ideas. He started reading everything he could to help him to understand his own personality. He is now a more tolerant person and does not lash out with painful remarks that cut at you. He can handle his emotions better and talk about them without feeling threatened. He now recognizes that other people have different feelings that are just as important as his and should be valued. He often jokes that it only took him forty-seven years to become a conscious person. I think that is better than never. We are all proud of how far he has come.

In these cases, divorced individuals, realizing that something had gone terribly wrong with their marriages, became self-reflective for the first time. They examined their past behaviors, motives, and emotions, and made psychological progress on their own. Other parents seek professional counseling, and this, too, is beneficial.

Susan McDevitt

My mom says that she survived the divorce mainly through counseling—lots of it. She feels that she came through the situation smarter than she was before, and more aware of the damage that it had caused her, as well as my brother and me. She developed more self-esteem and self-worth than she had when she was married. She feels happy with herself now.

Naoko Russell

With the help of a therapist, my mom changed a lot after the divorce. One thing she learned was to be more assertive. After the divorce, she experienced discrimination because she was a single woman. For example, she had no credit rating because her name had not been on previous accounts, even though she had paid the bills every month. Problems like this kept piling up and added to her stress and frustration. Finally she had a "breakdown." She was suicidal, suffering from major depression, throwing up daily, and rapidly losing weight. She realized that she needed help. She had to get into therapy. Therapy really helped her, not only with the depression and anxiety, but it helped her develop social skills as well. She learned the assertiveness and adjustment skills she needed to cope. She became more outspoken and learned to deal with people in her work environment, to incorporate a little more fun in her life, and to establish a social support network. Therapy even encouraged her to start taking college courses. If it weren't for the useful life skills she learned through counseling, she says she "wouldn't be here today."

These students' stories are a testimonial to the value of therapy. Research supports their observations. When a person is going through divorce and adjusting to being alone or to being in a new relationship, it is often a lifesaver to have professional help. Other students reported that their parents found that just getting out of the house and doing things helped their mental state.

Susan McDevitt
    After the divorce, my mom kept herself busy with activities like her church choir and "Amigos de las Americas," of which she was president for the local chapter. She walked every day with a friend, and that helped her, too.

Religion also has benefits for some parents.

Melissa Shipman
    My mom says that, after the divorce, prayer and her deep faith that "I can do all things through Christ who strengthens me" helped her get to overcome the pain of the divorce.

Having something motivational or spiritual to move yourself forward clearly helps in the adjustment to divorce. But as our students' stories demonstrate, there are many different routes to reaching a new plane and calmer state of mind after divorce. What is worst is when the person just stays in the same miserable condition, wallowing in grief and depression.

The Joys and Pains of Parenthood: Losing the Children

Another source of stress for parents after the divorce is losing contact with their children. Parents who do not have custody are likely to feel lonely and rootless, cut off from contact and control. The initial adjustment to divorce is harder for them than it is for childless adults or parents who have custody. Even if they have left the marriage and family willingly, their self-esteem drops and they confront identity issues. Compared with custodial parents, in the year of two after divorce, noncustodial parents feel more depressed, anxious, maladjusted, and guilty. They have poorer relationships with their children and with their ex-spouse. Parents who are denied visitation suffer most.

> Agatha Turner
> After the divorce, my brother and I lived with our mother and seldom saw our father. He says that that was the hardest part for him. He felt rejected and abandoned. The divorce made him feel like a complete failure. He missed my brother and me tremendously and felt completely cut off from our lives.

But although the loss of contact with their children has a strong, negative effect on noncustodial parents, they can eventually get over it.

> Staci Chen
> My mom felt a sense of loss and depression because she wasn't with her children after the divorce. Her grief lasted until she realized that we were better off with our father.

Adjustment for noncustodial parents seems to depend upon whether they can either retain a close relationship with their children or move on to a new life. If the noncustodial parent has frequent visits, continues to provide the children with discipline, and has some responsibility for both important and daily decisions about the child, rather than just acting like a visiting aunt or uncle, adjustment will go more smoothly. Alternatively, adjustment will be easier is the noncustodial parent can "forget" about the children from the first marriage and move on to a new life or a new family. Often, though, neither of these options is available to the noncustodial parent. He or she is not able to forget about the children from the first marriage, and the lack of contact and lack of regular visits continues to be a source of unhappiness.

The Joys and Pains of Parenthood: Getting the Children
In contrast to losing the children, having the children offers company and support to the divorced parent and gives meaning and grounding to their lives—at least this is the way it appeared to our students. Having the children helped the parents get through the emotional crisis a divorce brings.

Veena Sankar
We were my mother's main source of happiness and hope through the divorce. I believe that without us children, it would have been a lot harder for her to adjust to the divorce. Yes, she had to work hard to support us, but we were also a strong source of support for her.

Elisa Petrov
My mom managed to keep us together and keep us happy. We were never really unhappy. I know that the divorce affected her tremendously, but she had us to look after, we provided her with a goal for the future. I think that's what helped her keep an emotional balance. She dedicated her life to us; we provided meaning in her life.

Of course, there are also costs to having the children. Parents who have custody of the children often find that there is not enough time for both children and work, let alone time for themselves. They experience task overload, disorganization, and a chaotic lifestyle. Their interactions with the children become less affectionate and they are less able to offer consistent discipline. Parents who get custody often feel overwhelmed, trapped, and resentful. The children are always on their minds, and they may begrudge the fact that they have to bear the burden of daily child rearing alone.

Naoko Russell

The hardest part of the divorce for my mother was worrying about us kids all day. Because she was always worrying about us—if she could make it in time to pick us up; if we were safe at home when she wasn't there—it was hard for her to concentrate at work, and this affected her ability to get ahead professionally.

Jessica Turnball

Six months after the divorce my mom was still devastated. Dinner used to be family time with the four of us sitting around the dinner table—my mom, my dad, my brother, and me. Now my mom would look at my father's empty seat and cry. My brother and I did not understand, and we would say something like, "Are you going to cry again?" Or we would ask her a lot of questions, like "Where is Daddy?" We were the most important thing in Mom's life, but we definitely made everything harder for her. We required enormous attention and energy and she was always tired.

Because of the difficulties expressed by both custodial parents and noncustodial parents, one might think that the ideal solution would be for parents to share custody. Joint physical custody—in which parents share the children's time, sometimes up to a 50:50 time split—offers a continuing relationship with the children for both parents, as well as time off for each parent to recoup his or her energy and take care of personal needs. Research does suggest that couples who work out a joint custody arrangement on their own seem to adjust quite well. One has to take into account, though, that parents who have agreed on a joint custody arrangement may be more motivated, friendly, and cooperative with each other than those who file for and obtain sole custody. Thus, their better adjustment may be due to their higher commitment to the children and their better cooperation rather than the custody arrangement per se. Research also suggests that there is no lasting difference in psychological well-being between parents who have joint physical custody and parents who have sole custody. Probably more important than having a joint custody or an exact fifty-fifty split of custody is parents' ability to maintain a positive and cooperative relationship with each other where each parent has regular and unencumbered contact with the children.

The Overwhelming Importance of Money

Perhaps the major factor affecting parents' adjustment to divorce is money. The underlying cause of much anguish after divorce is not the loss of the spouse but—let's face it—the loss of the spouse's money. Money is a preoccupying concern for divorced men and women, regardless of their absolute income level—and for good reason. Two apart cannot live as cheaply as two together. How individuals adjust to the divorce is strongly linked to their economic situation, particularly to whether their income post divorce is lower than their income pre divorce and if they experience economic insecurity.

Abby Chen

After the divorce, my dad's income was cut in half. This meant that besides house payments, he was supporting my brother and me on half the income they had before. My mom took $12,500 out of the checking account and left two weeks before income taxes were due. My dad had to get an advance from his employer to pay the government $5,000 for income taxes. He was already struggling emotionally, but his financial worries made things only worse.

Kaylee Moore

Within a year after the divorce, the relief my mother first felt after she separated from my dad had worn off. Her new life was a burden. She could hardly pay her bills. She had been working in a series of dead-end jobs and she was exhausted. She was tired of moving (we had moved to six different houses within the year), and she was suffering from the stress of having to start over again and again and again. After ending a particularly bad relationship with a boyfriend, she decided it was time to move back to our former neighborhood. At this point my dad stopped paying child support. My mom had just taken on the financial obligation of moving into a new house, and then she was fired from her new job (for refusing to submit to her married boss's advances). Our phone was disconnected, the power was turned off, and there was nothing in the refrigerator. Times were brutal as Mom struggled to provide for us.

As this story aptly illustrates, it is impossible for adults to adjust to divorce emotionally when their very survival and the survival of their children is at stake. Money may not guarantee a person's recovery from divorce, but lack of money makes it impossible.

The Significance of Meaningful Work

The importance of meaningful work as a stabilizing influence in life also should not be underestimated. Research demonstrates that people with more stable and satisfying jobs after divorce (and this usually means before the divorce as well) experience less stress and make a better and easier adjustment to being single. People who work more hours and receive a higher salary, whose work is at a higher level, and who are more satisfied with conditions at work are better off psychologically after a divorce (and at any other time). Work is important not just as a source of financial support for the divorced individual, but as a source of psychological support. It gets people out of the house, gives them something meaningful to do, adds success and satisfaction to their lives, and brings them into contact with other people.

Kathy Lee

After the divorce, my father went through a period of anger and depression, sadness and confusion. But then he refocused on his business and began to build it up. His income increased about 25 percent and he made dramatic advances in his field. I think it was his work that saved him.

Gale Fisher

Eighteen months after my parents divorced, we moved to California. We rented a two-bedroom apartment, and my brother and I started school. Because we were gone all day, my mom was able to work. She did not need to work; she had her savings and the money my dad sent every month. She worked because she wanted to get out and do something, to meet people. Real estate was the perfect job for her because the hours were flexible. It made her feel competent and self-sufficient and got her thoughts off the divorce. She said it was a big help in her adjustment.

But of course there is a price to pay for working, too; it's not a panacea, as the following story shows.

Naoko Russell

In my parents' dissolution, there was a pretty even split of the property, the cars, and the other possessions. My mother also received regular child support from my dad. In addition, she had the benefit of keeping the condominium we lived in, which had a very low mortgage payment. Still, to cope with the divorce economically, it was necessary for my mom to get a job. Every day she forced herself through the daily responsibilities—getting up at 5 A.M., getting the kids ready for the sitter, going to work, rushing back to the sitter to get there before 6 P.M., and then the nightly routine of fixing dinner, spending time with the kids, and getting us cleaned up and ready for bed—only to start the whole process again the next morning. A couple of months after the divorce, she added to her daily list, throwing up every morning from the stress of being on this treadmill. She had no choice; she had to get everything done, but the anxiety of the day made her so "wound up" that that she had trouble sleeping at night. Needless to say, everything at this time (even minor things like being pulled over and given a fix-it ticket, or having to get car repair work done) was a terrible stress for my mom, who was barely holding it together. The worst time came when she noticed that the constant changes and the lack of having a good and consistent sitter for us kids were causing problems. She ended up quitting her job, which wasn't going well anyway, and going on welfare for about three months. She needed to try to stabilize us kids and herself and figure out what to do next. Food stamps also helped to cut down on the food bill, and we received medical insurance through MediCal. However, because food stamps are not accepted for non-food items, there were times when she was rolling pennies from our piggy banks to pay for toothpaste.

Work, especially unskilled work, can be draining, frustrating, and stressful, as it was for this mother. Working custodial parents often say they feel as if they are on a treadmill.

Sean Fitzpatrick

By the time they went to court for the divorce, my father had six counts of contempt of court against him and had hidden his income so well that my mother got no spousal support and only $425 a month in child support for my brother and me. Obviously, this was not enough for the three of us to live on, so after the divorce, my mother had to go to work. She had gotten married right out of high school and not gone to college, and she did not have any job skills because my father had not wanted her to work. It was a grueling struggle, economically. I remember the tears in my mom's eyes when we went grocery shopping and she would have to say no to extras we wanted. Finally, my mother got a job. She worked eight hours a day and then brought home four more hours of work to do every night. She worked very hard so that we could stay in our house.

The Psychology of Spousal and Child Support

One of the reasons that parents suffer economically after divorce is that they receive little or no spousal or child support. Support payments provide an income that can ease the custodial parent's financial struggle a bit at least. Students whose custodial parents received their child support payments every month without fail described their situation much more positively than those whose parents did not.

Deanna Knowlson

My mother did not have any big complaints about the financial situation after the divorce. We had to be careful about our spending, and we definitely couldn't afford any luxuries, but because my father was a doctor who faithfully paid the family support every month, we had a good and stable life.

The faithful payment of spousal and child support does more than just provide a steady income. It also helps the custodial parent and child psychologically.

> Jennie Lee Nolan
>   My father was excellent about making his child support payments. He never missed one. Of course, he only had to pay $100 a month for me from the time I was three until I turned eighteen. Nevertheless, it meant a lot to me and to my mother to know that he cared enough to send the money. It wasn't much, but it was better than nothing, my mother used to say.

Unfortunately, as we discussed in last chapter, child support is often not paid—even when the court has awarded it. Many noncustodial parents don't think they should have to support the children they seldom see, so they pay support only sporadically or not at all. In reaction, the custodial parent often denies them visitation, and then, if they haven't already, the noncustodial parent stops paying totally. In other families, the custodial parent realizes that the child support payments are inadequate and makes the noncustodial parent's visits miserable. In reaction, the noncustodial parent stops visiting and also stops paying. Without the regular payment of support, parents have difficulty adjusting to the divorce, and their relationships with their ex-spouse became even more strained.

> Sean Fitzpatrick
>   Each month it was a major conflict for my mom to get the child support from my father. He never paid it on time. He and my mother would yell at each other in front of us when he came to pick us up. Then, as we were leaving, she would ask us to ask him to give us the check before we came back. We felt terrible because we were caught in the middle. By the end of the weekend, Dad would write the check that no doubt didn't make

any kind of dent in his bank account but was absolutely necessary for my mother just to make it. He definitely used the child support payment as control. For instance, one weekend my mom forgot to pack underwear for my brother. My father spent five dollars buying him some and deducted it out of the child support payment. This was his way of continuing to hurt and control her.

Keeping support and visitation separate can have advantages for parents' psychological adjustment. In the following case, although the court tied the issues of support and visitation together, the mother overlooked this and continued to allow the father access to the children.

Judd Michaelson

When my parents got divorced, my dad only had to pay $100 a month in child support and no alimony. He refused to pay even this small amount, though, so my mom took him back to court. My dad told the judge that he wasn't paying because my mom wasn't allowing him visitation. Fortunately, my mom had brought proof showing that he had received all of his visitation rights—and the judge found him in contempt of court. When my mom and her new husband, decided to move to California so that my stepdad could start his medical career out here, my mom and dad decided they had better go back to court so that they could work out a new visitation schedule. When they were in court, the judge reviewed my dad's file and said that because he hadn't paid his support, he was a "deadbeat dad" and he wasn't to receive any visitation at all. But, because my mom didn't want to disrupt my contact with my dad, she told him that he could have visitation anyway. From then on, my dad got better about paying his child support.

In the following case, as well, the mother's fairness ultimately helped the father overcome his anger, stay involved

with his child, and continue to make child-support payments—
an outcome that would help all parents and children to better
adjust after divorce.

Sally Salow

My father wasn't always able to make his monthly
payments because he was a full-time graduate student
and the only money he made was from his job as
a part-time janitor. My mom wouldn't tolerate his
missing payments, so she went to the DA's office to seek
assistance. A minimum amount was set for him to pay
until he graduated. After he graduated, the amount of
child support went up to $200 per month. From that
point on, he was consistent with his payments. My dad
says that the way my mom handled visitation made a big
difference during this time. Even when he was late with
his child support payments, my mom did not forbid him
to visit me, but encouraged our relationship. This made
my dad feel good and helped him resolve the anger he
felt towards her.

Staying Friendly with the Ex-spouse

Another important factor in adjusting to divorce, which
the previous story hints at, is having a good relationship with
the ex-spouse. Couples who adjust best are able to relate to
each other in ways that are open and communicative, relatively
free of conflict, and not characterized by continuing romantic
attachment. It is beneficial to have separated without rancor,
by mutual agreement (as mutual as divorce can ever be), after
long and careful deliberation. It is ideal if neither spouse feels
like a victim and if both of them are able to continue friendly,
but not passionate, relations.

Jennie Lee Nolan

My father and mother remained friends after their
divorce. My dad would come over to our house on Saturday
mornings and we would all sit at the dining room table,

drinking tea or coffee and talking about me or them or whatever. They maintained their relationship for my sake, and I think it helped us all adjust very well to the divorce. I had friends in school whose parents—married and divorced—fought all the time, and I was so glad that I didn't have to go through that. If two parents have to be divorced, my parents would be a good example of how to do it well. They got along, for the most part, and I don't remember it as being bad at all.

In contrast, it is difficult for everyone when the parents can't get along and continue their conflicts even after the divorce.

Roxie Levine

My parents separated three years ago and have been divorced for about a year. But even though they are divorced, they continue to fight. My father just won't leave my mom alone. He gets in fights with my sisters and me and always ends up blaming it on my mother. He thinks that she says bad things about him behind his back and tries to get us to side against him. My father isn't paying child support for my younger sister even though it is written in the settlement that he is supposed to pay $200 a month. This week my mother and father went out for coffee. My mother explained to him that it would be so much easier if they were on good terms, because they're going to be seeing a lot of each other. There are five more years of joint child rearing for my younger sister, and then there will be graduations, weddings and grandchildren—so they better learn to get along if they don't want to make us all miserable.

This is so true! It is in everyone's best interests after a divorce to somehow rise above the conflicts of the past and behave with each other in a rational and neutral way. Everyone involved has an easier time getting over the divorce if the parents can just overcome their differences and develop a civil relationship. Couples who share children are bound to each other, for better or worse, forever. It really does not matter how much they like or dislike each other—they just have to do their best to get along. Not getting along means misery for both parents and children indefinitely.

His and Hers Divorces

In our students' stories and also in research on people's adjustment to divorce, one of the most consistent themes is that the effects of divorce are different for men and women. Men are more likely to have serious problems, like being hospitalized for a psychiatric disturbance or attempting suicide. These men suffer intensely from the emotional trauma of the separation. They feel pain and loss acutely and are more likely than women to go off the deep end.

Linda Green

Adjusting to life after the divorce was not extremely difficult for my mom. The pain of divorcing seemed like nothing compared to the pain she had felt during the marriage. Soon after the divorce, she began working more hours, trying to move up in the company she was working at. She started feeling some hope for the future and began viewing the divorce as a welcome relief. My dad took the divorce much harder. Throughout the divorce process he saw my mom become more independent and self sufficient, and he began to feel threatened by her new sense of confidence. He found himself drinking, not just socially, but after work, at home, and sometimes from a stashed bottle in his car, as he tried to sedate himself from the negative emotions he was experiencing. He felt angry at himself for allowing things to turn out as they had, angry at himself for the immaturity he had displayed, and angry at my mom for not giving him "another chance." He felt overwhelming sadness and grief, as he came to terms with the loss of his family. Most of all, he felt he was a failure—as a husband and as a father. It also didn't help that his own mother and father did not support the divorce and often expressed their disappointment in him. After the divorce, he experienced many physical symptoms like headaches and sleeplessness. He also suffered from depression, which he thought would never end. These emotions and the drinking to numb his pain continued for several years.

On the other hand, although women may not go off the deep end as often as men, they are more likely to struggle longer because of the changes in lifestyle precipitated by divorce. It takes women longer to adjust to divorce, because for them divorce is accompanied by a larger drop in income, a more significant change in work status, greater responsibility in child rearing, and greater loss of social contacts. On average, men get over the negative emotional effects of the divorce faster than women do. Research suggests that—on average—men take about two years to overcome the divorce "crisis" and get back to a "normal" life, whereas for women this takes about three years.

Deanna Nelson
My father adjusted fairly quickly to being divorced and was remarried a year later. Immediately after the separation he suffered a lot, but then he moved on and seemed not much affected. Adjustment for my mother was slower. She saw a counselor for at least a year after the divorce, and she waited a couple of years before dating anyone seriously. She eventually remarried a man she dated for four years before they finally got engaged.

Our students' stories were particularly poignant about their mothers' struggles to cope after the divorce. Of course they had more direct exposure to the mother's struggles, because most of them lived with their mothers.

Her Social World Shrinks While His Expands

Divorced women discover that the social world is like Noah's ark—they are not accepted without their mate. They are viewed as a threat by other wives, who worry that their own husbands will stray with the "merry divorcee." They feel lonely, vulnerable, and unwanted—socially and sexually. Usually, though, they do keep one or two close friends in whom they can confide. Men are less likely to have a confidant to talk over their feelings and frustrations with, but they are not treated like social pariahs. They usually experience less decrease in the size of their social network—because their friendships are based on contacts at work, because they—unlike their ex-wives—become desirable dinner guests, and because friends rally around men who have custody to help them out. After the divorce, men enlarge their social contacts, have a flurry of dating, and accept frequent social engagements as "eligible bachelors." They date significantly more often and with more different partners than their ex-wives. They go to singles' bars (which divorced women hate), pick up women at work, and join health clubs. They can afford these activities because they have more money.

Dianne Knowles

After the divorce, my father did not have much difficulty socially. Being fairly new in town, he and my mother had not established many friends as a married couple, and most of his acquaintances knew him, alone, from work. The divorce did not significantly alter his social network.

Traci Jones

After the divorce, most of my mom's couple friends disappeared rather quickly. They just stopped calling. Mom made an effort to call them a few times, but she did not pursue it when her efforts were not reciprocated. The exception was a few personal friends of my mom's. They continued their "girlfriend" activities with my mother—

shopping, lunches, activities with the kids—but they no longer included her in their social activities as couples.

She Has the Children

The fact that adjusting to divorce is hardest at first for those who lose their home and children may be one reason that men are more likely than women to have an intense initial reaction to divorce. Men are more likely than women to move out of the family home and more likely to leave their children behind. This loss of house and children, even if left willingly, precipitates anxiety and depression. On the other hand, the fact that women's adjustment to divorce is prolonged may be a consequence of the fact that it is women who are most likely to end up with the children—and it is custodial parents who feel trapped, overwhelmed, and resentful. As one mother described it, being a custodial mother of a preschooler is like being trapped in a child's world and married to Barney (what a thought!).

> Andrea Keller
>
> I think my dad's adjustment period was shorter and easier than my mom's because he did not have to deal with us daily and with our hurt and anger. We never shared our feelings with him and he had a lot fewer demands placed on him. This is not to say that the divorce was easy for him by any means. However, he seemed to get over it a lot quicker than my mom did.

He Has the Money

Over the long run, adults' adjustment to divorce depends on their economic security, and this is a major source of disadvantage for women. It's not that women are greedier, but after a divorce, it's usually women who are needier. Women are more likely to suffer loss of income and loss of economic security, because they can't get well-paying or permanent jobs, and because spousal support or child support, if awarded, is uncertain. Many women find themselves suddenly thrown into economic disaster, not knowing how they will support themselves and their children, certainly unable to do so at the level at which they have been living.

One of the most consistent outcomes of no-fault divorce is that in the first year after separation, for most couples, women's standard of living drops—sometimes drastically—while men's drops less or even rises. This is because, in traditional marriages, women focus on their family and men focus on their career. So, when they get divorced, women end up without the family, but men still have their career. Their work goes on uninterrupted (and in fact increases as family demands diminish). Many women are not prepared to support themselves, even if they had a job to supplement the family income while they were married. They have no money of their own, no assets except what they get in the property settlement, no career, few job prospects (employers discriminate against divorced women because they have no job history), limited earning capacity (women get paid only about 75% of the wages men get), and they are more likely to have children to feed and clothe.

The law, in divorce, treats women as if they are equal to men, but in terms of their earning potential and employment history, they are not. The law does not require men to share their salary equally with their ex-wife (men keep twice as much disposable income as women, on average, and more if they are affluent). The law does not require men to pay spousal or child support to the level of income at which the wife was living or even to the level necessary to pay for raising the children. Court-ordered support covers less than half the cost of child rearing, and two thirds of men ordered to pay it don't pay it anyway. The law does not require a man to cover the ex-wife's medical insurance, pay for the ex-wife's education to same level as his own, or share his future earning power. Many women suffer emotionally because of their bleak financial situation. Our students described this suffering.

Denise Leblanc

When my parents got divorced, my mom got no money. For a long time, she struggled paying the bills. She was depressed for years and had very low self-esteem. She occasionally had thoughts of suicide.

Sarah Beller

Several years after the divorce, my mother was in a deep depression. She felt that she was cheated during the divorce because she was not given half of everything to which she was entitled. For the first few years, she did okay financially, but then the money she had received from selling the house ran out. She found that she did not have the skills or the experience needed in the job market. Her standard of living dropped dramatically. She had not anticipated how hard it would be to make ends meet. She had a house payment to make but no money to pay it with, because my dad was not giving her any. She had no prospect of getting a good job, so things kept getting worse. I often came home from school and found my mother still in her pajamas, sitting in front of the TV, smoking, with all the windows and curtains closed in a dark, dreary house. Today, my mom is single and living alone. She still has severe depressions and terrible headaches. Her electricity is shut off because she still does not have the money to pay the bill. I pay the phone bill for her, but I am going to school and can barely make ends meet myself. Because the electricity is shut off, she has no TV, no radio, no refrigerator and no light. Fortunately, she has a gas stove to cook her food. She lives off noodles and macaroni.

For my father, adjusting to the divorce was initially very difficult because he did not have a house to live in and he did not have his daughter around. But in the long run, he adjusted much better than my mother because he had his business to keep him occupied and to provide an income. Now, fourteen years after the divorce, my dad is doing very well financially and emotionally. He has remarried and has a new family and lives in a beautiful house.

The economic aftermath of divorce is especially hard on three groups of women. One group is older homemakers. Women who are divorced when they are over fifty, after a lifetime of domestic duty, do more poorly than younger women in terms of both economic and psychological adjustment. Older women tend to be more bitter, lonely, angry—and poor—than younger women after divorce. Their husbands and society promised older homemakers that his income was also "theirs." But, in the divorce, the court says that the husband's income is his and that the ex-wife must find a job to support herself. What can a fifty-year-old woman who has not worked for twenty or thirty years and who has no education do? She can never get to a high level of employment starting at an age when many people are retiring. She may be required to begin work for first time, and the best job she can find may be as a short order cook or a file clerk.

Elisa Petrov

At 52 years old, my mother, who had never worked before, had to take up a job in order to support us. She was forced to accept any offer, and she started working in the kitchen of a restaurant. It was incredibly tiring; she would leave at 7 in the morning and come home at 9 at night. She wasn't young anymore, and this kind of physical work was devastating for her.

June Kim

After the divorce, my mother moved back East and took a job as a nanny and live-in housekeeper. I am still angry at my father because he did this to her. My mother is living a life well below what she was accustomed to. It is degrading. There is nothing wrong with being a nanny or a housekeeper, but it isn't right, given the way she was accustomed to living for twenty-seven years of marriage. She has gone from a life of being taken care of by nannies and having housekeepers of her own, to being one.

The second group of women for whom divorce is especially hard is women from upper-income families—because the higher up they are, the farther they fall. The drop in the standard of living after divorce is greatest for women whose husbands made the most money. The less the husband contributed to the household income, the less he can take away. Formerly affluent women who were dependent on their husband's income move down into a different social class. They lose their housekeeper, drive an increasingly decrepit car, and live on generic brand food.

Allison Rodgers

After the divorce, my mom was on her own after twenty years of marriage, with three kids to raise, no education, and no job experience. Her settlement from the divorce was the house and $3000 a month in spousal and child support. But my dad didn't pay—never on time and often not at all. She finally got a decent job after working three terrible ones (a sandwich place, Toys R Us, and a used office furniture place). But even then she had to make it on minimum wage. Before the divorce, she was a "corporate wife" and used to living well. Now, she no longer attends the Republican Convention, the Governor's Ball, or ritzy dinners. She doesn't fly in the company jet to vacations in Hawaii or Florida anymore, doesn't get her nails done, and no longer shops at Bloomingdale's. As a matter of fact, she doesn't shop anywhere. While my mom's life disintegrated, life for my dad was great fun. He still had all the perks that come with being a top lawyer. He has a great job. He lives with the girlfriend at the beach and has no responsibilities. My mom feels like a victim. It's been five years since the divorce, but money-wise she will never recover.

The third group of women who suffer most from divorce is mothers with children. These women have greater demands on their resources and less ability to meet them. Mothers with college-age children suffer because child support only lasts until the child is eighteen, not through college; and mothers of preschool children suffer because, if they work, they must find and pay for child care for their children. Divorce has created a new poverty class in the U.S.—single moms and children. More than half of the poor families in this country are single mothers with children.

Elizabeth Harrison

Looking back, my mom says that the decade after the divorce was a desperate and continuous struggle for survival. The worst part was the constant fear of not having enough money to support herself and me. She began working part time at a snack bar in a grocery store and was soon promoted to manager, earning $100 a week. Mom thought it would be in her best interest not to pursue my dad for child support because, based on what he had said in the past, it would be a battle. As I grew older and our financial needs were greater, my mom became a meat cutter, because it was the highest paying job she knew that did not require a college education. She did this despite the fact that it was such a strenuous and dangerous job.

To try to get out of poverty, some poor mothers make rash remarriages.

John Klinger

Less than a year after my parents' divorce, my mother remarried. Her second marriage was worse than the first. Her new husband was extremely lazy and sat around the house all day. He cost my mother more money than he brought in. After five years, she asked him for a divorce. Since then, my mother has struggled to make it on her own. She lives week-to-week on her paychecks and feels that she is fortunate to have health insurance and other benefits through the city where she is employed as a police dispatcher.

Adjusting to Divorce: How Long Does It Take?

How long does it take to get back to "normal" after a divorce? This is an impossible question to answer, because there is no single course to divorce adjustment. In general, though, over the course of the first year following the separation, extreme mood swings and intense ambivalence and confusion level off and reality sets in. Reality consists of role overload and a pile-up of stressors, often leading to further depression and anger. For most people, by the end of the first year, there has been no decrease in symptoms. The majority of people think the divorce might have been a mistake. They are seeing less of the ex-spouse and feeling less attached, but they are experiencing power struggles over children, money, and property. Interactions with children are at their nadir.

It takes a few years before routines are back to normal and the adult has adjusted to his or her new lifestyle—although not everyone is happy or psychologically well adjusted even then. By that point, psychosomatic symptoms have decreased, because the most intense stress is over. Severe depression and alcohol abuse may have declined. Most individuals are happier than they were earlier during the anguish of separation. Some people report that their self-esteem is higher than it was during the time they were married, because they feel they have more control over their lives and have gone through emotional growth. By this time, most people see the divorce as a positive event in their lives and believe that things are better than they were during the marriage. Of course, these people have just been through a severe emotional crisis, and anything even slightly better would feel good. Social activities for men have typically decreased to a normal level. The relationship between the ex-spouses has usually stabilized, and the couple feels indifferent or mildly friendly or somewhat resentful toward each other. They are no longer blaming each other and fighting over property and custody issues has decreased or disappeared, because these issues have so many years later become a moot point. The parental roles have been agreed upon. The custodial parent's relationship with the children has improved. Almost all wish they were on better terms with their former spouse.

Sandra Hayward

It is four years since my parents divorced. My mom says that her life is more peaceful now, because she is no longer under attack. She is more mature and her self-awareness has grown. She enjoys feeling cared about and validated by her friends and co-workers. She says that her experience going through the divorce helps her deal with people at work, where she is a marriage and family counselor. Her work experience is helpful because she now sees the value of getting help early on and she understands the effects of depression better. She says that she is just now finally feeling really adjusted and "back to normal."

This mother seemed to benefit from having a meaningful job that provided her not only with income, but also with valuable insights and a social network. Not everyone feels so much better only a few years after the divorce.

Elizabeth Harrison

It took my mother about a year to get over the initial trauma of the divorce, but she did not get over the pain of losing my dad until recently, more than eighteen years later.

Other parents seem to get over the divorce just fine—at first. But later, the emotional consequences of the divorce are revisited with increased anguish.

Iram Patel

After she recovered from the initial shock of the separation, my mother seemed fine. She got sad from time to time, but for the most part she seemed glad to finally be rid of the marriage. We could see that she wasn't really dealing with the situation, though, because she was caught up in selling the house, finding a new place to live, and moving. It wasn't until she heard that my father was remarrying that she broke down. She said she never expected that he'd go on with his life, because he had always been the one who wanted her to stay while she was always pushing him away. It wasn't until this time that she went through an emotional crisis. I don't think that it hit her until he got remarried that their divorce was actually final and their life together was really over.

On the other hand, some students reported that their parents' adjustment to the divorce was swift—because they had already put in their time suffering before the divorce occurred.

Sally Salow

Mom felt that the actual divorce was "anti-climactic." By the time the divorce was final, she had already been through all the emotional craziness. During the last part of the marriage, she was on an emotional roller coaster. The constant separations and reconciliations left her unable to eat and sleep. She cried every day and felt a tremendous anxiety about the future. Because my dad was frequently not there, she experienced feelings of loss and grief throughout their marriage. The pain of divorcing was nothing compared to the pain of the marriage.

The Benefits of Moving On

A number of students described the advantages of moving after the divorce, moving to a new house, a new community, and a new life. Research supports these observations, showing that people who move on are better adjusted than those who stay in the same place after the divorce.

Lauren Gordon

After moving back to the United States from England, my mom started to feel better about the whole situation. She was away from my dad, close to family and friends, working, and basically getting on with her life.

Kimmy McCardle

My mom got a good job in a new city, which offered her a fresh start with new friends, new schools, and a great area to raise kids. Starting fresh really helped her get her thoughts off the divorce and move on with her life.

Ending the Anguish of Alimony

Another factor that affects adults' adjustment to divorce is the issue of continued payment of alimony. We have seen the problems women experience because they don't get enough spousal support or because they don't get reliable spousal support. But what about the other side? What about the divorced husbands, who experience the difficulty of paying support? Our students' stories suggested that it is difficult to be truly recovered from the divorce until this anguish has ended.

Kristin Sanders

Although my father was the one to initiate the separation and divorce, he had trouble coping. He was angry and hostile. Not only did the constant thought of the divorce affect his performance at work, but he found it difficult to give so much money to a person he now felt so negative about. He found it enormously frustrating that my mother continued to be a part of his life. He wanted her out of his life, and the fact that she wasn't made him angry, frustrated, and depressed. He had to pay my mother alimony for five years. It was not until he quit writing her the alimony check every month that he was able to put his resentment aside.

Severing of the alimony artery can be good for the recipient as well as the donor of support, as the following student indicated.

Margaret Morrison
    Money was tight, and my dad did send support of $1000 a month for about two years after the divorce. By then my mom was doing well and planning to get married. When my dad told her he was having hard times and couldn't make the payments she didn't make a big deal of it—it was one less connection to him for her to deal with.

In brief, then, parents struggle through the period after divorce. Their path to adjustment may be paved by help and support from friends and family, work and money, or full of jagged rocks thrown up by disapproval, loneliness, poverty, and unemployment. Resentments against the ex-spouse may linger, stresses may continue. But for the fortunate ones, life returns to normal within a few years.

Lessons to Be Learned

The stories in this chapter paint a bleak picture of divorced adults struggling to get back on their feet. But certain aspects of experience did seem to prompt speedier recoveries. Some individuals adjusted more easily to their new circumstances because they were surrounded by supportive friends and relatives. They enjoyed adequate incomes and meaningful careers. They worked out joint custody arrangements that went smoothly for them and their children. To these individuals, we say "Bravo! You did well indeed." These people offer inspiring success stories. Even without these comforts, though, other people adjusted quite well because they were able to make new lives for themselves. This seemed to be the key to their recovery—off out with the old, on with the new.

1. Seek out new friends. After a divorce, it's terrific if friends stay loyal and family members are supportive. But if a person is suffering from a dwindling social network or being constantly criticized by carping relatives, the solution is to form new friendships and social supports. There are many opportunities to make new friends and gain acquaintances in groups like Parents without Partners, in service organizations like Big Brothers or Big Sisters, in activities sponsored by the church or the temple, in seminars at the Y, and in countless clubs—book clubs, garden clubs, cooking clubs, motorcycle clubs, sports clubs…. There is no reason to be lonely or wallow in misery. The secret is to get out and get busy.

2. Find new help. As a result of the frequency of divorce in our society, there are many kinds of help available. There are abundant books and tapes to provide you with twelve steps to recovery, for example. But the two sources of support that were mentioned as particularly helpful by our students were therapy and religion or spirituality. If you are having trouble adjusting to divorce, a well-trained professional can be a great booster and offer practical guidelines to adjustment and better relationships. Alternatively, immersing yourself in spiritual experiences can be a great comfort.

3. Develop your career and enjoy it. Being gainfully employed in meaningful work provides psychological support and satisfaction to individuals adjusting to divorce. It also offers social network possibilities. Furthermore, work has obvious financial benefits and offers self-sufficiency. The post divorce period can be a time for personal and professional growth. Many individuals use this time to reassess their educational and professional achievements and as an opportunity for development. Gaining new skills and reaching new professional heights are tremendous boosters for self-confidence and life-satisfaction.

4. Children—love them or leave them. Of course involvement in work must be balanced with responsibility to children; youngsters cannot be neglected during this critical period, and parents should not bury themselves in their jobs if they have children at home. But the lesson suggested by the stories in this chapter is that caring for children is not a one-way street. Parents find comfort and care in the company of their children and this helps them adjust to divorce as well as it helps the children. Parents and children should maintain close and loving relations during this challenging time. On the other hand, if it is absolutely not possible for one parent to continue to be involved with the children, he or she will recover faster by moving on to a new life rather than moping about in the background or battling the other parent in the foreground.

9

Goodbye to the Fairy Tale: Children Suffer Through the Separation

When parents separate, it turns their children's world upside down. Most children are shocked when they discover that their parents are breaking up and dismayed to find out that their happy family wasn't what it appeared. They are hurt and confused when their parents separate, and feel overwhelmingly anxious and afraid. They lose the family they knew, the lifestyle they were accustomed to, and, often, one of the parents they loved. In the aftermath of the breakup, they are frequently neglected as their parents struggle with their own problems. Their self-esteem plummets; they withdraw into sadness, they may become ill.

Lia Chen

It was a perfectly ordinary afternoon in April. I was twelve years old. As I walked home from school with my friends, I chatted about what we were going to do over the weekend. When I got to our house my little brother was waiting for me. Nobody was home because Mom was at work and Dad was out of town on business. I pulled out my keys from my backpack and opened the door. Jason needed to use the bathroom, so he ran in first. He was in such a hurry that he didn't notice that all the furniture was gone. I followed him into the house and stopped dead in my tracks. I stared into the empty living room feeling scared. I thought that we had been robbed. I yelled for Jason and he came running up the stairs. His eyes grew bigger when he saw the vast emptiness of the living room. Then he looked at me for an answer. I didn't know what to tell him. Jason was really scared, and I didn't know how to calm him. My heart raced at the thought that whoever took everything might still be there. I called a friend to see if we could stay there until Mom got home, then Jason and I went over there to wait. When my friend's mother got home, we went back to our house. My friend's mother found a note from Mom saying she had all the furniture, not to worry, and she would explain when she got home. Waiting for my mother seemed to take forever. I couldn't figure out why she would take all of our stuff—maybe she was having it cleaned.

Late that night Mom finally arrived. She told us that she was leaving my father because she couldn't live with him anymore. She really didn't give us an explanation. She just said that it would be better for everyone. She told us to pack some things because we were going to spend the night at her new apartment and she didn't want to be at the house when my father got back from his trip. She left him a note saying where we were.

We got in the car and drove for about 45 minutes in silence. Jason and I didn't know what to say. We were a little scared about what was going to happen. The uncertainty made me shiver. I wanted answers, but nobody could give me any. We arrived at the apartment around bedtime, so the first thing we did was to put on our pajamas. Then we explored the two-bedroom apartment. The place was sort of sleazy compared to our house.

Meanwhile, Dad's plane arrived, and when he got off, there was nobody there to greet him. He called the house and got the answering machine. He called again and again; still no answer. Giving up on us, he called a neighbor to pick him up. When the neighbor dropped him off at home, Dad walked into the dark house and headed straight for the kitchen. When he found the note, he was shocked. He couldn't believe what he was reading. He called the phone number Mom had written on the note.

Back at the apartment, we were watching TV, and we all got very quiet when we heard the phone ring. We knew who it was. Jason turned the TV down and Mom went to answer the phone. She talked for a little while, agreeing to meet Dad in a bar down the street in an hour. Jason and I lay awake in our sleeping bags as we waited for Mom to return from her meeting. It seemed like she had been gone for twelve years, but in reality, it was only an hour. She came in to check on us as soon as she came back. We pretended to be asleep.

The next day, Mom took us back to see our father. I thought maybe he would give us some answers about what was going on, but he couldn't because he didn't really know himself. All he knew was that things would never be the same again. Mom wanted nothing to do with him anymore. She wanted to start a new life without him—and, for the most part, without us.

Dad tried to reassure us the best he could that we didn't cause the breakup and that even though Mom and Dad weren't together they both loved us very much. No matter what anybody said, Jason thought that it was his fault for being a bad kid. He couldn't understand what was going on.

I was too busy trying to forget my own pain to really help him. The whole thing was too painful for me to deal with, so I just tried to forget about it. I cried myself to sleep at night, and I was so angry at my mom that I never wanted to see her again. I felt betrayed by her and abandoned. I became withdrawn. I focused on other things in my life, such as my friends, so I wouldn't have to face what was going on at home. I sort of pushed all my emotions to the side because they were too painful to deal with. I stopped feeling and loving so I wouldn't be vulnerable to getting hurt. I put up a wall so that nobody could get in and hurt me again.

Children Unprepared

Like Lia and Jason, most children—researchers say about 80 percent—get no warning at all that their parents are planning to separate. Children are better prepared for a tonsillectomy than for their parents' separation. Before they undergo a tonsillectomy, children often are given a booklet telling them about what will happen in a reassuring way; they may take a tour of the hospital; they are told that they will get ice cream when it's over. But they are seldom prepared for the event that turns their world upside down. Another student speaks of his experience:

> Bobby Yukon
> The last time I believed in God, Mom, and apple pie, I was a happy little ten-year-old walking home from school on a sunny spring day. I was the last one to get home that day, and as soon as I walked in, Mom said "Come on, everybody, we're going to Grandma's for a visit," and she piled us into the car for a fun-filled afternoon. I had homework to do, but it could wait until later. "Later" turned out to be a lifetime away. When we got to Grandma's house, Mom sat us all down in the living room and said, "Your father and I are getting divorced, and there are going to be a few changes in our lives. But it's all for the best. We'll be much happier now." Little did we know that she had already filed for divorce and, while we were on our way to Grandma's house, Dad was being served with the papers at work.

As in these students' families, parents rarely discuss the problems in their marriage or the possibility of separating before the event occurs. Perhaps they believe they are "protecting" the children; perhaps they are just too involved in their own suffering to think about the impact the separation will have on their children. Whatever their reasoning—or lack of it—parents typically spring the news on their children as they head out the door. This is especially true when one parent decides to leave the other one and that parent, too, is caught unawares.

Yolanda Sandoval

My parents had never discussed the possibility of a separation or divorce with my sisters and me. The day it happened, my mom dropped me off at school and said that she would pick me up after school as usual. In the middle of the day, though, I was called out of my class by the nurse and told to take all my things with me because my mother was there to pick me up. I was surprised and confused, because I knew that I was not sick and I did not have an appointment to go to. When I arrived at the nurse's office and saw my mom, she said she was taking me to the dentist. I noticed that she seemed kind of strange, and I got a little scared. I got even more scared when I saw both my sisters and a friend of my mother's in the car. When we got in, I noticed that my mother had packed some luggage. I demanded to know where she was taking us. She said we were going to go to someone's house until some problems were settled at home. My mom's friend dropped us off at a house in a strange city. My sister and I wanted to call our dad and have him come and pick us up, but my mom would not let us use the phone. As it turned out, my dad looked for us non-stop for four days. He called and visited hospitals, police stations, and even mortuaries trying to find us. He filed a missing persons report. When we returned, my mother told my dad that she had filed for divorce and that she was moving out of the house.

Children who are unprepared for their parents' announcement are stunned and shocked. They cannot believe what is happening. They fear for their own futures. They don't understand the reasons for the divorce. They are intensely worried and anxious. The word used most often to describe their reaction to the news that their parents are separating is "scared."

John Klinger

I woke up at 5:30 when my father's alarm went off, but he was nowhere to be found. When I went to tell my mom, she told me that my father was gone and not to worry about it. They were just going to live separately for a while. Worry was the first thing I did. I had no one to turn to, and I felt very alone and scared in the darkness of that early morning.

It is especially difficult for children when the news of the separation comes from out of the blue. When the parents have kept their disagreements hidden from the children and then suddenly they tell them "I'm leaving your dad," or "Your daddy's not coming home anymore," or "Mommy and Daddy don't love each other anymore," or "Your mother and I are getting a divorce," this can be incomprehensible and devastating. The children go into shock. When the world they thought they knew turns out to be a fantasy, children may feel deceived by their parents. It doesn't matter whether they are very young or old enough to "understand," children who are unprepared suffer a shock. Their shock can then turn into mistrust.

Tiffani Leach

About a month after I graduated from high school, when everything couldn't have been better, my mom told me that she and my dad were separating. That was it. No warning whatsoever. Nothing more was said. No explanation was given. No questions were asked. It turned out that they had decided earlier that they were going to separate, but they had waited for me to graduate from high school and my grandfather to die before they announced their decision. I was in total shock. I felt like I could never trust them—or my own perceptions—again.

Other children saw hints of trouble between their parents before the day of separation. Their parents acted different or dressed differently; they argued or fought. But the children denied or ignored the significance of these behaviors. They wanted and needed to believe so strongly that their parents would stay together that their parents' separation came as a shock to them, too. Remember Kathy Lee, the student whose story was quoted at the beginning of Chapter 5, the student whose mother left "shockingly and secretly"? This student had hidden her head in the sand until the day her mother actually walked out. She was old enough to have sensed the disintegration of her parents' relationship—her mother was going out at night looking beautiful, having fights with her husband and breaking dishes—but, being an adolescent, Kathy was living in her own world, oblivious to the implications of her parents' problems. Thus, even when there are clues that the marriage is in trouble, these children also may be unprepared for their parents' separation.

Besides breaking the news of their impending separation suddenly, parents often give the children inadequate explanations when they do break the news. They do not explain how the marriage has fallen apart, how they are going to survive, or what will happen next. Like the following student, the children are left to figure it out for themselves.

Gerry Schonfeld

My mother was not concerned about how my sister and I would deal with a separation. She just knew she had to get out, and so she asked my father to leave the house. We were never sure why they split up, and my mother

never sat us down and told us why. All I remember is
sitting with my sister on the couch crying because Dad
wasn't around anymore and we were afraid we would
never see him again.

Unfortunately, the fact that parents do not explain the
divorce to their children leaves them unnecessarily unsure
and afraid. These children are left in the dark, just when
they most need reassurance and information. "Why is Daddy
leaving?" "When will I see him again?" "What is going to
happen to meeee?" One reason that parents fail to explain
their actions and decisions to their children is that they don't
think the children are old enough to understand.

Morgan Dennison
I remember walking alongside a white wooden fence
on the way home from the grocery store with my mom.
I was seven years old, and I asked her why she and Dad
were getting a divorce. She told me, "It's none of your
business. I'll tell you when you are older."

It is sad, indeed, that parents take this escape route. Part of
being a parent is trying to explain the unexplainable to young
children. Parents have to explain what it means when the cat
dies, why you have to brush your teeth, and why you shouldn't
run into the street. They discuss "God" and being nice to old
people. They even talk about where babies come from and
what "safe sex" means. If they tried, they could find words
that would prepare their children for a separation and help
them understand the reasons that mommy and daddy will be
living in separate houses. They could offer extra support and
comfort and reassure the children that "everything will be all
right"—even if they don't believe it themselves.

Separation Is Especially Hard for Young Children
The news that parents are separating is especially
confusing for younger children. To a young child, parents are

everything, all-powerful, all knowing. When you're three, or four, or five years old, the sun rises and sets on your parents, and home is the place you want to be. At this age, a separation is most bewildering. Young children don't understand what is going on. They don't know what the words "divorce" and "separation" mean. Without the preparation and explanation that only their parents can provide, these young children don't understand why Daddy is leaving, why Mommy is crying. They are confused and bewildered.

Diana Denman

I was five years old when my father moved out. All I can remember is confusion. I did not know that my parents were separated. I remember asking my mother where Daddy was, one night, when I slept in her bed. She told me that he had moved out, but this was too difficult for me to understand. I just kept hoping that he would move back home soon.

Young children conceptualize a relationship only in terms of the person's physical presence. For the preschool child, love is being with the person. At this age children are frightened when the parent leaves—afraid of being left alone, afraid of being abandoned. If Daddy has left, who is to say that Mommy won't leave too? They are afraid about who will take care of them if Mommy does leave.

Kelsi Nogawa

After the separation, when I was four, my father would come to babysit for me while my mother had her meetings for work. There was one particular time that stands out clearly in my mind, showing my confusion about our family situation. My mother had just come home from her meeting, and my father was ready to head out the door. I ran to the front door and clung to him as tight as I could. I remember feeling the terror of pure abandonment. I didn't want him to go because I was afraid that I would never see him again after he stepped outside.

Many young children feel panic when their parents separate. Sometimes parents add to the young child's confusion by their own confused behavior.

Beni Yasunari
When I was four years old, my parents had a big fight. I saw my father hit my mother, and then he was gone. But the next thing I knew, he came home to stay with us, and my mother was looking after him. This was because he was in a car accident after he had been drinking. He was unable to walk without crutches and his left eye was completely swollen shut. As soon as he got well, my mother petitioned for a divorce. I was totally confused. I remember thinking after the "hitting incident" that I would never see my father again, and then, a few weeks later, he was at home watching television and asking me how my day went. Then he was gone again.

Young children have a very limited understanding of time—of the past, the present, and the future. They are easily confused when parents move in and out of the household. This confusion adds to their general uncertainty about what is going on in their universe. As we saw in earlier chapters, it is not uncommon for parents to separate and reconcile and separate again before they ultimately get a divorce. From the child's point of view, this is even more confusing than a simple break, and certainly it is more difficult for the parent to explain.

But Older Children React Too
As children get older, they can understand better what the words "separation" and "divorce," mean, but they may be just as shocked and just as afraid as younger children. Understanding does not relieve their pain or anxiety. They

still long for their intact family. These older children, too, experience grief and sadness; they yearn for their lost parents. They have greater awareness of their parents' problems and greater understanding of the separation—but not less sorrow, sadness, or fear at the end of marriage and family as they have known it. They often react with the same kind of anguish as younger children.

Dannie Dorado

When I was fifteen, my mom called us into the family room where she had been folding laundry. She sat us down and told us that she and Dad loved us very much and always would, but they didn't love each other anymore and couldn't continue to live together; my dad was moving out. I can't say I hadn't expected it. My parents had been fighting for years. But it felt as if someone had blown a hole in my stomach. That night my dad left. I sat on the stairs and watched through the railing as he packed his car. When he gave me a hug and told me he loved me, I told him not to go. His eyes started to water and he said he had to and that everything would be all right. He promised to call soon. Everything changed from that moment on. As his car disappeared down the street, I knew nothing would ever be the same. I cried all night long, sobbing silently into my pillow. I was scared—scared of the new life that was ahead of us.

Loss of Family and Father

For the adults who are getting the divorce, divorce offers some advantages. The woman may value the career she will now be able to pursue more actively; the man may want his freedom; they may both move on to other partners who are more compatible, with eagerness, and end the marriage with relief and hope for a better tomorrow. For them, the divorce, although painful, may be a net gain. But children seldom see a gain in the divorce. For them, the end of their parents' marriage is nothing but a loss. Student after student, whatever their age at the time of the divorce, expressed their feelings of loss.

With divorce, children lose the family they have known for their entire life. Even in a family that has been wracked with conflict, a "divorced" child feels the loss of family unity, the loss of security and love, and the loss of the fairy tale fantasy of happily ever after. Children generally are not able to take their parents' perspective and admit that the divorce might be a good idea. They are egocentrically concerned about having their own needs satisfied. The following student was so grief stricken she became physically ill.

Kristin Sanders

My parents separated when I was in the sixth grade. In retrospect, when I try to picture my family and how we interacted before my parents split, I realize how miserable they were and how much they fought. But regardless of how unhappy they were, I did not want them to divorce. Not only was I terribly hurt, I was embarrassed. I had taken great pride in the fact that my parents were still together while all my friends' parents were divorced. My parents' separation was the most devastating event in my life. I remember getting sick after I was informed of my parents' plans. I was sick for weeks; all I did was sleep and vomit. In fact, I remember vomiting for about a month after my parents separated. My parents' explanation was that I kept getting the stomach flu.

Another student, discovering she would be losing her family, expressed her strong opposition to her parents' divorce.

Dakota Dale

My first reaction, when Mom sprang the news on us that she and Dad were getting a divorce, was how could she do such a stupid, thoughtless, selfish thing, ruining our lives like that? So what if everything wasn't rosy between her and Dad. Sure they argued a lot—in fact, really horribly a couple of times. Dad would get jealous of other men looking at Mom; Mom would yell at him for drinking and threaten to leave him; and then Dad would cry. It wasn't "Leave It to Beaver" or anything, but I never thought it was that big a deal. After all, didn't everyone's parents fight? Why couldn't she just drop it and let us go back home? Dad wasn't such a bad guy anyway. He was always kind and loving to us kids, and he never screamed at us or hit us like Mom did. I loved him so much. To think of spending every night and day without him was almost more than I could bear.

This student was angry at her mother for precipitating the divorce. As she viewed the world, from her own egocentric perspective, it would be better—for her—if her parents stayed together. She could not bear the thought of losing her dad. And losing her dad was indeed a strong possibility. When parents divorce, children not only lose their "family," they also often lose a parent. Usually it is Dad who disappears. Sometimes, the father disappears immediately and entirely.

Gale Fisher
    After my dad moved out, he would come by the house for things. My brother and I would be playing in the back yard, but he would not want to see us. After that day, we didn't see him for an entire year.

Other fathers fade away more gradually. As we pointed out in Chapter 7, father visits frequently dwindle so that within a year or two, less than half of the children in divorced families see their fathers at all, and less than one fifth see their fathers as often as once a week. This makes children sad and frustrated. Many children deplore their lack of contact with their fathers and feel that their fathers just don't care about them.

Diana Denman

By the time I was in high school, visits with Dad had almost stopped, and after I went away to college, almost all communication ended. Today, my dad pays for my tuition and housing, but he does not call or write. I call every so often to update him about my activities and let him know how I am, but I never hear from him. I think it is sad that it has to be this way. Even though his lack of attention has been pointed out to him, he hasn't changed, and I guess he never will.

As children lose contact with their fathers, they lose the feeling of closeness they once had. They become more and more distant and estranged. The lack of contact becomes a two-way street; they no longer want closeness and foresee a future without their father.

Tracey Sanchez

I used to visit my father at his apartment, and then the visits became fewer and fewer. I still do not understand why I lost that connection with him, and it's so sad. I feel guilty that I don't have the desire to be close to him, and when I do have the desire, I just can't. Now I feel it is so far gone I don't know how to ever be close again.

Even if the father doesn't disappear entirely, his visits are often sporadic and unpredictable. Children hate the fact that they don't have regular visits with Dad. They feel unloved by a dad who disappointed them, and they continue to yearn for more—more time, more contact, more attention...more love.

Sean Fitzpatrick

I remember when I was young, after my parents' divorce, I always wanted my father to love me. I could never figure out why he would go skiing or camping with his girlfriend on the weekends we were suppose to stay

with him. I cried a lot and was always saying I wanted to
live with my father.

The children often find that the activities they share
with Dad during their times together—whether regular or
sporadic—are unsatisfying. Because of the rareness of the
visits, the father does not want to spend his time in routine
parenting. He does not want to use "his" precious time for
mundane activities like shopping for shoes or onerous tasks
like supervising homework. Instead, he fills the hours with
entertainment—going to Disneyland, McDonald's, the
movies. This can leave the child feeling empty and emotionally
disconnected from the father. The focus on "his" time
may reflect the father's self-centeredness or his continuing
resentment toward his former wife. Time with the children is
seen as getting "his" share, not as a time to be a parent. These
fathers ignore the fact that it is the children's time, too. They
do not understand that their children's childhood is being
adversely affected by their abdication of parenting.

Lauren Gordon
My dad used to take me out for Disneyland trips—
shopping, to the movies, restaurants—and I would always
come home with something new and wonderful that he
had bought for me. But looking back on those weekly
visits, they were really empty, because my dad never really
talked to me about anything important. We would only
talk about surface things. After my mother and I moved
to California, his phone calls and visits soon dwindled to
nothing.

With their contact restricted to Disneyland visits, children
lose a father and gain a "pal." They no longer feel close to
their dad the way they used to when they lived with him and
he was a parent, putting Band-Aids on their boo-boos and
telling them when it was time for bed. Some children respond
to this new paternal role negatively.

Judie Myers

Once visitation was established—every other weekend and Wednesday night—Dad became a Disneyland Dad. He tried to keep us entertained by going to amusement parks and buying us toys. He took us to the movies, out to dinner, and to the mall. But we never felt comfortable with him. We never liked to go to his house. We felt we did not know him. He acted like a "buddy" instead of a father.

Other children eventually got around to valuing their father—not as a father, per se, but as a good friend.

Kelsi Nogawa

After the divorce, my dad was one of those fathers who wanted to shove a lifetime of memories into a day of play. Often I would end up with a stomachache at the end of our time together. We developed an unusual relationship. He never attempted to be much of a "parent" figure to me. When I got older, we talked of politics, future goals, and the loves in both our lives. In other words, he was a really lousy father but a pretty good friend.

Mothers are not as likely as fathers to disappear after the separation. This is true not just because mothers are more likely to have custody, but because even when they do not have custody, they are more likely to have continuing contact with their children. Of the children in father custody, research suggests, about one third continue to see their mother at least once a week (whereas this is true for less than one fifth of the children in mother custody), and nearly all children in father custody see their mother at least once a year. Mothers, thus, are more likely than fathers to continue to be involved in their children's lives.

Keith Barnett

I was happy that I got to stay in our house with my dad after the divorce, because this meant that my mom had a place to come and visit me. She dropped in almost every day on her way home from work. Sometimes we had dinner together; sometimes she helped me with my homework. She made a special effort to go to all my school open houses. I always knew she was there for me.

Of course, this is not always the case. Sometimes children are taken away from their mothers by their angry fathers. This experience can leave deep wounds as the dramatic story of the following student shows.

Kyonghui Seong

I remember the night it happened. My dad was pounding on the door and it woke me up. He stumbled in after a night of drinking. I started to cry and looked for my brother and my mom, but they were not there. I thought they had run away. My dad must have had the same idea because he started to yell, "Where did she go with my son?" He asked me if I knew where they were. He was asking me, only four years old, if I knew where my mom had gone. But I did know. They had gone to her best friend's house, which I knew was near a street with a big hill. We immediately went after them. When we got to the house, my dad knocked on the door and as soon as it opened, he went after my brother. I ran to my mother and held on. I was clinging to her back. My dad was screaming at her. Then my dad called for me to go with him and my brother. He tore me away from my mother. I was crying, screaming, and kicking. As I turned around one last time to see my mom, her back was turned to us, and that is the only image of my mom that I have with me now.

Fortunately, such dramatic partings are rare. More commonly, the loss of the parent—or parents—is gradual and psychological, as in the following story:

Kristin Sanders
Until the divorce, I had always been very close to my father. I was "Daddy's little girl" and I was not that close to my mother. She was irrational and had problems with drinking. These problems became worse after the marriage ended and my father left the house. Not only did I lose the physical presence of my father, I lost both my parents emotionally. They both became very self-involved. They were so involved in their own lives that they minimized and dismissed my pain. During this vulnerable and difficult period I needed my parents more than ever, yet they were less available and less accessible than ever before. My father was preoccupied with living his life as a single man. He purchased a new sports car and started dating a lot. My mother's drinking increased and she started having an affair three days after my father left the house. Within weeks, the man she was having the affair with moved into our home and drove my dad's Mercedes around as if it was his own. My mother made no attempt to hide her affair from me. Today, I do not have a close relationship with either of my parents.

Children Unparented
In the initial period after separation, most divorcing parents are distracted, suffering their own pain, involved with their own problems. At the same time as their children are seeking more attention and reassurance, these preoccupied parents have less to give them. Because divorcing parents are often emotional wrecks, many children go "unparented" in the first year after the separation.

Kate Ferris
My mom was always crying and taking things out on us. She was a wreck and we were wrecks too. She was too worried about herself to think about how we felt.

This lack of parenting, and the parent's emotional distress, can take a severe toll on the child. In one extreme case, the child had to provide emotional support for her depressed mother and it made her, literally, sick.

Sarah Beller
After the divorce, my mother was severely depressed. This made me totally depressed. Then somewhere along the line, my mother and I switched roles. I became her emotional caretaker. I was trying desperately to control my feelings and the situation around me. It got so bad I remember feeling like I was going to choke whenever I was eating. For about five months, I had trouble every night at dinner. I could hardly get the food down.

In extreme cases like this, the children feel like they have changed places with the parent—that they have become the caretaker and the parent is the child. It is common for them to recollect that after the divorce they had to assume more responsibility for their own care because their parents were distracted or depressed. When there are younger children in the family, the older children often have to assume the caretaker role because their parents are not up to the job.

Susan Ford
My brother, Billy, who was four, would cling to me and ask me where Daddy was and if Mommy was going away too. I held him and hugged him and told him everything was going to be okay. Mom couldn't be bothered with Billy or any of us, so we just kind of took care of ourselves. We had no money, no real home, no father to turn to when Mom got upset. She had to go to work to feed us

and pay the rent. At one point we were so poor we had to go on food stamps. Because I was the oldest girl, she piled everything on me. I was only eleven, but I had to do all the cooking and clean the house every day. Mom was hardly ever there to take care of anything. She was working, going to court, going out with her friends, or complaining about Dad. I also had to baby sit for Billy and my younger sister, Valerie. Before the divorce, I had been getting straight A's in school. But now, if either of my siblings was sick, I had to stay home and take care of them so Mom could work. And with all the other things I had to do, I didn't have time to do my homework. So who cared when my grades went from A's to D's and F's? Little Billy really needed a mother more than the rest of us, and I was all he was going to get. He even called me Mom sometimes. I began to realize that my mom couldn't even take care of herself. She needed me to take care of her too.

This student provides a poignant description of what happens in many households after divorce, when the custodial parent is engrossed with his or her own activities and concerns and leaves the children to rear themselves. This is a real burden for the older child and a cause for lasting resentment. It is developmentally impossible for children to truly appreciate their parents' plight, and it is an imposition on their childhood to expect them to take on the emotional and practical tasks of an adult.

In the months following a marital breakup, because of the parent's distraction and distress, household rules, routines, and discipline are typically thrown into disarray. The household loses structure and organization. There are fewer bedtime stories, family meals, and play times. Children have irregular bedtimes and mealtimes. They are more often late for school. They lack supervision. It is easy for them to get into trouble.

Kerry Purdue

I had no supervision after the divorce. My mom was always off at work or out with friends. At the time, I appreciated the freedom; however, in retrospect I think it was dangerous and irresponsible of my parents to offer me no guidance when I was so young. I took advantage of the situation and threw parties every weekend and had people over all the time. Everyone liked my house because my mom had no control. When my mom tried to regain some control, I got mad and went to live with my dad. He was never around either. He was either out or watching TV or working on the computer. So I had parties all the time at his house, too. He would be downstairs, and about twenty kids would be in the house, and he never even knew.

Besides neglecting their children, some divorced parents are so focused on their own survival and well-being, or so relieved to be free of their unhappy marriage, that they act like adolescents themselves. This sets a poor example for the children, and the children do not like it.

Terry Bodette

After the divorce, my dad dated a lot of women and drank heavily. He would call me to pick him up late at night and tell me about all of his conquests, like I was a college buddy. It made me sick.

Loss of Lifestyle

Besides losing their parents, children of divorce also lose the lifestyle they have enjoyed. If children lose their home, their friends, and their neighborhood right at the time they lose a parent, this is particularly difficult. Even if it might feel better for the parent, immediately uprooting the family after the separation is not best for the child. This is so for two reasons. One reason is that it is difficult for children to cope with transitions in general. The second reason is that the transition in this case is likely to be in a downward direction. Even if their families were relatively affluent, children whose parents divorce almost inevitably experience the loss of material things—from cars to computers—and a decline in their standard of living. It is often necessary for them to move, and unless the parent is moving in with a new mate with money, the move is not to a better house. Parents no longer have the same budget for their children's wardrobes, vacations, food or entertainment, because divorce is expensive and family income is reduced. In addition to the loss of material objects, children also suffer from the humiliation of moving to a tacky neighborhood or going on welfare.

> Brett Knowles
> I lived in a big, beautiful home in Rancho Palos Verdes, where I could walk outside into the backyard and see the ocean as it met the horizon. It was a stunning and wonderful place to grow up. The day we moved from that house, I sat in my empty room and cried. The truck outside was ready to go. I unplugged the phone that sat in the corner on the floor, gave one last look at my room with its blue and white flowered wallpaper, and went downstairs. As we drove away I looked back and wished I'd walked into the backyard to see the ocean one last time. I still miss the ocean every day. We moved to a small, rented house a few miles away. It was old and needed a lot of repairs. It wasn't bad, but I felt cheated and angry. I didn't want my friends to come over and feel sorry for me. I changed from a private school to a public school, and every day I felt like I wore the scarlet letter on my chest—a big "D" for divorce.

One of the reasons that mothers and children lose the lifestyle to which they have been accustomed is that child support is seldom set at a level high enough to maintain their standard of living—and, as we have noted before, the father often doesn't pay the support payments.

Brittany Roberts

My mother was supposed to be receiving child support from my father, but he never kept a job long enough to afford to make these payments. In total, he paid only three or four monthly payments in the six years they were ordered. So my mom had to work longer hours to make more money. I hated it. I felt like she was never home anymore and that making money was more important than spending time with me.

The battle to capture the child support checks can also be demoralizing to the child, and, when fathers don't pay up, they lose their children's affection and respect. Even worse, the children may lose respect for themselves.

Annette Vanderhoof

Right before we left for our weekend visit, my mom would say, "Tell your father I need my check." The "check" was her support check. My dad is very stingy with his money and he would always moan and complain on Sunday when I asked him for Mom's check. This made me feel really bad inside, and I remember thinking to myself that if I had only never been born, my dad wouldn't have to pay money to my mom.

It is particularly difficult for children to deal with the loss of family income and lack of child support if the father is living an affluent lifestyle. This can make the children furious and resentful—whether they are three years old or twenty-three.

Diana Denman

My father wanted to pay as little as possible for child support and he did not want to pay for anything else. I remember a time when my brother and I went to his house to swim and we forgot our bathing suits. My father blew up at us, saying that it was not his responsibility to buy us clothes. We could not understand why he could not take us to get another because he had so much money to spend on himself and his new wife. Another time, my mother tried to charge some clothing for us on my dad's credit card. Unbeknownst to her, the card had been canceled, and so the clerk cut it up in front of us. It was very embarrassing and humiliating for my mother. The next time we saw our father, my brother, who was only three at the time, yelled at him that he stole our clothes and that we did not have enough money.

Children's Reactions to Separation: A Recap

In brief, then, their parents' separation sends children into a tailspin. They are unprepared and confused; they do not understand what is happening, and they are anxious and afraid. Young children especially are bewildered—they do not even have the concept of "separation"—but older children and adolescents also react strongly and negatively to the news that their parents are parting. After the separation, the children are acutely saddened by the loss of the family and lifestyle they have known. Their contact with their father diminishes and this leads to even greater pain and anguish. They often experience a period of emotional and physical neglect, as their parents try to deal with their own problems and issues. The household is thrown into disorganization, and rules and routines are in disarray. This, too, takes a toll. Some children are required to shoulder a huge caretaking burden, caring for younger siblings and often a suffering parent as well. The unfortunate irony is that, just at the time children most need their parents' support, the parents are least able to give it. Parents, struggling for survival themselves, ignore their children's need for information and reassurance. They do not see the children's profound feelings of anxiety and loss and fail to appreciate the depth of their suffering.

Lessons to Be Learned

The decision to separate is made "of the parents, by the parents, and for the parents." It is almost never made "for the sake of the children." So parents must make special efforts to protect their children as they are break up their marriage. Here are some things that parents can do to alleviate their children's suffering:

1. Prepare the children. Children suffer more if the separation is unexpected and they are unprepared. They are more shocked, scared and distraught if their parents spring the separation on them with no warning and no explanation. So the first lesson is that, after parents have decided that their marriage is over, they should discuss this with their children, calmly and rationally, instead of having one parent leave home in a huff. This discussion should be gentle, gradual, and probably repeated. It will be painful for everyone to talk about, but parents are adults; they need to draw on that maturity to deal with this excruciatingly difficult situation "for the sake of the children."

2. Explain in ways children understand. When parents discuss the separation with their children, they should provide an explanation that is specific and at a level the child can understand. There are age differences in what children can comprehend, but no child is too young or too old for an explanation. It is most difficult for children when parents only say, "Mommy and Daddy don't love each other anymore." A vague explanation like this increases children's fear that their parents will stop loving them, too, and that both parents may abandon them. It is better if parents are honest and specific: "Father drinks" or "Mother has a new boyfriend." Children need and deserve an explanation they can understand.

3. Spell out the implications for the children. It is important to let children know what the separation is and what it is not. They need to know who will live where, when they will see each parent, and how they will all manage. If parents throw up their hands and wail, "I don't know what's going to happen. I don't know how we'll manage," the child's anxiety level goes through the roof. Parents should keep their own anxieties and fears to themselves as much as they can. It can be helpful to involve children in age appropriate decision-making, for example, they can decide the color of their new room, which toys to have in which house, or the best new neighborhood bakery.

4. Reassure the children. It is also essential that when parents discuss the separation with their children they assure them that both parents will continue to love and care for them even though they will not all be living in the same house. Children's reactions to the separation are most severe if, at the same time as they lose the presence of a parent, they worry about losing the parent's love. It's bad enough that they are losing their "family"; they need to be told—and shown—again and again that their parents are still there for them emotionally. Parents should concede that the separation will bring changes but assure their children that in the long run they will be okay and that the parents will be okay, too.

5. Encourage children to express their feelings. A separation is difficult for the parents, who feel sad, angry, lost, anxious, but it is even harder for the children, who have less ability to understand and talk about their feelings. Parents need to encourage their children to talk and ask questions about the separation and to express their concerns and uncertainties. Children should be able to express their feeling of missing their other parent without feeling guilty about it. It is natural for them to long for the "good old days" and yearn for the missing parent. Parents should let children vent their feelings in a supportive environment and should minimize the children's feelings of loss by continuing to provide contact with both parents.

6. Continue to be a parent. It is not uncommon for parents to underestimate what their children are going through— because they are absorbed by their own difficulties and don't have the energy to pay attention or the clinical experience to recognize the child's problems. If children are not weeping or wailing, parents may think they're fine. But probably they are not fine. They are likely to be suffering inside. It is particularly important, therefore, for parents not to neglect their children at this time of heightened vulnerability and pain. It is vital to find time to be with them, to maintain family routines and traditions, to keep their lives predictable. Parents need to make a concentrated effort not to leave their children "unparented" at this critical time.

7. Minimize disruption in the child's life. The more changes children have to go through and the more extreme those changes are, the harder it is for them. In particular, when parents go through repeated separations and reconciliations, it makes children even more confused and upset. Parents should realize this when they are "trying on" the idea of separation, and they should make sure that their decision to separate is as final as thinking and planning can make it before anyone actually moves out. They should also be aware of the number of changes that the separation will cause for the child. The more changes that get piled on at once, the more stress this creates. Children who lose their mother to employment and their father to a new girlfriend at the same time have a harder time than if the new job and the new girlfriend wait until after the shock of the separation has passed. Children who lose their home, their friends, and their neighborhood when they lose their "family" feel more overwhelmed by the separation than if they continue to have the support of familiar teachers, friends, and relatives. Immediately uprooting the children and moving to a cheaper place may have advantages for the parents, but it is not beneficial for the children. For the sake of the children, parents would be well advised to wait until the immediate adjustment is over before moving on and beginning a new life in a new place. If parents give their children psychological help and support during the separation, the transition can be easier for everyone.

10
Hello to the School of Hard Knocks: Problems for Children of All Ages

Clearly children have strong immediate reactions to news of their parents' separation, and they experience a strong sense of loss—of family, of father, of lifestyle. But after the shock and the immediate aftermath of the separation, do children bounce back, or do they continue to suffer? What are the psychological consequences of the permanent termination of their family "unit"? How do they feel in the period after the divorce, and are these feelings different for children of different ages? What our students' stories suggest is that divorce brings psychological turmoil for children of all ages.

The Youngest Victims
It is often assumed that divorce itself will not have a strong effect on babies who have little attachment to the parents they will be "losing." There need be little noticeable change in the infant's routine and little stress experienced by the infant after the divorce. Even if the infant is attached to the father and loses contact with him after the divorce, he or

she should get over it, as long as the mother continues her nurturing care. Nevertheless, infants are vulnerable because they are helpless; they survive and thrive at the whim of the environment. Our students' stories suggested that infants could have a strong reaction to losing a parent, a reaction that lasts for months—if the mother herself is stressed.

Clarissa Cambridge

At the time of my parents' divorce I was only eighteen months old. Because I was so young, I don't remember anything about the divorce. My mom tells me, though, that the effects on me were awful. No matter who I was with, if I was leaving anyone or if anyone was leaving me, I threw a tantrum. The fits I threw could go on for half an hour, and this kept up for more than a year after the divorce. I was surprised to hear that at such a young age I showed such emotion. I asked my mom what she thought about my behavior, but she could not explain it. "I just didn't understand how you knew to get upset," my mom said. "We would just be going to the store, but somehow you acted as if I was taking you from your dad."

What was the emotional context in which a toddler had this reaction? Clarissa's story continues…

After the separation, I spent equal time with my mom and my dad. My mom's job often took her out of town, and my dad took care of me while she was gone. My mom had a new apartment, but we spent most of our time at her new boyfriend's. Soon she discovered that the boyfriend had problems. This was the first time she had ever experienced his "silent treatment," and she could not understand what had come over the man who had made her happy enough to leave her marriage. She had just taken a huge stand to be with him, and now he was treating her like dirt. She had hurt many people to be with him, and now he was hurting her. The relationship turned out to be a really bad one. One night, in fear, she and I left her boyfriend's house and went to stay with my dad.

It is not surprising that, in this emotional context, the infant was throwing tantrums. She herself was experiencing repeated separations from both parents, and her mother was the victim of pressure and physical abuse from her new partner. Of course, the child was suffering. In this student's case, the suffering was fortunately short lived. Her mother left the abusive boyfriend and recovered from the divorce, and Clarissa was able to have a positive relationship with both her parents. But things don't always work out so well.

Elizabeth Harrison

It has always been extremely painful knowing that I have a father who is alive and perfectly capable of acting like a parent, but who does not care about me. As a child, I was often depressed and acted out. Around the age of four or five, I had severe temper tantrums. As I grew older I had very low self-esteem. In junior high school, I was very introverted. Although I was very successful academically, I felt like I belonged with the "loser crowd." Throughout my high school years, curiosity about what my father might be like was eating away at my concentration. I also felt guilty for all that my mom had to go through for me. I compensated for that guilt by always trying hard to make her proud of me, and I deprived myself of much of the fun of childhood and adolescence by devoting all my time to trying to become the best for her. Even when I was the best in something, it was not enough for me. I still felt inadequate. I never told my mom how I felt about my father for fear of hurting her. I got really good at holding my feelings inside: so good, in fact, that it became difficult to express myself even when I wanted to. After I graduated from high school, I decided that I finally needed to fill the emptiness in my life by finding out at least a little about my father. I was seventeen when I found his number and called to see if he would be willing to talk. After a long pause, he agreed. We met and spent the day together. He has called me regularly ever since. Today I am able to better understand what I was feeling all those years. Now I am able to say without guilt that the absence of my father caused me much pain. I no longer feel abandoned, but many of the scars still remain. I still have not been able to bring myself to call him "Dad."

Young children, as well as infants, are vulnerable to continued emotional distress after a divorce. The stress of divorce often leads young children to regress to earlier levels of functioning—a reaction to stress and a return to happier times. It is not uncommon for children of this age to regress in terms of their toilet habits. Their play behavior with peers also is less mature; they stare at the other children instead of joining in the play. They are whiny, act out, or have temper tantrums. They have nightmares about monsters. They become afraid of separating from their parents, although earlier they had separated easily. They suck their thumbs, cry for their cuddlies, and cling to their mothers.

Alex Peterson

After my parents' divorce I had intense nightmares. I was paranoid about closets and robbers coming through open windows. It was months before I could sleep soundly.

Chelsea Kim

After my father left, I couldn't sleep alone. I slept with my mom and wet the bed almost every night for months. I was afraid, but I did not know what I was afraid of.

Leah Frank

After my parents got divorced, I remember waking up in the middle of the night crying, and I remember crying every time my mom left me at kindergarten. I had never done this before. All I wanted was to be with my mom. I think I just wanted to make sure I never lost her.

These young children were expressing fear and anxiety, whereas once they had been outgoing and sociable.

Ginny Rook

Six months after my parents' divorce I started kindergarten. Socializing was no longer my favorite activity. I was very insecure, shy, and frightened. I didn't have enough self-confidence to talk to new kids. Walking home from school, I was terrified that someone would kidnap me, so I would run all the way home. My mommy and sister were the only two people that I trusted. My mom's boyfriends posed the biggest threats; there were many different men, and I could never speak to any of them. I remember saying to my mom, "You know we're doing just fine, Mommy. I don't want you to ever get married again." Throughout this period, I remained a withdrawn, shy little girl, who didn't think very highly of herself.

Preschoolers also may feel guilt, as if the divorce is their fault. They reason as follows: a person who doesn't like someone goes away; Daddy went away; so Daddy doesn't like me; so it was my fault. They may act super good to bring Daddy back, or they may deny that Daddy has left. They make up stories about seeing Daddy or talking to him on the phone. If they do see their father, they may feel torn in two: They miss their mother when they are with their father, and they miss their father when they are with their mother. Preschool children don't have a good sense of time, so a week is like forever. They don't understand blood ties, so they think the departed parent may find another son or daughter to replace them. They are afraid that the parent will forget about them when they're gone. As one child put it, "When I'm with one parent, I always think the other one is dead." Children's reaction to a divorce is like their reaction to the death of a loved one. They experience stress, guilt, loneliness, and sadness. These feelings and diminished functioning can last a long time, and even years later there may be residual effects. Some studies suggest that this young age has particular difficulty adjusting to the divorce.

Judie Myers

I was four years old when my parents divorced, and I felt confused and bewildered. I started sucking my thumb and withdrew from activities at school with other children. I was very fearful about being abandoned by my mother, and I did not understand why I was being forced to see my father. I felt I did not know him and was angry at him without understanding the reason. I remember only feeling really "safe" in my mother's presence. She was the only person I could trust. The anxiety I felt while I was with my father surfaced more and more as I got older. I think that deep down I knew something terrible had happened, but I could not understand what. In my early adolescence, the lack of a consistent, everyday father figure in my life became a source of many problems. Because I felt deprived of a quality relationship with a man, I tried to satisfy this need by starting to date very young. I was desperate to please every boyfriend, and this often led to promiscuous behavior. I was anxious and seductive in my interactions with males. It seemed like no matter how hard I tried I could not make these relationships work. Just as with my dad—no matter how good I was, my father remained emotionally unavailable. I still feel a lot of anger. As a young woman, now, I am continuously struggling with these issues trying to get my life together.

Sometimes the stress of the divorce and its aftermath caused the child to develop strong defenses to escape the pain. These defenses later turn out to be dysfunctional.

Sean Fitzpatrick
After my parents divorced, when I was five, they were constantly fighting whenever they had contact with each other. I remember my mother always yelling: "You're such a liar!" and, for some reason, each time she said it, I pictured a lion. I learned a valuable defense during this time, and that was to shut things out—like thinking of a lion every time my mom called my dad a liar. I was able to focus on that thought and not the fight. I also began to daydream quite a bit. That was another way to shut things out. Often I dreamed that we would not have to see Dad's girlfriend anymore. I always dreamed of my parents getting back together. Years later, they did get back together. They even got married again. But it did not last long. Their constant fighting resumed. Within a year, my father was living upstairs in the spare bedroom and our living situation was worse than ever. All they did was fight. This is when my ability to shut things out became really valuable.

Shutting things out may have been necessary for this child, perhaps; but it is not "really valuable." Unhealthy patterns of escaping and avoiding negative emotions that have their roots in family conflict when children are young may contribute to the person's inability to confront and deal with conflict in their own marriages.

Older Children Don't Escape the Effects of Divorce
Compared with these "youngest victims," children who are of school age when their parents divorce are less likely to express their grief and sadness. These children struggle to master and control their feelings of depression. They try to

bury their unhappiness. But still they, too, suffer psychological consequences. The most common emotional reaction at this age is anger. Rather than focusing on sadness, these children express intense anger. Adjusting to the divorce is probably easier at this age than earlier, but these children don't realize it. They're too mad—and they let their parents know it. They are vengeful and try to hurt their parents.

Annette Vanderhoof

After my parents separated, I became a little brat. I misbehaved all the time and talked back to my mother constantly. I was angry at my father because he had left us, and I was angry at my mother because she was there.

One reason these children are angry is that, in their view, their parents have broken the rules—and following the rules is very important at this age. Another reason they are angry is that in their new world order, they have to work harder.

Morgan Dennison

After the divorce, my mom worked, so I had to watch my one-year-old sister. This made me angry because it interfered with my activities. I became very aggressive and mouthy with my mother. I never did what she asked without giving her a good argument first.

Children are especially angry at the parent they believe is to blame for the divorce or for the other parent's suffering. They openly express their animosity and even hatred.

Thuy Ngoc

A week after my mom left my father and we moved into our new house, a strange man started appearing. At first, my mother told us he was a friend from work. But when she told us his name, a bell rang. This was the man my dad had been yelling about. I became intensely angry with my mom because she had not only ruined my dad's life, but also the family and me. At that moment, I was so frustrated with my mom that I would have done anything to make her life miserable. My performance in school dropped just to spite her, and I began to stay out late purposely to make her worry. I was unfriendly to her "friend." I hated the man and blamed him as well as my mother for breaking up my family.

Of course, just because these children express strong anger doesn't mean that they are not feeling sad. They just keep that sadness locked inside. They don't want to act like a baby.

Sarah Beller

I kept all my feelings in and I never let my parents know how much it bothered me. I would cry in the school bathroom privately, and I would cry when I got off the school bus when I was alone so no one would see me. I made sure to wipe off all my tears before I got home. At home, I would lock myself in my room and cry. The only reaction I let them see was when I vented my anger on my mother.

These children don't just take out their anger on their parents. They also take it out against anything else that gets in their way.

Kurt Leinbach

In my intense rage, I would often lock myself in my room and hit and break objects.

They also are likely to internalize their anger. Psychosomatic symptoms of stress—headaches, vomiting, dizziness, sleep problems—are common in this age group.

Kurt Leinbach

I had stomach problems and threw up almost every morning before school because of my anxiety, stress, and anger.

They also take out their anger at school. As a result of the divorce and its aftermath, their school achievement often declines.

Nicole Raffaella

My sister and I both had delayed achievement in school for a year after the divorce. She had to repeat first grade; I failed math, which had been my best subject, and I was removed from the advanced math class.

Even more serious, school-age children whose parents divorce exhibit behavior problems at school. They are twice as likely as children from intact families to be suspended from school. They make up more than half of school truants and nearly half of school dropouts. Their teachers report that they are aggressive and disobedient and that they lack self-control. Our students who were of school age when their parents got divorced, also, confessed to bad attitudes and problem behavior.

Julia Garcia

I was eleven years old when my parents separated. I tried not to let myself feel any of the pain surrounding the breakup of my family. I coped with it in two ways. First, I developed a serious attitude problem with all of my teachers. I talked back, didn't listen, and did anything I could to disrupt the class. When I graduated from eighth grade I was voted "teacher's nightmare" by the other kids at school. And in fact I was. A teacher in junior high told me he would not allow me in his class because he lived in my neighborhood and had heard "what goes on in your house." The other way I coped was by eating everything in sight. By the end of my eighth grade year, I weighed 180 pounds. I was extremely unhappy. I was so shut down emotionally that I couldn't feel close to anybody.

The anger these children feel can last for years.

John Klinger

I was angry at my father for hurting my mother and I was angry at my mother for throwing him out. I began having serious problems at school. I rebelled and did whatever I could to ruin my life. I didn't care about school anymore, and I never did my homework—simply to spite my mother. I would have dropped out of school if I could have. My entire childhood, I just wanted out. I contemplated running away, suicide, and even killing both of them if it meant getting rid of my pain.

Tom Lee

Even now, I have a short fuse when it comes to my mom. I know I haven't forgiven her for dumping my father for another man. I still haven't accepted that other man. I still hate him. I hope that one day I can release all the torment and anguish that is bottled up in me and calmly tell my mother how I feel about the divorce. Part of me died when she and my father separated, and unfortunately, some of my love for my mom died too.

These stories describe the heart-wrenching persistence of the children's anger toward their parents following divorce.

Divorce Hits Young Adolescents Hard

Adolescence is a vulnerable time at best—a time of shaky self-esteem and autonomy issues. It is a particularly risky time for parents to divorce. When their parents divorce, adolescents often overreact with unrealistic anguish and anxiety. In their adolescent egocentrism they can see only their own needs and they feel that the world's eyes are on them. So they lash out at their parents, "How could you do this to me?" Rarely do they understand their parents' perspective. To make matters worse, their parents give them added household and child care responsibilities and urge them to take on odd jobs to make some extra money. In addition, these young adolescents see their parents in a new light, becoming aware of their weaknesses and failures, and often having to listen to them as they unload their feelings of misery and frustration. As a result, the entire divorce experience may give young adolescents a sense of "false maturity." They identify with the custodial parent and take on the role of the departed parent: an adolescent son becomes the man around the house; a girl becomes the parent's confidante. As one of our students, put it, "I played soul saver for my mother." This early push for maturity comes with a high price tag. Being cast into a role for which they are not ready may lead young adolescents to be depressed, sometimes suicidal. It is all too much for them. They cannot hide behind the confusion of the young child or erupt into the angry outbursts of the school-age child. They understand all too well what is going on, but they are helpless to stop it.

Tracey Sanchez
Every Saturday my father would take us to the beach and he would always say, "You seem to be adjusting to the divorce very well." I think this was his way of relieving his own guilt. I began to pull away from him. I hated him for leaving ME to be the spouse and parent. I was the one who was there for my mother when she cried every night for one whole year straight. I was the one who slept in bed with her every night for that whole year. I was the one who comforted her. I was the one who was strong for my brother. Yet I felt no one was strong for me. I was lost and day dreamed about suicide.

As well as becoming depressed, young adolescents dealt with being thrust into the role of the divorced parent's confidante by developing strong animosity toward the other parent, who had victimized their "friend." Remaining loyal to both parents was not an option; these young adolescents took the side of the one who confided in them. They saw and shared that parent's pain.

Andrea Keller

I was just starting eighth grade when my parents separated. I was instantly forced into a multitude of roles including caretaker, confidante, advisor, supporter, housekeeper, and cook. My mom would show me letters my dad wrote her or let me listen to their conversations on the phone. She confided in me and valued my opinion. So I tried to tend to her needs and everyone else's. But I had nowhere to go to vent my own feelings. I would cry myself to sleep; I was extremely depressed and often had suicidal thoughts. And most of all, I hated every second I was with my dad. I only saw him because I had to. Twice he took me to a therapist to work out my anger, but I couldn't do it. I was angry because I shared my mother's pain. I saw my father humiliate her in public by grinding nachos in her face. I saw him break through our garage window with his hand so that he could get his tools, and then I watched her wash the blood off our driveway in front of the neighbors. I saw the hurt in her eyes as she tried to explain the incident to my younger siblings. I saw her suffer the threat of having the house taken away because she had no money. I saw her turn away when we kept bumping into his new "girlfriend" everywhere we went. I saw her cry like a baby. I lived everyday watching my mother's and my brother's and my sister's pain.

To resolve their depression and their anger, adolescents might shut down emotionally. They cannot deal with the emotions for which they are not developmentally ready. They cannot foster their own emotional development, and there is no one else to do it for them. So they suppress their own needs.

Gerry Schonfeld

After my mother asked him to leave, my father moved into an apartment about twenty minutes away, and we visited him every other weekend. I looked forward to the weekends at first, but after a while I just felt sad. My father started to open up about his feelings and exposed us to a side of him we had never seen. He would ask us to help him write a poem for my mother or to bake something for her. I felt sucked into emotions I was not ready for. I always stayed up late crying with my dad telling him that mom would take him back soon and to just give it some time. My family problems were so severe I stopped thinking about what I needed to do for myself. Even now, seven years after the divorce, I try to avoid getting hurt by shutting out my emotions and going "dead" inside. Eventually, I pushed all my feelings about the divorce out of my head and became numb.

Their false sense of maturity also makes it more likely that these young adolescents will engage in risky behaviors. This is another negative consequence of enduring a parental divorce during early adolescence. Looking for love and attention to cover their pain and loss, seeing their parents involved in dating, and lacking close parental supervision, some young adolescents are thrust into premature sexual activity—just as they are entering puberty. Together these factors are responsible for a higher rate of pregnancy among girls from divorced families. These factors also propel adolescents into other risky behavior like using drugs and alcohol, which lead to problems in school and trouble with the law.

Marcy Graham

When my parents divorced, I was fourteen. Soon after my dad left, I remember sitting in my room feeling

so alone. I felt like a martyr and wanted to do something
that would make people pay attention to me and feel my
pain. I took 60 aspirin tablets. Then I got really scared
because I didn't feel well at all. I told my mom and she
took me to the emergency room. They said too much
time had passed for them to pump my stomach, so they
had to regulate my potassium with an IV and keep me
in the hospital over night. I found out later that I almost
died because my potassium level was so low. I know that I
did not want to die, I just wanted attention, but everyone
treated it like a suicide attempt. By the time I was fifteen,
I had run away and was staying with a friend's family.
I had gotten involved with the punk kids and become
my mother's worst nightmare. I was rebellious and
wild, getting drunk and smoking pot all the time, even
at school. It felt really good to be able to forget about
the pain in my life. I looked to boys for the love I wasn't
getting at home. I would go out with anyone who asked
me—regardless of whether I liked the guy or not.

Relationship troubles are another common outcome for
young adolescents whose parents divorce. Some of these
adolescents rush into marriage prematurely; others avoid
it like the plague. Often they worried about making a
commitment, about getting into a bad marriage, about going
through a divorce.

Jack Soderburg
    Even today, ten years after my parents split up,
I still find myself trying to overcome the effects of the
divorce. There will always be scars. I have a pessimistic
view of marriage and hope to avoid it as long as possible,
if not entirely. I am afraid of putting my future children
through the same problems I had to face.

Many of our students chronicled histories of problematic
and failed relationships. It is clear that their experience

with their parents' problematic and failed relationship and their feelings of loss and abandonment influenced their own behavior in a dysfunctional way.

Melissa Shipman

I began dating right after my parents separated, when I was fourteen. My sister was constantly telling my dad that I needed a curfew and that I was too young to date. I, of course, rebelled. One day my sister came home and found me making out with a guy in our bedroom, so she went and told my dad. She said that I was becoming the slut at our high school. I had no rules and basically did what I wanted. I went to a lot of parties and drank, just like my friends. I was sexually active. At one point, my mother, not liking how my dad was handling things, moved back into the house and tried to change the rules. I stormed out and went to my boyfriend's house. I did not come home that night, and when I came home the next night, she was gone. When I was nineteen, I got pregnant. I dropped out of school, moved in with the man, and worked full time. Five months later, I got married. The first time I realized how much my parents' divorce had affected me was when my husband entered an outpatient drug and alcohol clinic. It was during one of the family group meetings, when I shared that I was ashamed of myself for staying with my husband during many emotionally abusive episodes. I realized then that my ex-boyfriend had taken advantage of me, too, by cheating on me while I was away at school, and I had also taken him back. All of a sudden I began putting the pieces together. I began to understand why I held on to bad relationships: I was afraid that a man would do to me what my mother did—leave. It is this fear of being abandoned that I need to resolve in my adult life.

The risk-taking described in these stories—indulgence in drugs, sex, overdoses, and abusive relationships—is a common theme for young adolescents when their parents divorce. When they lack adequate parental guidance, authority, and appropriate role models, these young people express their unhappiness in these self-destructive ways.

Psychological Problems for Older Adolescents

Their parents' divorce may not be as earth shattering for older adolescents as it is for younger adolescents, because their egos are more mature. They are more involved in their own activities; they may not even be living at home anymore. Nevertheless, even these older adolescents often reported psychological problems. They felt abandoned, anxious, and depressed. Their use of drugs and alcohol increased. They had problems sleeping and eating. They were unable to focus on their work or their studies.

> Susan McDevitt
>
> My grades at college during the quarter when my parents split up were the worst I've ever gotten. I couldn't concentrate on schoolwork at all. I went to a lot of parties and drank to get drunk. When I was drunk, I did not have to worry about my parents' divorce. I had horrible insomnia and rarely got to sleep before three in the morning. When I did sleep I would have nightmares and wake up with my shoulders so tense they hurt. During finals week, I got strep throat and mononucleosis. I missed all my finals, flew home and spent five weeks in bed. I lost twenty pounds and almost did not go back to school in winter quarter. I tried to get hold of my dad during the week of Christmas and could not because I didn't know where he was. When I finally did talk to him, he told me how sad he was that I hadn't even sent him a card. He didn't even ask how I was.

Older adolescents, too, had problems with their interpersonal relationships. Their sexual activity increased, but they were not satisfied in their relationships. They felt vulnerable and concerned about their future or present marriage. Their self-confidence had been severely undermined by experiencing their parents' divorce.

Allison Rodgers

My parents' divorce, when I was a senior in high school, made me grow up—fast. I watched my mother become an emotional wreck, my father go wild and crazy dating and drinking, my sister try to kill herself, and my brother develop phobias. My boyfriend, Ryan, became my life. But Ryan was trouble. He was popular and handsome—and wild. I was on the student council, the school newspaper, and the honors list, and he was struggling to get through the week to make the weekend parties. He started getting physically abusive. He hit me hard enough to bruise me. He said he loved me, but he took things out on me. He got into cocaine. The whole football team was on it. He would call me with hallucinations and keep me up all night. I also had friends telling me he was out with other girls. It was hard, but I ignored it. I thought he loved me. We almost got married. I felt I needed him, and in a sense I did. I think I needed an escape from my family life. Thank goodness we didn't get married. He reminded me a lot of my dad, and I think that's why I loved him. It would have been a disaster. When I got to university, Ryan and I broke up, and I started dating college guys. Again, I picked up the wrong kind of guys. I was almost date raped twice. I loved the guys that everyone wanted and who treated me like dirt. Today, I am dating a really nice guy. Nobody realizes I have problems. Everyone thinks I am happy. I dress nice and drive a nice car. Everyone thinks I am pretty and secure with a good head and going places. They think I can manage things well. Well, I try hard to make them believe it, but I am not. I have many masks, and I don't really think I know who I am. At home, I am the strong confidante who listens to my mom's problems. At school,

I am the happy student who works hard. In the sorority, they call me the guy magnet and party girl. At work, they call me a manager with an excellent selling record. My boyfriend loves me, but I always dread that someday he might see who I really am…. scared and insecure about my future.

Older adolescents are preoccupied with issues of their own identity. This is the time when they try to figure out who they are. They need to develop a self-image as a unique person, so that by the time they end adolescence, they are ready to enter adulthood with self-confidence and a clear idea of their personal goals and values. When parents divorce, especially if the divorce is unexpected, this can throw the adolescent's developing identity into chaos and undermine their self-confidence and their faith that they will have a permanent, committed relationship themselves.

Tyler Small

I was seventeen when my parents announced their plans to divorce. I remember feeling disbelief, anger, and sadness. I could not believe that this was happening to me—to our perfect family. I was angry at both my mother and my father. I thought that they were hypocrites: they had always taught me that divorce was wrong. I was angry because they had stopped trying. I thought that they were just taking the easy way out. I was sad because my world was falling apart. I had just begun my senior year of high school and had been accepted to all but one of the colleges to which I applied. I was involved in a steady relationship. I was anticipating the senior prom, graduation, and college. The separation and divorce affected all these areas of my life. But the most significant effect was that the divorce weakened the foundation of my identity—my Christian faith. All my life I had been taught that divorce was wrong and so when my parents divorced, I questioned the validity of my faith. I left the Church and made some poor decisions. By the time I was twenty, I was pregnant and married. Our marriage has not been easy. I still feel guilt, anxiety, loss, and doubt: guilt because I disappointed myself and I disappointed God; anxiety because of the overwhelming responsibilities of a husband and a baby; loss because I gave up my career goals; and doubt because I question the strength of my marriage. The fear of divorce always lurks in the shadows.

As these stories clearly demonstrate, there is no good age for parents to divorce. Divorce affects children's mental health in different ways at different developmental periods, but children of all ages, from infancy through adolescence, are at risk for long-term sadness and dysfunction. In the next chapter we will discuss some of the factors that determine whether that risk is realized.

Lessons to Be Learned

The lessons to be learned from the stories in this chapter suggest that the effects of divorce on children call for different sensitivities at different ages: protection for the youngest children, patience for those of school age, guidance and good examples for adolescents.

1. Protect young children from emotional turmoil. The youngest children are likely to feel anxious and afraid, sad and guilty, when their parents divorce. It is important that parents (and other adults) become aware of these feelings and act with particular sensitivity toward these young ones who cannot yet express their feelings well in words. There is a real danger that angry, depressed mothers (assuming that these youngsters are living with their mothers) will pass on their own emotional turmoil to their children, just as, during pregnancy, they could pass on toxins (environmental poisons, alcohol, drugs) to their unborn child. After parents divorce, children need to be protected from divorce "toxins." At the same time, they benefit from continued contact with the parent with whom they are not living, so that they continue to feel that they "own" both Mommy and Daddy. It is far easier for adults to move on to new lives and new partners than it is for children, who are irrevocably tied to their parents. Therefore, because it is important not to expose young children to parental conflict, if parents can't stand to be in the same room with each other, they should arrange for children to get together with the other parent on neutral ground.

2. Be patient with older children's outbursts of anger. School-age children may act out with destructive and vengeful force, destroying prized possessions, beating up on siblings, failing in school. Adults should realize that these outbursts hide inner sadness. They should not reject the children, carp about homework, constantly criticize, or pile on extra chores. They should not flaunt the new honey that was the reason for the divorce. All of these adult behaviors will just exacerbate—and justify—the child's anger.

3. Provide guidance and good role models for young adolescents. With young adolescents, the negative fall-out from divorce may be that they are pushed into a false maturity and adopt risky habits like drinking, taking drugs, and having sex at a young age. Adults need to be sure that their own actions are not promoting these undesirable behaviors. They must provide young adolescents with advice about values and warnings about the consequences of undesirable behavior. Most important, they must set a good example with their own behavior. Adolescents who see their parents drunk, disorderly, or promiscuous will think that's an acceptable form of behavior. Parents also need to attend to the developmental needs of the young adolescent. Early adolescence is a challenging age at the best of times—when children find themselves in changing bodies and new social circumstances. These young adolescents want to be able to lean on their parents as they navigate the storm and stress of adolescence; they don't need their parents leaning on them. If parents are not able to offer adult-sized strength, they should find some other supportive counsel for their children.

4. Don't pull out the rug from under older adolescents. Older adolescents feel undermined and uncertain when they find out that the family they thought would last forever has come apart. At an age when they are searching for identity, these older adolescents discover that the beliefs they held to be self-evident are false. They lose their footing; they don't know who they are; and certainly they don't know about marriage anymore. Their belief that their family was happy, or at least stable, turns out to be untrue; their parents' sermons about the evils of divorce ring hypocritical. They are left without an anchor, a foundation, and without confidence in their own judgment. What is the lesson here? Perhaps it is that parents should be more honest with their children if they are having marital difficulties. They should not keep their differences a secret until the day they file for divorce, and should not condemn divorce with the fervor of the righteous. Certainly it is damaging to spring a sudden separation on children at any age; waiting until they leave home to go to college does not help.

11
What Works, What Doesn't: Helping or Hindering Children's Adjustment

In the previous chapter, we discussed how the effects of divorce on children's psychological well-being differ depending on the child's age. But age is not the only factor that determines how children respond to a marital breakup. What happens before, during, and after the divorce also makes a difference. Some fortunate children bounce back in a few months or years to basically the same children they were before the divorce, as if nothing had happened. Others experience serious long-term consequences because of the divorce and its aftermath. In this chapter we examine the factors that help or hinder children's adjustment to their parents' divorce. In the first story, the children were clearly losers after the divorce—physically, even, they were wrecks—and the reasons they were suffering included financial insecurity, lack of contact with their father, conflict between their parents, and their mother's unstable emotional state.

Susan Nomura

For ten years I have watched my parents battling. When they were married, one thing they constantly battled about was money. My father claimed that my mother spent extravagantly, but he offset her hundreds of dollars in clothing with thousands of dollars for computers and exercise equipment and a Jeep Cherokee. Their fights escalated until finally they decided to separate. My father immediately stopped paying the bills and declared bankruptcy.

That was three years ago. Since then I have been in a state of anxiety, waiting to be evicted from our home, wondering if there will be money for next quarter's tuition, dealing with my mother's constant crying. I have not had any contact with my father, except through my mother. She continues to talk to him on the phone, but it always ends in fights. She leans on me for support and is constantly expounding on my father's mistakes and how miserable her life is. As a result of this stress, I have been plagued with health problems. I was diagnosed with a peptic ulcer and then developed a spastic colon and lactose intolerance. Now, in periods of stress—which are frequent—I become sick to my stomach. Between Thanksgiving and Christmas, with the stress of the holidays, I stopped eating altogether and lost about twenty pounds. I had to take a leave of absence from my job to stay home and rest. I have had two relapses with the ulcer; the last one, just five weeks ago. I have also been diagnosed with endometriosis, a condition aggravated by stress. I have had two surgeries to remove cysts and scarring. I take strong painkillers regularly for the pain of my ulcer, the pain of endometriosis, and the pain of migraine headaches. I have tried biofeedback, relaxation tapes, meditation and self-help books, but my body is still a mess and my anger toward my parents is a savage undercurrent.

Parental Conflict: A Major Risk

As this story suggests, parents' anger can be contagious and its effects pervasive and permanent. This story illustrates one of the saddest outcomes of divorce, the havoc parents' hostility wreaks on their children's mental and physical health. Descriptions of parental conflict leapt dramatically from the pages of our students' stories, offering many striking examples of marital conflict when the parents were still together and many illustrations of conflict that continued after the parents separated. Almost two thirds of our students reported that they had seen their parents fighting—sometimes violently. Parental conflict before the separation has both immediate and long-lasting effects on the children. Continued conflict over many years during the marriage is especially damaging. These children are unlikely to recover.

Wendy Farran

When I was a child, conflict between my parents turned my home environment into a torturous nightmare. I have no happy memories of childhood. I was six when my mother filed for divorce the first time. In her bitterness and anger, she had an affair openly in front of me. It made me sick to see a man other than my father touching my mother. But my parents did not go through with the divorce. When I was fourteen, my mother told me about my father's infidelity and showed me the pictures she had found in the trash. The house was a terrible place then, with my mother screaming and throwing things around. She swore to divorce my father this time. But she did not follow through. Finally, five years later, they did get divorced. My parents' dark journey was over, but mine had just begun.

Exposed to my parents' flaws at such a tender age, I created defense mechanisms to protect myself from the terrible, emotionally abusive surroundings of my childhood. Now, those defense mechanisms are dysfunctional. A few summers ago, I became seriously anorexic. I was passing out at work, and my bones poked out, and I slept all day. I believe that my anorexia is the manifestation of all the powerlessness I ever felt as a child victim of a dysfunctional marriage, sucked into the middle of my parents' conflict. Another legacy from my parents' behavior is my inability to form close relationships with men. For many years I have felt adrift and trapped in a cycle of dependency with negative men. I doubt that I will ever recover from the wounds that began the day I was born to an unhappy couple.

When fights between the parents are persistent and pervasive, divorce is not the worst thing that can happen to the child. Researchers confirm that, in general, overt parental conflict is worse for children than parental divorce. Children suffer more in a conflict-ridden family than in family that successfully navigates the shoals of divorce. The longer, more egregious, and more physical the conflict between the parents during the marriage, the more likely are problems for the child. When children witness parents physically attacking each other, researchers say, they manifest aggressive behaviors and achievement problems in school age and delinquency in adolescence. In the stories of our students, we found that additional consequences of parental conflict were profound and prolonged unhappiness, frozen emotions, and serious, psychologically driven physical ailments.

Should Parents Stay Together for the Sake of the Children?

Often, unhappy parents ask whether it is better to stay together, even in an unharmonious marriage, "for the sake of the children." The answer most experts would give is that if parents are in frequent open conflict, it is better to divorce than to stay together. If the parents can keep their conflicts hidden from the children, it may be better for the children if they stay together. A number of our students voiced their opinion on this issue. Living in a divorced family, they said, was better than living in a pre-divorce war zone.

Veena Sankar

I felt happy about the divorce. Life with my father had been a nightmare. To this day, I remember all the horrible things he did to my mother. It was hard after the divorce, because there was no money. But it did not matter because now at last we were away from my father. Our problems after the divorce were nothing compared to what we went through living with him.

Martina Nunez

If my parents had stayed married, I think one of them would have ended up killing the other. I was glad that they got divorced. It was better because the brutal fighting stopped.

By the second or third year after the divorce, the disruptions of the family transition have usually ended and things have settled down. If the family is going to have to move, it has done so. Parents who previously were not working have usually found some sort of job. A pattern of visitation has been set. Support payments have been established. Family routines have been re-established. By this time, although life may be pretty grim, it is at least more predictable than in the first year after the separation. Sadly, though, if conflict between the parents continues, this undermines the children's psychological well-being. If parents continue to fight after they divorce—about money, possessions, custody, new relationships—or if they can't get over their pain and jealousy, children continue to suffer.

Brad Dawson

When my dad found out that my mom was dating, he went berserk. After each weekend we spent with her, he grilled us. He wanted to know if her "boyfriend" was there, and if he was, he insisted that we tell Mom we did not want him there on "our" weekends. He constantly took out his anger and frustrations about Mom on us. We dreaded there are weekends because we knew he would open the door and start in on us. Anytime we mentioned wanting to spend time with Mom, he would belittle her—and us. It is now thirteen years since the divorce. My dad has never forgiven Mom, and his anger still consumes him. I still suffer from my exposure to my parents' consuming conflict. Because of their terrible relationship, I have not been able to make a commitment to a serious relationship myself.

Sometimes, when parents continue their conflict after the divorce, they deliberately use the children to make things miserable for each other. This was true for the following student and her siblings.

Marcy Graham
My mom always went out of her way to bribe me and my brothers and sisters to stay with her when it was time to go with Dad. When he showed up to pick us up for his visits, she would say that we didn't want to go and he couldn't make us. Or she would take us out and leave a note on the door saying we didn't want to see him. If we did go with him, she would make us cry and scream, just to show my dad how much we hated him.

Research confirms what our students' stories suggest: that children who experience parental hostility are "at risk" for psychological problems. In fact, continued parental conflict is the primary predictor of children's maladjustment after divorce.

Is There a Best Custody Arrangement?
Another question that divorcing parents often ask is whether there is one custody arrangement that is best for

helping children adjust to and recover from divorce. Joint custody? Mother custody? Father custody? Does one type of custody guarantee that the child will come through the divorce unscathed? Does one type of custody ensure that the child will maintain closer relationships with both parents? In recent decades, joint custody has been touted as offering children a better chance for recovery, and all other things being equal, it is frequently the arrangement imposed by the court. It has the advantage of ensuring the child's continued contact with both parents, and, on the face of it, it looks the most like the family before the divorce. It is a way of keeping fathers involved and invested; it is a way of giving mothers support and respite. Researchers have found, however, that the consequences of joint custody are not all rosy; it, too, has pros and cons.

When the parents have mutually decided on joint custody, they are more satisfied with the custody arrangement. Mothers like it because, compared with having sole custody, joint custody gives them time off to pursue their own interests. They feel they can be better parents because they are not overwhelmed by the constant burden of being a single parent. Fathers like it because they get to see their children more than they would if the mother had sole custody. Parents who have a joint custody arrangement are more likely to make their child support payments. When joint custody was freely chosen and not imposed by the court, it has also been linked to lower rates of relitigation. The same is not true for court-imposed joint custody. For children, the advantage of joint custody is that they continue to have steady relations with both parents. When parents choose joint custody, are able to cooperate as parents, and live near each other, this is probably the best arrangement for all concerned.

Unfortunately, however, not all parents can reach this agreement and not all can cooperate as parents—even if the court tells them to. Only a tiny minority of parents report that they have no problems with joint custody, and problems are particularly salient if the parents were reluctant participants to begin with. There are problems with transitions, with pick-ups and drop-offs. Joint custody limits parents' options. They can't leave town for long periods of time or move to a new community. There is also a serious psychological cost of dealing with the ex-spouse every week and needing to be "nice" so that the ex won't take them back to court and sue for sole custody. Joint custody won't work if parents have conflicting lifestyles, contradictory values, poor communication, inconsistent child-rearing styles, and are not committed to providing child care despite their own differences. When joint custody is imposed by the court or when divorced mothers and fathers in a joint custody arrangement are not able to cooperate, joint custody is associated with the poorest adjustment for the children. It is most risky if children are emotionally insecure or very young.

But even when children are not emotionally insecure and when the parents can and do cooperate, joint custody can lead to anxiety and confusion on the child's part. In the following stories, students described their experiences of joint custody—from a child's point of view.

Amanda Killian

I remember going back and forth between my parents' houses. At first, it was one week at my mom's house and one week at my dad's house. Then, after a while, we stayed at each parent's house for two weeks to a month at a time. When we got tired of the rules or the stepparent at one house, we went to the other. I remember both liking this arrangement and also feeling burdened by it. I liked having two homes because each was a different experience and I never had to stay at one house long enough to stick to a task that I didn't want to do. We knew that we could use one parent against the other to get around the rules and to get what we wanted. But it was hard to be going back and forth all the time.

Although this student notes the difficulty of the frequent transitions, she also describes one of the positive aspects of joint custody for children. It offers an escape hatch when things start to get tough at one home and provides fresh adult ears to listen to the child's pleas when the other parent has said "no." This can be a good thing when one parent is stressed, irritable, or unavailable. But it can also mean that children grow up with inconsistent parenting—whenever they don't like the rules, or demands, or chores in one house, they shift to the other—in essence escaping any consistent parenting throughout their childhood.

The next student reported that she and her brother were confused by the inconsistency between their two homes.

Maria Schaefer
In the divorce, my parents agreed on joint legal and physical custody for my brother and me. We started out staying with our father most of the time until my mother found an apartment in a nearby town. After that, we switched between staying at our father's house and staying at our mother's apartment every few days. Then we switched every two weeks, then every month, then every three months, then every six months. This was very difficult for my brother and me because our mother was strict and our father was permissive. There were completely different rules and ways of acting at the two places. We were very confused and depressed.

Even worse that inconsistency, joint custody may create loyalty conflicts, as children have to divide themselves between their parents, and pragmatic difficulties, as they have to divide their time.

Cheryl Wade
It was 4:30 a.m. and the light from the hallway crept under my bedroom door. It wouldn't be long till Daddy cracked the door open and picked me up from my warm

bed to carry me to the cold van. Then it would be my
sister's turn. He would lay each of us down in the bed he
had made for us in the back of the van. Then he would
make one last trip into the house to get our overnight
bags full of clothes, homework for school, and, once a
month, a child support check in an envelope to give to
Mom. The donut shop was next. Daddy would stop there
every morning to get himself a donut and coffee. Once a
week he would surprise us and leave us a white paper bag
crumpled at the top with two sprinkled donuts inside. At
about 5:00 a.m. we would arrive at Mom's house. Daddy
would once again put each of us over his shoulder and
carry us in. Erin, my sister, and I would walk to our bunk
beds and try to go back to sleep until 6:30 a.m., when it
was time to get up for school. Mom packed our lunches
and delivered us to school. Then Daddy would be back
to pick us up from school when he got off work at 3:30.
We would have dinner with him, finish our homework,
pack our bags, go to bed, and then the routine would
be repeated. This happened five days a week, from the
time I was six until I was fourteen. On the weekend, we
would spend one and a half days with Mom and one and
a half days with Dad. I don't remember ever being asked
if I liked this way of splitting our time exactly down the
middle. The one time I remember questioning it, my
dad criticized me harshly and told me I was selfish. I felt
horrible afterwards, because I had hurt my dad, but I
just wanted to sleep through the night in one bed like
any other child. After that, I never spoke about it again.
The only positive thing about this custody arrangement
was that I knew I had two parents who really cared about
me. Otherwise, everything that happened was extra
difficult because it had to be divided—where we went for
holidays, who we sat with at school banquets, how school
picture packages were divided up, who we went with to
school open houses, who congratulated us first after a
school performance, where we had birthday parties, and
at whose house we kept our souvenirs and awards. The

cumulative stress was enormous because I was so worried about hurting one parent's feelings and because I was always thinking about how I was going to divide myself.

As this student describes, joint custody can mean not just dividing your time, but dividing yourself. As a result, children learn to become good at doing what they think other people want them to do; but they become stunted in their ability to express or even identify their own feelings.

The other question in trying to determine the best custody arrangement is whether children in sole custody are better off in the custody of their mothers or their fathers. Research indicates that there may be advantages of being in father custody. In an analysis of all available studies using objective measures of children's well-being, one researcher found that children in father custody had fewer problems than children in mother custody. In a study that we conducted as well, children in father custody—especially sons—were doing better on a variety of measures of psychological well-being and self-esteem. It would be premature, however, to conclude that all children should be placed in father custody. Custodial fathers who choose the full responsibilities of being the custodial parent tend to be more emotionally invested in their children and to be more effective parents. As we have already mentioned, there is no one best custody arrangement for all children. Custody determinations must be made on a case-by-case basis.

More important than the formal, legal custody arrangement for children may be feeling that they are wanted wherever they are. The following student experienced pain and uncertainty and negative consequences, because she felt that her parents were just shuffling her back and forth to suit their convenience, not to facilitate her "best interests."

Annette Vanderhoof
      My parents would always rearrange the visitation schedule to fit their own personal schedules. If my dad

couldn't take us on his weekend, he would take us for the next two weekends in a row to make up for it. I always felt like I was being bounced around from place to place, and I didn't have a whole lot of self-esteem. When puberty hit, I went wild. I would have sex with boys just to be held and feel like somebody cared about me. I wanted to feel like I belonged somewhere.

Children Need Contact with Both Parents

It is easier for children to adjust to their parents' divorce if they don't both lose their parents—whatever the custody arrangement. Children who have continued contact with both parents feel better about themselves and their parents. They are better adjusted, happier, and do better in school. They have closer relationships with their parents, are less anxious, and have higher self-esteem. These observations from research were confirmed in our students' stories.

Martina Nunez
    After the divorce, I lived with my mom, but my dad always remained close. I never felt that I had lost a parent—because both of them were always there. I knew both of my parents loved me and I knew that it didn't stop just because they didn't live together anymore. The long-term effects of my parents' divorce on me have been minimal.

The contrast between this student's cheery recovery and the pathos of students who lost a parent is profound. It was particularly difficult when the parent just disappeared. It may also be more difficult when it's the primary parent—the mother—who disappears, as happened to the following student.

Emily Gray
    "Today was terrible. I wish Mommy was here. I feel so sad. If Mommy was here everything would be happy.

Mommy went to Aunt Jennie's house and she took a lot of her clothes. Today was hot and we went swimming. Oh Mom, please, Mom, come back. Now on I'm gonna be good. God let Mom come back."

This was an entry I made in my diary a week after my mother left us when I was nine years old. I remember their last big fight. I was in bed praying the fight would stop. I climbed into my sister's bed and we held each other. In the morning our mother was gone. She left without saying goodbye or explaining what was happening. I was heart broken. We didn't hear from her for two months. For more than a year I kept writing in my diary asking God to bring back our mom. I made deals with God. I promised that I would be really good if He brought our mommy back. But two years later, an entry in my diary shows that things had not improved.

"Today was terrible. Nobody wants us. Mommy doesn't want us. Daddy doesn't want us. Nobody does. I'm so sad. Sometimes I wish God would take us away to heaven. Then we could be happy and loved. I wish I could be happy and have a happy family. But I know it's only a dream that can't come true."

This student felt that she been abandoned by her mother and was not wanted by her father. Her emotional life was a disaster. The next student was abandoned by her father and left with an incompetent mother and no resources. This also was a disaster.

Anna Nguyen

Nothing was worse than when my father walked out on us. We woke up and he was gone. We had no idea where he was. I was suicidal. Along with my dad, went all our family income. My mother didn't work, and she was addicted to gambling. She gambled until there was nothing left. We had to sell the house and move to a one-bedroom apartment. Imagine seven people in a one-

bedroom apartment. I told her how much she hurt me
and how ashamed I was of her. I told her that I would
disown her. I constantly agonized if we would make it.

These stories are extreme. Most of our students had good-
enough mothers. But still they wrote poignantly of their
persistent longing for their absent father—longing strongly
tinged with anger. Most of them felt ambivalent toward
their absent dad. They longed to know him, they wanted
explanations for having been abandoned, yet at the same
time they rejected the parent who had so callously rejected
them, in a child's version of "You can't fire me, I quit!"

Leah Frank
    I didn't think much about my dad for many years
after he left us when I was four. I just hated him for
abandoning my mom, my brother, and me and never
giving a damn about us. I had zero contact with him,
not even a birthday card. But when I graduated from
high school, my mom and I decided to send his parents
a graduation announcement. The next day, he called
and asked to talk to me. Fortunately, I wasn't home.
When I heard that he had called, at first, I was angry.
I thought what nerve he has. I don't hear from him for
fourteen years and now he expects to talk to me. Then
I started thinking about what I would say to him. Since
then, I have been agonizing over whether I want to see
him. I don't think he deserves to be part of our lives, yet
I can't seem to get over the desire to see him. I can't help
thinking about the dad who left me. He is always an ache
in my heart.

Feelings about the absent parent clearly persist into
adulthood and color special occasions, like a wound that will
not heal. Another student finally gave in to her longing to see
her absent father, but even that was not a satisfying balm for
the ache in her heart.

Shiva Ghosheh

When I was about seventeen, I began a kind of inner quest. I was searching for something deeper, and a big part of this search involved the void from my childhood. I realized that I had never known who my father was and why my parents were not together. I tracked down my father and began asking him questions about himself— about his relationship with his parents, his childhood, his philosophy, his beliefs. I had this incredible need to know everything about him. What I found was disappointing. He is a negative and pessimistic person. His only words of wisdom to me were: "Life is unfair, kid. People are evil." Gee, thanks, Dad! He says he is sorry that things didn't work out, but I cannot forgive him. I can't forget that he is my father, but neither can I forget that he was never there for me.

Children in mother custody who continue to have a close relationship with their father are less likely to have behavior problems and developmental difficulties. If the father doesn't visit, children feel abandoned and rejected, as these students did. But even when the father does not disappear entirely, the amount and kind of contact he has with the child makes a difference. It is better if visits are longer and more frequent so that father is not just like a visiting uncle or a "Disneyland Dad." Children usually want more and longer visits, particularly overnight visits, with their dads, and so do the dads. It is also important that the same level of contact be maintained over the years. When the number of hours with the father decreases over time, this predicts problems for the child, especially for school-age children, who are more accustomed to spending time with dad. But close contact is not just more frequent visits. As our study of elementary-school children shows, close contact derives from meaningful visits, like spending holidays together and doing regular parent-child things like homework and shopping and chores, not just being entertained and eating out. Clearly, as research and our students suggest, it helps children adjust to divorce if they maintain close, frequent, meaningful contact with both parents.

Quality of Parenting Is Critical

Another factor that determines how children adjust to their parents' divorce is the quality of care they receive after the separation. After divorce, the parents are often emotional wrecks, oblivious to their children's needs. When this happens, children feel neglected and overburdened. In addition to tackling the tasks of growing up, they must become responsible for their own care and, often, for the care of their parent. They feel that they have no one to turn to for comfort, guidance, or supervision. They may be treated inappropriately, like a grown-up, by their parent.

Morgan Dennison

> Even though I was young, my father confided in me about his problems. He did not realize the burden he was placing on my shoulders. I did all I could by listening, but inside my heart was breaking. I always felt so helpless because there was nothing I could do to help. I was a child who was forced to grow up faster and wiser because I was exposed to the pressures of the adult world. My veil of ignorance was torn away as he dumped on me his feelings about divorce, alcoholism, lying, cheating, and dejected hopes.

Another kind burden came in the form of parental neglect and the chaos it engendered.

Kurt Leinbach

> After the divorce, life at our house was chaotic. My mom was busy having fun with her new man and ignoring problems at home. My brother and I would have friends

over to watch movies, and in the middle we would be interrupted by the sound of squeaking bedsprings from my mother's bedroom. Meal times were up to us. Dinner usually consisted of a bowl of Cheerios and a layer of white sugar.

Among our students' stories were terrifying descriptions of the tragedies that followed divorce when the custodial parent was not in control and could not provide the kind of parenting and authority that children need.

Brian Hoolihan

When the divorce was final and my dad moved away, all the problems should have been solved. Instead, I watched our family self-destruct. Mom worked endless hours and was never around. She also developed a little drinking problem, so supervision of us kids was out of the question. My older brother and sister turned to drugs. I remember watching them and their friends shoot up heroin and smoke PCP. They were out of control, but what could my mom do? She was in the same boat. I would go to my mom to narc them off, only to see her plowed on wine and muscle relaxers. There was no authority in the house. There was no bedtime; no one made me dinner, no one washed my clothes; and, mostly, no one gave a shit. I was fending for myself at age nine. Every day was a challenge and I spent as much time away from the house as I could, Eating at friends' houses was the norm. Minute by minute, I lived in uncertainty and fear. I would wait up every night because I was afraid my mom would crash her car and die, and I couldn't fall asleep until I heard her pull into the driveway. One day, my mom promised to take my younger brother out on the weekend to go to the comic book store. But when the weekend came, she slept the whole time. Monday morning, in a stoned haze, my older brother ditched school and took my brother to the comic book store. As they ran across the busy intersection, my little brother lagged behind. My older brother told him to hurry up, and as my little brother ran to catch up, he was hit by a car and killed. The death of my little brother only escalated the problems in the family. I just sat back and watched everything go downhill into the darkness of drugs, drinking, and reckless behavior.

In this story we see what happened when the mother abdicated her responsibility—older siblings took over the care of young children, with disastrous results. In the following story, too, the older children in the family made life hell for the younger one.

Christy Klein

After the divorce, my two brothers were both very angry with me because I had supported my mother's decision to get a divorce. Every Sunday they spent with my dad seemed to intensify their hatred. They laughed and talked together and did guy things. They played rough together. My mom and I hated to interact with them because they were so rough. We planned secret escapades to the mall. We would tell my brothers that I had a doctor's appointment and we'd take off on a shopping spree. We loved the adventures and simply being together. The challenge was to sneak the bags of new clothes past my brothers. This was a dangerous task because both of them were bigger than my mom and me and they used that to their advantage. Bobby would hold the door shut to keep us from getting in or he would bang the door down to get inside and beat on us. My mom would literally beg—as she had with my father. My brothers gained complete control of the house, and it was as if they were role-playing my father. I had a chain lock on my bedroom door to keep them out of my room so they couldn't steal my belongings, destroy my room and cut up my clothes. I was powerless and so was my mother.

In the following case, neither parent provided adequate care for the child.

Allison Rodgers

After the divorce, Mom was a wreck and so were we. My sister, who was fourteen, was hanging out with us juniors and seniors. She started dating older guys, smoking, and partying. Mom couldn't control us, so we moved to Dad's house. He was seldom there, and when he was, he was abusive. There were many times when my sister and I would come home and our stuff would be in trash bags because my father's girlfriend had convinced him to kick us out. If the girlfriend was there, he would make us sleep in our cars. A year and a half after the divorce, my sister attempted suicide and then was locked in a hospital for two months.

Is it possible that our students were exaggerating their problems? Are parents really this bad? Among the children in one long-term study, 60 percent had parents who were evaluated by the researchers as rejecting; they thought of their children as a burden. We conclude, therefore, that these students were not just imagining their parents' rejection; it was real. When parents are loving and supportive, the contrast is profound.

Morgan Dennison

My sister and I are incredibly blessed, because we have survived a divorce and still have wonderful relationships with both our parents. The turbulence of divorce, the anger, and poverty, all these crises can be conquered with the love and support of both parents.

Perhaps this sounds trite, but our stories and the results of research as well suggest that parents' continued positive involvement and consistent parenting are in fact the keys to children's surviving their parents' divorce. The more reassurance, nurturing, and guidance parents give the child after the divorce, the better it is for the child's adjustment.

Continued Change Presents Obstacles

Another factor that affects children's adjustment to their parents' divorce is the extent to which the divorce is followed by change and uncertainty. The more changes they endure and the less stability they have in their lives, the harder it is for kids to settle down and get on to a happy and productive post-divorce life. If children move often, this makes the task of recovery more difficult.

Marianne Griffith

By the time I was in sixth grade I had attended eleven schools. The constant moving made me exceedingly shy and withdrawn. It was hard to make new friends at each new school. The lack of stability was very difficult for me. As I got older, it was even harder to leave my friends and start over at another school.

Moving is difficult, but when it is combined with a changing cast of characters in the home, this makes matters even worse.

Gerry Schonfeld

After the divorce, my sister didn't bounce back. I think that moving twice in two years really made things much worse for her. Changing schools and making new friends was difficult, and she often made poor choices. She began to hang out with the bad crowd and started sleeping around. She skipped school, stole, and lied. Then my mother's boyfriend moved in with us and made our lives worse. Meanwhile, my father married a woman who had a son and a daughter and very shortly the two of them had a child together who was born with cerebral palsy. It seemed as if the hard times would never let up. My sister got deeper and deeper into drugs and alcohol.

At an already vulnerable time in life, these children had to cope not only with their parents' divorce but also with the many changes that followed. In this case, the changes were too many and too overwhelming to cope with.

Emotional Support from Others Helps Children Adjust

Finally, the last factor that made a difference in how well our students adjusted to divorce was the help they received from people other than their parents. Sometimes the help came from a school counselor.

John Klinger

After I nearly dropped out of school, my counselor suggested that I be put into a group with other students whose parents were recently divorced, and we met once a week with a psychologist. The group really helped, and by the following year I felt that I could stand on my own. I got out of the bad circle of friends that I was with and started to put some effort into my life.

Sometimes the help came from a psychological counselor or therapist.

Susan Nomura

I have seen five different counselors to try to deal with my stress. The most positive experience was when my mother took me to a Divorce Recovery Workshop, which offered a three-week session for children of divorce. There I learned more about how our family operated. It was helpful to learn the term "surrogate spouse," which described my role in fulfilling domestic responsibilities, raising and disciplining my sister, and acting as confidante and partner to my father. It also helped explain why I felt so betrayed when I found out that my father had had an affair. I had worked so hard to maintain his home and his family and it still wasn't enough for him. It felt as if he had cheated on me and left me as well as my mother. I am still seeing the counselor who headed the DRW workshop, and I am still recovering.

Counselors, therapists, and school programs for children from divorced or divorcing families can all be helpful. They offer opportunities for children to talk about their experiences and learn specific skills related to interpersonal problem solving, communication, and expression of anger. Positive results have been reported in terms of teachers' ratings of children's problem behavior, parents' reports of their communication with the children, and the children's reports of decreased anxiety.

Social support from friends and relatives can also have a positive influence on children's adjustment. A supportive social network can provide help, a sense of comfort and stability, and the feeling that somebody cares. Even when parents are unavailable, children can still thrive if they have the support of extended family, friends, or teachers, as did the student in the following story.

Kurt Leinbach

Fortunately I had my friends, my teachers, my grandparents, and my brother to help me through the whole crazy-making time after my parents' divorce. The most important people were my brother and a teacher I had in sixth and seventh grades. My brother was important because he was the only constant in my life; we shared every experience. My teacher was important because she took an interest in me and showed me compassion. My grandparents also offered consistent support. They gave my mother money for rent and food and paid for private schools for my brother and me; they were like second parents to us.

Lessons to Be Learned

This chapter describes a number of factors that help or hinder children's adjustment after their parents' divorce; knowing about these factors leads to six lessons that are worth learning.

1. Shield children from conflict. Children clearly suffer if they are exposed to conflict between their parents before or after the divorce. If parents frequently fight in front of the children before the divorce, the consequences can be dire. Therefore, if the marriage is irretrievably and visibly broken, parents should not stay together "for the sake of the children." Watching their parents tear each other apart causes deeper wounds than if the parents terminated the marriage. Continued conflict after the divorce then continues the dire effects on children. Conflict is the strongest predictor of children's post-divorce maladjustment. It is critical that parents stop fighting.

2. Use custody as a means to an end. There is no one-size-fits-all custody arrangement that is best for all divorcing families. It depends on the circumstances and the individuals. What is important is that the parents work out an arrangement that meets their needs and their children's and not use custody as a further battleground. Children feel dreadful when they are pulled between their parents in a custody fight. Custody should be a means to an end, and that end is that children get the best possible care. Sole mother custody is not the only possible arrangement, nor necessarily the best; there may be advantages to father custody—for one thing, both parents are more likely to stay involved with the children. There may also be advantages to joint custody—if parents choose it, can cooperate, live close to each other, and are compatible in their childrearing styles. It is worst when the court or the child has to decide and when the arrangement is arbitrary and inflexible.

3. Ensure meaningful contact with both parents. Children need continued contact with both their parents after the divorce. Most parents know enough to tell their children at the beginning, "Daddy and I are getting a divorce. Daddy isn't divorcing you." "Your mom and I can't live together anymore, but I'm still going to be your dad." But after the words are spoken, the effort to make them true begins. Even if one of the parents was the "bad guy" in the divorce, children still need to maintain contact or they feel bereft, and if contact diminishes over time, they feel rejected. Moreover, the nature of the contact has to be more than holiday cards and afternoon outings. Contact should entail spending holidays together, doing regular routine activities, and having deep talks.

4. Offer the best possible parenting. It is almost always difficult for divorced parents to provide their children with the nurturing and the control they long for and need after the divorce. But if the parents abdicate their role, children will be damaged. It is critical that parents, no matter how much they are suffering themselves, pay attention to their children's needs, treat them like children, not adults, and provide them with authoritative supervision and guidance. This is not the time for parents to disappear into drugs, drink, or dates. Parents need to stabilize themselves so they can support their children.

5. Provide stability. Children need a stable place to live and an unchanging household while they adjust to the divorce. Repeated moving adds to their difficulty adjusting to new life circumstances. To the extent possible, this is a time to stay put and begin to build a new, stronger family.

6. Seek out sources of emotional support for the children. Because it is so difficult for parents to adjust to divorce themselves, it is expecting too much that they alone provide all the emotional support for their children. There are other sources of support—school counselors, therapists, workshop leaders, friends of the family, and extended family members. This is a time to call on those resources. This is a time for other adults to step in and offer children friendship, counsel, reassurance, and just plain help. Children can benefit from having someone else outside the situation to talk to, someone with experience, someone who cares.

12
Stepfamilies: The Plot Thickens

Of the people who get divorced, about three quarters remarry, most of them within a few years. Remarriage sounds like best outcome for all concerned, but it also can be fraught with problems. We found many examples in which students talked about their "wicked stepmother" or "cruel stepfather" and described their lives in ways that sounded like Cinderella's before the fairy godmother saved her. Many children experienced their parents putting their own desires for a new mate before the children's needs—and they resented it. On the other hand, for some children, the stepparent was the best thing that ever happened to them.

Being in a stepfamily changes the child's life and ideas in many ways. It brings with it a new mother or father and perhaps new siblings and sibling rivalries. It brings a feeling of finality about the divorce: children whose mother or father has remarried can no longer entertain the hope that their parents will get back together again. But remarriage is no guarantee that the child or the parent will be better off psychologically. Research suggests that remarried parents are likely to feel less lonely, and they appreciate the help with parenting they get from the new spouse, but they may still feel depressed, angry at the ex-spouse, and dissatisfied with life. Remarriage does not provide a sure fix for a "broken family." It is not a guaranteed cure for the blues. If individuals are unhappy and maladjusted before they remarry, a new spouse is not likely to improve their mental state. Under the best circumstances, remarriage can create a richer, more gratifying life that includes the child; under the worst circumstances, remarriage leads to neglect, abuse, and instability for the children.

We open this chapter with one of the most extreme examples of stepfamily instability reported by our students. In this case, the children suffered tremendously at the hands of both their stepparents, as they bounced back and forth between them, year after year, searching for a home where they felt loved and secure. Their stepparents were just adolescents themselves, only twenty years old when they got married. They were immature and not even ready for marriage let alone stepparenting six children, the oldest of whom was only nine years younger than they. This was a recipe for disaster, and disaster followed.

Scott Mallard

When my parents got divorced, they were 32 years old and had six children. I was the youngest, three years old at the time. By the time they were 34, they had both remarried, to partners who were both twenty years old. I was the ring-bearer at my father's wedding, and I remember standing there for an eternity, holding the little satin pillow with the rings. We weren't invited to my mother's wedding. They didn't invite any of us. That summer, I had this little music toy that sang "Puff the Magic Dragon." It was a very sad song to me, but for some reason I just loved it. I played it over and over. I think that I related to the dragon who had been abandoned by his best friend.

My first reaction to my parents' new partners was positive. I particularly liked my stepfather, Tory, because

I lived with him and my mother, and he played with me a lot. I really loved him. I didn't have much time to get to know my stepmother, Glenda, until we all went to live with her and my dad, when I was in the fifth grade. That year, I discovered that she really didn't care about us kids. She never played with us, not once. All she did was discipline us. I remember one time she washed my mouth out with soap because I gave my brother the finger. My older brothers and sisters had already taken a disliking to her. On the day Glenda married our father, she told my sisters Kate and Mara that if they stayed out of her way, she would stay out of their way. Later, Kate overheard Glenda saying that she didn't want us kids to be part of her life. That year, living with Dad and Glenda, my grades dropped.

The next year, I went back to live with Mom and Tory. I was in the sixth grade. Then the problems with Tory started. Tory was a drug addict. He had drugs in the house all the time, and my brothers and sisters and I learned to steal them. He knew that we did this, so he was mad at us, but there was nothing he could do about it except smack us in the back of the head. He did that a lot.

In eighth grade, I was back living with Dad and Glenda. They were very disappointed with me because I wasn't doing well in school. Glenda was always on my back for something. I could take the discipline and the punishments for my grades, and I did enjoy waking up before school every day to swim laps in the pool with my father. But Glenda also thought that I was trying to kill her son. We fought quite a bit, it's true, but I would never have intentionally hurt him. He is my little brother and I love him. One day, there was a big family gathering, about a hundred people, and my little brother and I were playing in the pool. My little brother's two front teeth were loose; that was common knowledge. As we were playing, I threw him onto a foam pool mat and he landed on his teeth and they immediately popped out. He wasn't hurt, but when he saw the blood, he started to scream, like any six-year-old. Well, Glenda ran into the poolroom and immediately started yelling, "What did you do to my son?" She told me to get away and not come near him. This all happened in front of all of my relatives, who were there for the party. I was feeling so humiliated, I did not know what to do. Our live-in nanny saw what happened, and she tried to defend me. Glenda yelled at her in front of everyone, too. I spent the next hour in the pool finding the teeth, but that was not appreciated one bit.

When spring break came, I decided that I could no longer take it. I felt like such a rotten person. I told my father that I was going back to live with Mom and Tory in Idaho. He was very upset. He told me that I would be a loser for the rest of my life and never amount to anything if I left. I cried a lot. My little brother cried too when I told him that I was leaving. My sister Mara was also upset, but she said that she understood that my problems with Glenda were only getting worse. My dad took me to the airport. He didn't even look at me when he said goodbye. When I got to my seat on the plane I started crying, and I didn't stop till we landed. When my mother and Tory picked me up at the airport, they didn't even hug me or say that it was nice to see me. I guess they were still bitter that I had left them to go to my dad's.

I stayed with my mother and Tory until I graduated from high school. Tory continued to be upset at me for having left. He didn't really have anything to do with me except to discipline me with a smack in the back of the head or a kick in the rear with his cowboy boots. The smacks in the head really hurt because Tory had one big ring on his finger that always left a lump on my head. After I finished high school, my mother divorced Tory. But by that time, I also had become a drug addict and an alcoholic.

The risks of "solving" the divorce dilemma by leaping into remarriage are evident in this student's story. With family dynamics like these, it is not surprising that stepparents often "fail." They are thrown into a situation for which they have little or no preparation and they must sink or swim. In this case, the situation was particularly challenging—there were six stepchildren—and the stepparents were particularly inexperienced—they were only twenty years old, had never been married, and had no parenting experience. What is clear is that the step situation is difficult for everyone—parents, stepparents, and children.

First Reactions

For the children, the struggling and suffering started as soon as the "I do's" were spoken. Just as children's first reaction to the idea that their parents are getting a divorce is usually negative, so is their first reaction to the idea that their parents are getting remarried. For one thing, they fear further loss like the loss they experienced in the divorce. They are afraid that the stepparent will "steal" the one parent they have left.

Connie Phillips

Five years after the divorce, my mother sat me down to tell me that she was getting married again. I got very upset and started to cry. I tried to talk her out of it, but she said that she had made up her mind. I am still not sure to this day why I got mad at her about getting remarried. I had known her boyfriend for four years and we always got along fine. I used to think that it was because he was trying to take my father's place. Now, I think it was because I was afraid of losing my mother. I had lost everybody else and I was just getting used to there being just the two of us. I did not want to have to share her with anyone else. I did not want anyone to steal my mother.

Children may also be upset at the idea of the parent's

remarriage because it means that their "absent" parent is being replaced by the stepparent. They don't want a "new" dad or a "new" mom.

Tom Wise

After the divorce, my mom married the first man she went out with. This was the start of a very long war between my mother and me. I didn't like the idea of having a new dad, and I treated him like an intruder.

Children of divorce, who already have had to make a transition from family life with two parents to family life with a single parent, abhor more changes and transitions. A new stepparent represents yet another challenge in their already complicated lives. After all the turmoil and loss they have experienced, they don't want to lose the sense of stability they have just regained, as tenuous as it may be. They resent the stepparent as an intruder into their relationship with their parent, and often they feel as if their parent's new mate has replaced them. Custodial parents often form strong bonds with their children after divorce. Remarriage and the introduction of a stepparent changes the nature of this relationship, and children often resent the new parent, who, in a sense, replaces them and diminishes their central role in the family.

Tracey Sanchez

I was sixteen when my father began dating. I acted like it was no big deal, but it was scary for me to think of another woman replacing me. No longer did my brother and I have our father's full and undivided attention. Now, we had to share him with this other woman. They dated for about two years and then got married. She's the nicest stepmother anyone could have, but it was very hard for me to accept the whole thing.

The fear of losing the parent and the jealousy the child feels when a new adult enters the family scene can be quite severe and even express itself in physical symptoms. This is what happened to the following student. He was literally sickened by his rival for his mother's love.

Andrew Chan

It hurt me deeply to know that my mother loved another man. I remember when he started to come around I would always get sick. I would go into my room and start to cry. And when my mom came to look after me, I would tell her that my head hurt and that I needed to throw up. I must have done this a hundred times. Only later, did I realize that the man wasn't trying to take my mother from me.

Other children were more direct in their efforts to sabotage their parent's new relationship.

Rachel Hall

Two years after my parents' separation, my mom started to date a man named David. I believed it was my duty to help my father by running David out of my mom's life. I was very nasty to him whenever I got the chance. I always ignored him when he tried to make conversation and refused his invitations to go out. One time, I remember, I even hammered a nail into the bottom of his shoe. I guess I wanted him to suffer too.

If children are to have a positive reaction to their parent's remarriage, they must overcome the feeling that they are losing a parent and see that they are gaining a stepparent. They must get over their fear and learn to appreciate the value of the stepparent. This takes time, as the following student describes.

Anabel Sayers

When I turned seven, my mother remarried. Our standard of living increased dramatically. My mother was a happier person because the stress of being a single parent was over and she had the help of a wonderful new husband. The adjustment for my sisters and me, however, was difficult. We were used to having Mom's full attention, and the thought of sharing her was unbearable. We also did not trust another man because of our terrible experiences with our father. After about a year, we realized that this man was going to be a permanent part of our lives. Slowly, we began to really like him. He furnished our entire house and took us to nice restaurants. He always referred to us as "young ladies" and made us feel very special. Most important, he helped our mother by giving her the love and support she needed and deserved.

Children, like this one, can recover from their initial negative reaction to the remarriage—if the stepparent works at it. But the road is filled with hurdles, and many stepparents trip.

Instant Families

A stepfamily is not like a regular "natural" family. It doesn't grow and evolve gradually over the years. It is an "instant family." Suddenly, without years of getting used to each other, parents and children discover they are part of a new family constellation. A stepfamily may look like a family, but to the child it doesn't feel like a family.

Frances Sinclair

My parents were divorced when I was two and my brother was one, and because we were so young we naturally stayed with our mother. But when I was nine and my brother was eight, our father remarried and our parents decided that it would be good for my brother and

me to go to live with him and my stepmom. We became
this little instant family. We got a cat and a dog, joined
Scouts, and went to church. We looked like a family, but
we didn't feel like a family. We did things together and
had "family fun," but it wasn't "real." I always felt uneasy. I
felt as if I had to ask if I could take a shower or get a snack
from the fridge. It was as if I was out of place, a guest
in what was supposed to be my own home. I had a part
to play but I didn't know what it was. My brother and I
were confused and out of control. This father person was
very scary, and my stepmom, a huge threat. We hated her.
Before the year was over, we were back with our mother.

In this case, the shock of the "instant family" was particularly
severe because the children had been living with the other
parent until the father got remarried and they moved in with
him. Nevertheless, it illustrates one of the problems inherent
in stepfamilies—the problem of becoming a full-blown family
without the time to grow into the roles of parent and child.

Complicated Relationships

Another problem with stepfamilies is that life is complicated
because of the sheer number of people who are involved.
Children and their parents are hit with a cast of new players as
stepparents, stepsiblings, step-aunts, step-grandparents, and
step-friends enter the scene. This modern family is complex
and problematic and the cast of characters is extensive. One
of the difficulties this creates is that children have trouble
balancing the competing demands of their two sets of parents
and relatives. For the following student, this was a lifelong
problem.

Connie Phillips

The problem with stepfamilies is that you can never
make all your parents happy. When my sister got married,
she wanted both our father and our stepfather to walk
her down the aisle on her wedding day. This made my

father mad because he felt that it was his right to give her away and that he should not have to share it. But, because my stepfather and mother were paying for the wedding, my sister felt that our stepfather should be involved. She would not budge on the issue. In retaliation, our father sent the invitation back and did not come to her wedding. My sister and he did not speak to each other for years. Now my graduation is coming up. My father has never been to any important celebration of mine, but a couple of weeks ago he called and said that he and my stepmother are coming. I should be excited, but this just makes things more complicated. I am going to have an after-graduation dinner celebration at my mother's house and she, being gracious for my sake, has invited them. I know, though, that things are going to be tense. It may sound selfish, but in a way I wish they were not coming, because this is supposed to be a happy day for me.

As this student points out, it's difficult to make all your parents happy. It is expecting a lot from children to be able to negotiate the treacherous shoals of competing parental demands—when the adults often can't even work it out themselves.

His and Her Children: The Problem of Stepsiblings

As previous stories reveal, adding a stepparent to a family where parent and child are settled and stable is hard enough. It is worse when the new stepparent brings children from a prior marriage into the new blended family. Stepsiblings are often resentful and jealous of each other, and the child's life in a stepfamily is complicated when stepsiblings are added to the mix. As our storytellers reveal, the demands of dealing with stepsiblings as well as a stepparent adds a level of complexity, confusion, and competition that can often be nasty for all members of the new family. In the next story, children from both side of the aisle hated their new stepfamily.

Brenda Depner

Bob seemed to offer my mom the stability and security that was lacking in her first marriage. After they had been dating for a year, we moved in with him and his daughter. But our "instant family" brought with it a new set of problems. Mom was now faced with rearing a resentful stepdaughter and a biological daughter who ignored and sneered at her new husband. The conflict at home became unbearable. Before they got together, Mom and Bob each lived with one pretty well adjusted kid; now, they had two children who both hated the new family arrangement.

In other students' experience, the problem was that the stepparents favored their own children over their stepchildren. This may be natural sociobiologically, since we supposedly all want to protect most those who share our genes, but it's tough for the children who feel discriminated against, and it's a constant source of conflict for the couple.

Penny Packer

My father got remarried the day after the divorce was finalized. The woman he married was also recently divorced, and she had three children of her own, two boys and a girl, who were about the same ages as my sister and me. As the months went by it became clear to us that our stepmom's kids always came first, and my sister and I always got blamed for things we did not do. When we got in trouble, we always got a harsher punishment than her kids. When there were presents given out, theirs were bigger and better. We wanted our dad to stick up for us, but he always backed down when she gave him "that look."

New Babies, New Problems

A third reason that stepfamilies have problems is that often the marriage leads to the birth of more children, who are the biological offspring of the new couple. This complicates relationships in the family even further:

> Tracey Sanchez
> Soon after they got married, my dad and stepmom had two babies of their own. They are adorable little boys. But, oh, how this brought a flood of emotions I had never felt before—jealousy being the first. I felt very guilty and immature to be reacting like this at twenty years of age, but I couldn't help it. It brought back all the feelings of disappointment and pain and loss I went through when my father left my mother.
>
> It is difficult for children whose parents remarry to accept the new children their parent produces. They almost inevitably experience envy and revisit old feelings of pain and rejection. It is not surprising, therefore, that remarriage often leads to the "disappearance" of the remarried parent.

When Dad Remarries: Dad Disappears

It is typical that after a parent remarries, only one family remains actively involved with the child. Most often it is the dad who remarries and becomes less involved with his "first children." This may occur because relations between the families are too difficult. It may occur because the father just wants to forget all about his first marriage and get on with his new wife and his new life. Feeling this way, fathers find ways to distance themselves from their children.

> Paul Woo
> After my father remarried, he invited my brother and sister and me to visit him in Louisiana. The catch was that we had to address him as "Mr. Woo." "Don't call me Dad," he said, because his in-laws were visiting and he had not told them he had been married before.

This kind of behavior makes children feel rejected. Dad wants to leave his first family behind, and the children come to feel this way too. Even if the father doesn't deliberately reject the children, when he is too taken up with his new life to pay them any attention, the end result is the same: They feel rejected.

Judd Michaelson

When I was growing up, I spent the summers with my dad in Montana. But I always felt that when I went to visit him I was going on a vacation. I would go there to fish and hunt, not to visit my dad—because he was never around. He had remarried, and he had two young kids and a wife to look after. I know that those kids were his responsibility, too, but all I wanted was a little time alone with him. It became blatantly obvious after a few years that this wasn't going to happen. My mom thought that it was important for me to visit him so I could stay close to him, but it just didn't work out that way. He always seemed like a distant uncle, not a dad. He promised to give me a car when I turned sixteen; he didn't. He didn't call me on my eighteenth birthday. He didn't call to congratulate me on graduating high school, and I honestly don't think he knows where I am going to college. He didn't even send me a birthday card on my 21st birthday. How could a dad not care enough to send his only son a card on his 21st birthday? It hurts to know that a father can just turn his back on his son.

Sometimes it is the second wife who initiates the father's estrangement from his first family. She wants her husband to make his new family his first priority. She doesn't want any reminders of his first family around. She doesn't want to think about his ex-wife. She may resent and resist the father's continued contact with his first children.

Chandra Simons
  One source of conflict in my parents' marriage was my father's two children from his first marriage. At first, they spent their summers with us. But there was a lot of tension between them and my mother. My mother disliked them and resented their presence in "her" family. She was not willing to make room for "outsiders" in her new home. They were a constant reminder of my father's past marriage. Finally, after my mother threatened to leave, my father decided he could not be an active part of these children's lives. He resigned himself to a role of providing money and detached himself emotionally.

These children lost contact with their father after his remarriage, but at least he continued to pay for their support. They were lucky. Often the remarried dad claims he has trouble making payments to his first family because now he has a second family to support, and his new wife complains if he is paying to support his ex-wife. In addition to these battles of the budget, the first wife may be angry and jealous of the second wife and vice versa. In one study of divorced couples, those families in which the mother had custody and the father had remarried were the most likely to have continued conflict long after the divorce. At times, the first wife tries to punish the father by keeping him from the children, or she may act so antagonistic that he can't stand to be around her. Other times, the second wife tries to boot the first wife out of "her" husband's life, even out of his children's lives. She competes with the children's mother and tries to provide them with a "better" home than the biological mother can offer. Whatever the dynamics, it is common for remarried fathers to withdraw from their ex-wives and children to avoid the increased strain in their new family.

When Mother Remarries: Dad Disappears
Children also run the risk of losing Dad when the mother remarries. One reason for this is that the mother is more likely

to deny the father access to the children after her remarriage because now she has an intact family situation and doesn't need him. Another reason is that she may believe it's better for the children just to have one family. Yet another reason for the father to disappear is that the two dads may become rivals. They may be rivals over the mother.

Maria Schaefer

My father was so angry when my mother moved in with our future stepfather that he came over and pulled his knife on him. He was lonely and he still wanted her, even though they were divorced. After she married the man, my father was so angry that he sold his gun because he was afraid that he would end up using it.

Alternatively, the two dads may become rivals for the children.

Jonathan Bekarian

The first thing that our new stepfather said to my brother and me when he and my mom returned from their honeymoon was that we were to call him "Dad" instead of "Mike," and the first time we slipped up, we would be sent to our rooms. Our father was furious about that. From then on, he was always attacking Mike, and Mike was always attacking him.

Yet another reason that children lose contact with their father after their mother remarries is that they prefer being with their mom and new stepfamily to being with their dad.

Sandra Wilson

Three years after the divorce, my mom got remarried. At first, I felt guilty whenever I did things with my mom and John. Was I being disloyal to my dad, I wondered? As time went on, I made new friends near my mom's place. The hour drive to my dad's house started to be really irritating. I began going only once a month. I still spent half of each holiday with him, but things were changing. I really liked spending time with my mom and John. John is a very patient and caring person and a lot of fun. I preferred being around a healthy happy marriage rather than seeing my dad alone and bitter. The times that I did go to visit, I couldn't wait to leave.

Thus there are many reasons for the children of remarried parents to lose contact with their fathers—animosity between the ex-spouses, rivalry between the two wives, competition between the two dads, hostility among the children, and, as in this last story, "natural selection." Whatever the cause, for many children, remarriage often means losing dad irrevocably.

Positive Consequences of Remarriage: Solid Stepfamilies
As this last story suggests, though, sometimes the stepfamily works out for the best and is clearly preferable to the original divorced family for both the children and the parent. Our students' stories included a number of cases in which children benefited from the remarriage. In the majority of them, it was a wonderful, reliable, and supportive stepfather who transformed the child's life and became "Dad."

Karen Carlson
Within a year of my parents' divorce, my mom met Ray. He totally changed our lives. Economically, he ended our poverty. Emotionally, he filled the void that my invisible father had left. He cared for me and helped me with my homework. He encouraged me and cheered me on at soccer and volleyball games and track meets. He clapped for me in school plays. He supported me at music camp, paid for voice lessons, and attended all my recitals. He bought me a horse and encouraged my equestrian endeavors. He told me how lucky he felt to have me, and how my father was missing out on so much through his

neglect. He continues to tell me how proud he is, that my achievements are amazing, and that he has complete faith in my abilities. Ray is my dad.

A number of our students shared their stories about wonderful stepfathers who became their "real" dads. In all these stories, the children's biological dads were jerks and the children were young when their mothers remarried. Intuitively, it seems easier to develop close bonds between stepparents and stepchildren when the children are young. But our students also provided a few testimonials to the transforming power of wonderful stepmothers who joined the family when the children were not so young.

Kristin Sanders

My stepmother, Bonnie, has raised me since I was twelve years old. In my mind, she and my father are my parents. I think of myself as being from a happy intact family, not a miserable divorced one. If my parents had not divorced, my stepmother would never have been part of my life. The lack of her presence in my life would have been a tragedy because Bonnie is the best thing that has ever happened to me. I could not love her more if I were her own flesh and blood. My father and I seized the opportunity the divorce offered us and achieved a higher level of personal growth and satisfaction because of it.

These students were fortunate. Their stepparents were committed to their task of step parenting. They were interested in the children and cared for them; they accepted the children and supported them; they were available and involved. As a result, these children developed wholesome relationships with stepparents who were mature enough to form supportive families where children could flourish. Unfortunately, the opposite situation was more common in our students' stories, as the following tales reveal.

The Evil Stepmother

Getting along in a stepfamily is particularly trying for girls and stepmothers—just ask Cinderella. When researchers have asked stepparents to describe their relationships with their stepchildren, stepfathers say they are treated like a parent or friend, but stepmothers say their relationship is like that of an aunt, an acquaintance, an adult friend, a servant, or a rival. Stepmothers are dissatisfied with their roles as cook and chauffeur and resent not being given a "real" parent's authority. They have to put up with rejection, because they have replaced the child's mother and are often, like Julia Roberts, in the movie "Step Mom," younger and prettier than she. They are confused about the stepmom role, and, not being sure how to manage the children, they sometimes wield a heavy hand.

Kathy Kelley

From the beginning, my stepmother was mean to me. She would do things like make me stay in the bedroom when company was visiting. She was so mean that she actually told me that she hated children and would never have any. That was traumatic for me, because, even though she was mean, I always tried hard to make her like me. I spent all my time when I was at their house doing chores. When I was at my mother's house, I was not allowed to call my dad before eight o'clock in the morning or after nine at night. I remember how sad I felt when my father told me this. I pictured my stepmom standing over him and making him choose between her and me. She controlled everything, including him. He always took her side. That really hurt.

The stepdaughter-stepmother relationship is especially trying if the daughter is an adolescent. By that time it is difficult for a new person to enter the family and start acting like a parent. Adolescents are ready to rebel against the parents they already have; they do not need and will not accept a pseudo parent telling them what to do.

Nicole Raffaella

When I was fifteen, my dad remarried. A year later, I moved in with him and his new wife, Phyllis. It was really fun at first, but the good times didn't last. It was during the summer, and I was working in a bakery. But Phyllis thought I wasn't making enough money, so she tried to get me a job as a waitress. I really didn't want to work as a waitress, but she wouldn't let up. I never did find a job, and she was upset all summer. She began making house rules so strict I could barely stand to be there. For example, I wasn't allowed to use the shower between before 9 a.m. or after 6 p.m. because she would be disturbed. Phyllis and I became enemies.

It exacerbates the child's negative feelings when the stepmother is the "other woman," who was responsible for the parents' divorce. This starts the stepfamily off on the wrong foot and it may never recover if the stepmom is a home wrecker as well as a hateful person.

Morgan Dennison

The main reason for my parents' divorce was that my dad was having an affair. He married the woman immediately after the divorce. I hated her for that, and soon I hated her for herself. She was a moody and unpredictable person. I lived in fear of her. I remember waking up at night after a terrible nightmare, which I often had, and lying in my bed listening to the people walking down the hallway. I was trying to pick out my dad's slow and heavy footsteps rather than my stepmom's quick, short steps. I didn't want her to find out that I had a nightmare. I knew she would make fun of me.

The Abusive Stepfather

It is not just daughters and stepmothers who suffer, of course. Our stories also included abusive stepfathers who inflicted great pain on their stepchildren.

Mark Tran

When my mother met my future stepfather, Ky, a former pilot in the South Vietnamese Air Force, she thought he was honest, lovable, and just the right person to be a dad for her eight-year-old son. Three months into the marriage she found out that he had divorced his wife and left his three children just a month before he married her. She wanted to divorce him immediately, but by then she was pregnant. She didn't want her second child to suffer the same pain as I had, growing up with no father, so she swallowed her anger and continued on with the marriage.

By the time I was twelve, both my mother and stepfather were working, and because I was the eldest child, I was given the responsibility for taking care of my half brothers and sisters. I was expected to act as their parent, brother, friend and maid. I did just that all through school. I cooked and fed them, bathed them and guided them through their education. I also did house chores and worked for my stepfather in his shop from 6 p.m. until 1 a.m. every school night and on weekends. I basically had no life. If that wasn't enough, my stepfather would physically and mentally abuse me by saying that I had no potential to go any higher than a high-school degree. I recall once I came home late after a university partnership meeting, and he kicked me and whipped me with a steel hanger as though I was an animal. He said I shouldn't waste my time in club activities and should worry more about my house chores because I am stupid and useless. When, with my mother's help, I enrolled in college, he was so angry he kicked me out of the house because I was not his biological child.

In this sad story, the student was rejected by his stepfather because they lacked a biological tie. Over and over, our students' stories illustrated the old adage that blood is thicker than water.

In other stories, children suffered at the hands of their stepfather not because they were competing with his natural children, but simply because these men were abusive. Fortunately, this kind of story was rare. But it clearly shows how parents may be blind to the pain and torture their new spouses are inflicting on their children. It is discouraging to see how often parents' loyalty is devoted to the new mate instead of the children—at least until the scales fall from the parent's eyes. And in that time, a great deal of damage can be done.

Masayasu Lawrence

When I was six, my mom began to date Edward. He gave me the creeps pretty early on. Before they even got married, he had a moving sale. He took our toys and told us we had to sell them. There were some that I wanted to keep, but he said, "No, they have to go." I had a little rubber dog named Henri that my mother had given me. I didn't want to sell Henri, but Edward put a piece of masking tape on him marked 25 c and put him out with the rest of the stuff. Edward caught me trying to rescue Henri and took him away again and set him back out. I snuck Henri into my pocket. I still have Henri today, except now I don't have to hide him. I think this incident should have been a clue for my mom not to marry Edward; it was a clue for me. What kind of grown-up argues with a six-year-old over a miniature rubber dog? I knew life was going to be rough.

They got married when I was seven and my younger sister was five. Then, Edward started in with all his rules and chores. One of his rules was "Your mother is not responsible for the cleanliness of this house, you are."

So my sister and I vacuumed, mopped, climbed ladders to wash windows and ceilings, and dusted constantly to avoid Edward's wrath. Another rule was "You will finish eating all the food on your plate or you won't get anything the next day." If we accidentally put our elbows on the table during the meal, our hands were tied behind the chair with rope, and Edward would decide when we were to be untied.

As the years went on, life got worse. For some reason, he really didn't like me. He told me I was "an ugly kid" and stupid. Most of the time he called me "nigger" or "you little shit." He took a knife and carved the word "nigger" into my bed so that I would see it every day. It got so bad, that every day after I got home from school I would hide under my bed, holding my breath, hoping he wouldn't hear me. I would stay like this for two or three hours until my mom got home. Then I would watch my mom leave my side and go to him. He had complete control over her. He would regulate when I was allowed to talk to her. He would also regulate how many phone calls I was allowed (two per day), and I was never allowed to have any friends over. Sometimes I would go to my mom and tell her the crazy things Edward had done; she would always support him. This made me hate my mother. I felt very much alone. I couldn't believe that she could allow us to be this miserable. I kept hoping and praying that one day Edward would go too far and then my mom would have to leave him.

That day came one morning when I was eleven years old. I was debating about whether or not I should sneak into the kitchen to get a bowl of cereal. My mom had already left to take my sister to school. I didn't want to have to deal with Edward, but I was hungry. As soon as Edward heard me, he came out of his room, drunk, with a glass of whiskey in his hand. He started insulting me and taunting me as usual. Suddenly he took his whiskey glass and threw it through one of the kitchen windows. Then he picked me up and threw me too. I landed in a pile of shattered glass. My cuts were only superficial, but I was terrified. Edward told me that I couldn't go to school until I picked up every piece of glass with my fingers. I waited until he went inside to get another drink, then I climbed over the fence and ran all the way to school. I ran into my sixth-grade class screaming. Mrs. Winston, my teacher, saw the blood on my hands and called the police and then called my mother.

As this story shows, it is the children who are facing and coping with the greatest challenges after their parents remarry, because they have no control and are completely dependent on their parents. They have no say in their parents' breakup and no choice in their parents' remarriage. But they have to make do, and often more than that. They are pressured to conform to stepparents' rules and needs, and, in the process, their own needs often get railroaded.

Instability of Second Marriages

Not surprisingly, remarriages often end in divorce. More than half of all remarried couples split up, and the probability that a remarried couple will get divorced within the first five years of their marriage is 50 percent greater than after a first marriage. Why? One reason is that divorced individuals, still smarting (but not smart) from their divorce, rush into remarriage, and the same factors that cause rushed first marriages to fail operate again—the only difference is that the issues the family faces are even more complex.

Sandi Rodriguez

My father got married right after the divorce was final, but the marriage lasted only three months. He discovered on their honeymoon that his new wife had lied to him about almost everything. I remember going to my father's house for dinner on Wednesday night soon after they returned from their honeymoon. My father said he had a surprise for us. It was an empty garage; Jan was gone. We never heard from her again. We were glad.

Stepfamilies create complex problems with intricate relationships and demanding roles. Loyalty conflicts within the stepfamily are common. There may also be conflicts because of pulls and demands from the first family. Stress comes, too, from the clash of family cultures, rules, and ideas about how time, energy, goods, and affection should be shared, when two families are blended. In addition, stepfamilies may suffer from the same problems that arose in the parent's first marriage. Parents seldom have a chance to learn to overcome or sidestep the issues that plagued them in their first marriage before they are embroiled in parallel problems of the second. They also don't have time to get to know each other well and work out household issues before the kids are born and the pressure starts. Just as leaping into marriage often proves unworkable the first time around, leaping into remarriage is even riskier.

Suzanne Knowles

Two years ago my dad got remarried to a woman with four small children, and it was deja vu all over again. He had the same financial problems as when he was married to my mother, because they rented a huge house in Palos Verdes that they couldn't afford. He began using the same tone with my stepmom about finances and how to discipline the kids as I had heard all too often with my mom. The few times I did go to visit them they were fighting about the kids or the house. It sounded like old times to me. I wasn't at all surprised when they separated after a year of marriage.

In the following story, the student describes the unraveling of one stepfamily in detail. In this story we see how the demise of a stepfamily can be as emotionally difficult for the child as the divorce of the child's family in the first place. The marriage ground painfully to a halt, and the child (by then a college student) was as traumatized as she had been the first time around.

Tiffany Maurer

Lonely and unhappy from losing his home and his children, my father found the happiness he had missed the first time around with Cheryl—or so he thought. Cheryl was ten years younger than my dad and was living alone trying to take care of her son, Christopher, by herself. I clicked immediately with this young woman, who was interested in many of the same things I was.

Unfortunately, not long after they got married, Cheryl and my dad's relationship began to deteriorate. Christopher had always been a problem child. He lied, ran away from home, and failed in school. My father, although not wanting to overstep his bounds as a stepfather, had to be tough on Christopher because Cheryl never punished him. So Dad and Cheryl began to argue. Their arguments became louder and more frequent. The more Cheryl yelled, the colder my father became. The colder my father became, the more Cheryl yelled. Unable to communicate her feelings of unhappiness and discontent to my father, Cheryl turned to me as her confidante.

When I went away to college, Cheryl was devastated. She felt that I was deserting her just when she needed me the most. They began marriage counseling, but after a few sessions, Cheryl told my father that she wanted a divorce. He couldn't believe it. He felt like his world had collapsed. He became deeply depressed. I talked to him every night on the phone, trying to explain to him what Cheryl had been feeling all those months. Then Cheryl told him that I did not love him, that I was going to move in with her, and that it was my encouragement that had made her decide to get a divorce. That was the most painful part of the ordeal. In the middle of finals week, I got a call from my father. He was crying and accusing me of destroying his marriage. I was shocked, hurt, and angry that Cheryl would have said that to him. It just wasn't true. I had encouraged her to be independent, to speak up for herself, and to have more respect for herself. I never told her to divorce my father, or that I would move in with her, or that I did not love him. The day after the phone call from my dad, I had to go to the hospital because I had a severe asthma attack and almost stopped breathing. I have never had asthma before, and I know it was because of all the stress.

This student's visceral reaction was not unique. Other students also described deeply negative consequences after the divorce of their parent and stepparent—consequences that persist into their adult lives. The following student provided one of the clearest descriptions of how children are affected by their parents' serial relationships and by their experience of a series of broken family attachments.

Steven Goodrich

First there were my parents whom I loved very much. Then they divorced, and although I was little, I hurt. For years after the divorce, I was always playing house, and I would build my own world with the perfect family with a mommy and a daddy and a nice big house and a dog. I also drew hundreds of pictures of families, which always included a mommy and a daddy. I remember envying a friend of mine who had all that—a mom and a dad, a brother and a sister, a dog, and a nice big house. Oh, how I wished I could be him. Instead, I lived with my mom in a small apartment and saw my dad every other weekend. I still loved both of them, but I kept wishing for the perfect family.

Then when I was seven my mother remarried. And how lucky I was. My new stepdad was a wonderful man and best of all he brought along a brother and a sister who were my age. We moved into his big and really nice house with a pool. I instantly connected with my stepbrother

and we became best friends. My new family also came
along with a dog, "Jumper." I loved our life. I finally had
what I had always yearned for. On Sunday mornings we
kids would make breakfast for my mom and my stepdad
and serve it to them in bed. Then we would all get on
their bed and eat, and talk, and roughhouse. It made
me feel good that my stepdad said he would always be
there to take care of me. This lasted until the night that
my stepsister inadvertently blurted out that my stepdad
had had an affair the week before my mom and he got
married.

The result was that my mom ended her second
marriage five months after it had begun. The unraveling
of her first marriage to my dad had been traumatic,
and she was not going to live through another string
of disappointments with my stepdad. I never saw my
stepbrother again. This hurt me very much. For a long
time I kept asking to see him, but my stepdad did not want
his kids to have contact with me after my mom divorced
him. When I saw my stepdad, he was cold and distant. I
tried to hold his hand the way I used to, but he shook it
off and walked away, pulling a resistant Jumper along on
the leash. I had also lost the privilege of petting the dog.

As it happened, at the very time my mother married
my stepdad, my father remarried too. I was a little bit
dismayed because my stepmom was twenty years younger
than my dad, but soon I discovered that her age had
certain advantages. She was a whole lot more fun than
my dad. We would go to the movies together (all the
movies my dad didn't want to see) and she took me to
video arcades. She also often protected me from my
dad's crankiness and criticism. Although I loved my dad,
at times he could be irritable and unpleasant. So it was
nice to have my stepmom in the house as an ally and a
playmate. This lasted four whole years. Then my stepmom
left my dad because he was, after all, too irritable and
egotistic for her taste. She had found a much nicer and
younger boyfriend. When she left, she assured me that

her differences with my father had nothing to do with me, and that she would always keep in touch with me. I have never seen her again.

Currently, both my parents are on their third marriages, and there is yet another round of stepsiblings. My stepbrother on my stepfather's side is a year older than I and really nice—if a bit nerdy. My two younger sisters from my stepmother's side I don't particularly care for. They wreck my room in my father's house when I am not there and are so noisy and demanding that I don't get much time with my dad when I visit. My mother seems to be happy. In fact, she just announced that she is going to have a baby. That took my breath away. I don't know why. I have always wished for a brother or sister but now the thought stirs up tremendous anxiety. I think I should be happy but really I feel like crying. I feel completely overwhelmed. I have always had to adjust to whatever circumstances and characters were in my life. It wasn't just the stepparents and stepsiblings; I also had four sets of step grandparents and numerous step uncles and aunts. I chose none of them; I just had to accept them. In my short life I have experienced so many demands on me from strangers who descended and, in a flash, became intimately involved in my life, and I have experienced so many disappointments and losses and betrayals, that the thought of one more new relationship is numbing.

Children are presented with a formidable challenge when they must adapt to their parents' new partner(s) and the transformed circumstances of their lives and then let them go again when things don't work out. Along with the broken relationships that result from serial divorces come children's broken hearts. Their parents believe that they are making the right choices. They are hopeful and in love when a new relationship begins and believe that it will lead to better things for themselves and their children. When it ends, they are once again in despair. Preoccupied with their own emotions they often do not realize the toll the breakup is taking on their children, as they lose yet another parent, sibling, close friend, and sense of hope. They do not realize that their children are developing superficial emotional bonds out of self-defense, as a way of protecting themselves from further heartbreak. Serial remarriage presents serious risks for children.

Stepfamilies can provide the best of times or the worst of times. In the best of times, stepparents offer children love, support and opportunities that they would not otherwise have had. In the worst of times, stepparents are cruel and the children are hateful. The stepfamily never jells and animosity continues and grows. Often that animosity continues right into divorce court. It is not surprising that second marriages often end in divorce, when one considers the strikes they have against them. They are complicated and stressful from the start, and it takes an unusual level of acceptance and maturity from all the adults involved to make them succeed.

Lessons to Be Learned

What lessons can we learn from these students' stories of stepfamily successes and failures? Are there ideas here that can help us avoid remarriage mistakes?

1. Don't jump into remarriage. The clearest lesson of all is probably that it is just as risky to rush into marriage the second time as it is the first, and the consequences are just as dire. Make sure you know your spouse-to-be long and well before you say "yes." You've already been through a trial run of marriage and divorce; learn from your experience. Look for maturity and experience in your new mate, too, not just youth and beauty. According to research, the most important factor in the success of a second marriage is the choice of a mature, stable, supportive spouse, with good problem-solving skills. You remember the issues that destroyed your first marriage; look for a new partner with whom the same problems will not be repeated. Give your spouse-to-be plenty of time to get to know you and your children, as well. Don't marry someone who isn't willing to take your children with the package, someone who doesn't get along with your children. Your aim should be to provide stability for your children, not an emotional roller coaster. So before you remarry, make sure this union has the greatest possibility of being permanent. (And don't think that living together is the solution, either. Breaking up a cohabiting arrangement is just as painful for the children.)

2. Prepare children for the change. Don't spring the idea of remarriage on children suddenly and expect them to rejoice. Children need to feel they are part of the decision. They need to be assured about what the marriage means for them. It may not always be possible to take the time necessary to get children on board when a marriage breaks down, but there is no reason anyone has to embark on marriage the second time around without adequately preparing the children. Most important, make it clear that the marriage does not mean that the child will lose one or both of his or her parents.

3. Go slow in forming the blended family. When you do remarry, don't expect a fully functional family instantly. It takes time to grow a stepfamily. Let it unfold gradually. Give it time. Help your new mate form a genuine and sincere relationship with your children, rather than rushing in with big words ("I love you"), big promises ("I'll always be there for you"), and big demands ("Show me respect. Call me Dad."). Work out your new roles in the stepfamily with much sensitivity.

4. Dads, don't disappear. Make sure that the children continue to have close contact with both their natural parents. The stepfamily should be an addition to the child's life, not a replacement for his current relationships with mom and dad. Children should not feel that they have lost a parent (or parents) but that they have gained a stepparent.

5. Have reasonable expectations of the stepfamily. A stepfamily is not the same as a "natural" family, and relationships within it may never be as close. Parents and stepparents should accept this and not make unreasonable demands on the children to love and obey the stepparent. Nor should they make unreasonable demands on each other to "love my child like your own"—provided that the stepparent's behavior is generally positive, caring, and fair. A close relationship between stepparents and stepchildren may develop, but if it doesn't, you can't push it. If stepparents enter the scene when children are already adolescents they should not expect too much. What they should aim for is to become a good and trusted friend, not necessarily a parent figure.

6. Stepparents, tread lightly. Stepparents should not undermine biological parents' roles and demand status equal to that of a parent—especially with older children. It is the stepparent's responsibility to find ways to become the child's trusted friend. Treat stepchildren with courtesy and respect and expect the same in return. Don't treat them like servants or nuisances. Persistent verbal abuse and exercise of control is not the way to become friends. Verbal abusiveness is also not undone with occasional playfulness or protestations of love. In fact, the latter only make the relationship more confusing for the children and the attacks more painful. It's better all around to let the children's parent bear the brunt of disciplining them. So manage the children with a light hand, and don't expect them to love you or obey you in the same way they do their parents. Encourage and support them. Show them you care. But be prepared not to be the central parental figure in their lives.

7. Parents, do not abdicate your parenting responsibilities. It is still the "real" parent who is responsible for rearing the children, even though there is another pair of hands to help. Insisting on help, making many demands on the stepparent to take over the chores of your parenting will imperil the marriage. And parents are responsible, as well, for protecting their children if those other hands are ever raised in anger. There's a good reason that fairy tales, cultural stereotypes, and newspaper headlines feature wicked stepmothers and abusive stepfathers. There is a genuine risk that stepparents will mistreat their stepchildren. Parenting is a challenging task under the best of circumstances. It's hard enough for parents to curb their anger and treat their difficult children with kindness and patience. It's much harder for adults who did not decide to conceive or adopt the child, who lack a "blood tie" or genetic similarity to the child, and who do not have a natural parent's history of "bonding" with the child in infancy and childhood. They are presented with a child whose problems they are not responsible for and probably don't understand. It will be hard for them to learn to deal with your children. So it is imperative that parents monitor how their children are treated and protect them from erratic or cruel behavior.

8. Don't put the children in the middle. Stepfamilies are complicated, and children can easily find themselves in the middle of conflicts and complications when parents remarry. Take care that demands from the increased cast of adults in authority are consistent and compatible. Children should not have to choose between their families for special occasions, important events, or routine activities. It's up to the adults to make sure that children's welfare is assured by a shared schedule that all the adults can agree to and that the parents are not fighting over the child's time.

9. Treat all of the children equally. When the stepfamily includes children from both sides of the aisle, and even more, when new offspring are born into the family, it is inevitable that children will think that the other kids are getting better treatment than they are. So it is important for parents and stepparents to bend over backwards in their effort not to favor one set of children (theirs) over their spouse's when treats or punishments are distributed. It's important not to take sides with some children and to scapegoat others. In a stepfamily, even though they were not "created" equal, all children should be treated equal.

10. Children, give your stepparents a break. Finally, the "success" of a stepfamily is not just the responsibility of parents and stepparents. The children contribute too. If you are an adolescent or young adult in a new or struggling stepfamily, look for ways that you can help. Be positive. Look for the silver lining. Is your parent happier? Do you have more money? Have you acquired some great new cousins? Do you get more presents on your birthday? Is your stepdad a terrific cook (so he can teach you how)? Does your stepmom know all about history (so she can help you study)? Try to look at this new arrangement as offering great new opportunities. You have that much more adult expertise to draw on. Give your stepparent the benefit of the doubt. Make him or her feel welcome in your family. Do friendly activities together. Step-parenting is a really hard job, and life will be easier all around if you cooperate.

13

In the Long Run: Relationships, Survival and Personal Growth

These stories illustrate a fact that researchers have discovered again and again with bewilderment, that, in the case of divorce, time does not heal all wounds. Some of our students and their parents had not fully adjusted to the divorce years—and sometimes decades—later. Finalizing the divorce did not finalize all the problems; the old problems persisted, and often, new ones arose.

Adults' Lingering Pains and Belated Insights

The parents in our stories often experienced some growth and some emotional relief from the divorce, but they also told of lingering regrets, persistent anger, bitterness, and many unresolved issues. The following student described her parents as still being affected by the divorce years later—because they regretted the divorce itself and suffered so much going through it.

Deanna Knowlson
    Today, sixteen years after the divorce, my father has regrets. He now admits that he wrongly blamed

my mother for a lot of things that weren't her fault. He realizes that marriage isn't perfect, no matter whom you marry. He says that if he knew then what he knows now, he would have tried harder to make the marriage work. He no longer believes that divorce is the solution. My mom, although she is happily remarried now, says that she will never completely adjust to the divorce either. She feels she has accepted her new identity and can be civil towards my dad, but the divorce was so hard for her that even now, all these years later, she is not over it.

Another student's mother experienced persistent regrets about the divorce; because she lost the happiness she had early in her marriage and was left with nothing but blame and bitterness.

Edwin Ferguson

My mom regrets the divorce because she and my father did have a wonderful marriage—for a while. The divorce left deep scars that she fears will never heal. She still feels sad and resentful because she worked so hard to put my dad through school and she was left with almost nothing. She still feels angry that her parents helped pay for so many things and my dad never paid them back. She is bitter because my dad blames the divorce completely on her. She is sorry because she had many close friends on his side of the family and now they are gone. She is hurt because her parents tried to stay close to my dad's family, but my dad's family always snubs her. Because my mom still has these feelings eighteen years after the divorce, I believe that these issues will never be resolved and she will suffer from them forever.

In another case, the psychological problem was that the man repeated an unhealthy pattern of relationships—rushing into marriage, without adequate preparation and knowledge of the new woman in his life. This is a problem that divorce clearly does not fix.

Maria Schaefer

A year after my parents' divorce, my father got married to a woman he had known for two weeks. After the wedding, he discovered that she had a troubled past, and when he found out that she was also having an affair, they separated. He went through several other relationships for about four years before one girlfriend (thirty years younger) moved in and took control of his life. She helped him finalize his second divorce and write a will that included her. She drained his finances by running up charges on his credit cards, paying off her student loans, and buying expensive art. In her last semester of college she moved out (clearing the house of its valuables) after my father discovered she was having an affair with an ex-boyfriend. But even after this string of messy relationships, my father was not cured. He searched through a worldwide magazine of potential brides, and last year he married a woman from Peru. Not surprisingly, they are having problems—financial, cultural, and communicative.

The financial loss that comes with divorce is another way in which the impact of old problems can persist and continue to cause new problems even years after the divorce. One reason that emotional turmoil persists is that the perceived problems of the past were never resolved—so they keep eating away at people, draining them of energy and impairing their ability to move on in life.

Jennifer Weinstein

It was not until my father's death three years after their divorce that my mother began to recover. She began to feel stronger and more worthwhile. She no longer thought of herself as a doormat. The divorce forced her into action and proved that she could survive on her own. I still worry about her though. She still has so much unresolved anger toward my father, which may never be resolved now that he is dead. She never dates and doesn't even socialize much outside the immediate family.

This inability to establish a new intimate relationship and commit again to another was one of the most common long-term outcomes described in our stories.

Children's Lives in the Long Term

It was not only parents who experienced long-term consequences from the divorce. Some children continued to suffer, too—especially children who were old enough to have seen the unhappiness of their parents' marriage and to understand the implications of their parents' divorce.

Marcy Graham
I feel that I will never completely recover from my parents' divorce. I believe that I will never feel whole.

Some of our students described delayed negative reactions that surfaced or became worse only years after the divorce. These students found themselves haunted by the divorce experience

Adrianne Coman
Today, seven years after my parents' divorce, I suffer from depression. I build barriers between myself and those who are trying to get close to me. When I am feeling helpless or hurt, I become extremely agitated to the point of panic. Lately I have been experiencing anxiety attacks and I am thinking that I should see a psychiatrist.

Another common long-term effect described in our students' stories was that children, especially daughters, were afraid of relationships, had no trust in the opposite sex, and had already experienced in their own relationships the effects of not having a positive role model for a healthy relationship.

Melinda George

I cannot trust men. Every time I date a guy I think he will cheat like my father did. I want to make sure that I don't get hurt. I always look for the bad in situations. I think that if I can figure out the bad stuff quickly, I stay in control and can get out without hurting too much. I have resigned myself to the fact that I will probably get divorced someday.

Sometimes, though, with their parents' negative model in mind, the children were able to create a better situation for themselves and for their children. This is how the following student learned from her experience and was able to move beyond it.

Marcy Graham

My parents divorced when I was fourteen, but their fighting continued. When I was seventeen, I met a guy, and we moved in together. I couldn't wait to be on my own. I thought I was so mature. We were married the next year and our daughter was born nine months later. But then I discovered that my husband was an alcoholic and a drug addict. We separated, and I went through a wild period, just as I had in high school. I went to bars every weekend and drank heavily. I met another man, filed for divorce, and got remarried, within a year. Looking back, I can see that I felt helpless without a man. I was so needy for what I felt I had not received from my parents—attention and love. My second husband and I had two children together, and then, we grew apart, and eventually we divorced. My parents didn't give me much to work with in terms of setting a good example of a loving relationship, but their actions during the divorce were a shining example of how NOT to act. From them,

I learned never to speak negatively to my children about their father. My ex and I have always made a point to be pleasant to each other. We handled our divorce without attorneys and without court battles. My children are not suffering the way my siblings and I did. My experiences helped me give my children a better chance to survive divorce.

Who Is a Winner?

For some fortunate people, after the divorce, there was a clear sense of "winning." They seized the personal-psychological crisis of the divorce as an opportunity for achieving a higher level of personal growth and self-actualization. They stopped blaming the ex-spouse and accepted responsibility for themselves. They moved on to new successes and put past failures behind them. This was the most optimistic outcome of divorce. For some individuals, reaching this happy outcome was helped by a new marriage.

Jenny Messerman

Five years after the divorce, life for our family was pretty good. My brother and I had gotten more independent; we were doing well in school and had lots of friends. My mom's job was going well and she was making a good income. She was dating regularly and had a lot of single friends. Then, she met a wonderful man and our life improved immensely. Now she sees that the divorce was best for everyone and that, because of it, she became a stronger person, capable of facing challenging tasks. My dad, also, happily remarried someone with whom he shares many interests. So all in all, things seem to have turned out for the best for both of them.

Another predictor of being a "winner" after divorce is being a woman. In the long run—a different story from what happens in the few years immediately after the divorce—it is women rather than men who are likely to be winners.

Divorce leads to more psychological change and growth in women. This is because, in this society, women are generally less powerful, less confident, less educated and consequently less economically secure than their husbands, so divorce presents more opportunities for improvement in women. Women achieve improvement in many ways. The economic devastation that comes with divorce pushes many women to enter the work force, to get more education, to improve their standing in the business world, and to gain more self-confidence. Women are also more likely than men to reflect on their relationship problems after the divorce—frequently with the help of a counselor—and, as a result, experience more healing, more insight into their own behavior, and more personal growth.

Meredith Berman

My mom says that she spent the first two years after the divorce reflecting on her life and her marriage and what she wanted out of her future and how she needed to change. She resolved not to let another person control her, as my father had done. She opened her own stained glass store and succeeded in bringing in her own, independent income. She believes that the divorce made her a stronger and better person.

Eternal Enemies

Couples who continued to fight after the divorce were never "winners." They continued in relationships marked by strife and became "eternal enemies." Other couples managed to behave politely and cooperatively with each other and acted like "civil colleagues." Roughly 15 percent of our students' parents fell into each of these two groups. The remaining 70 percent were a diverse group, who at times acted like eternal enemies and at other times managed the jump into civilized territory. The following story describes one couple that ended up "eternal enemies."

Emma Wozniak

Twenty years and seven months have passed since my parent's divorce, but to this day the battle between my parents continues. They never stopped fighting, not during the two decades that have passed, and not even during my father's three remarriages. My father took the divorce as a personal war waged against him and proceeded to fight with all the energy he had. He told my mother, "I am going to punish you for this for the rest of your life. I am going to make your life a living hell." And he has.

Eternal enemies were characterized by ongoing battles over the children, money, new relationships, old problems, new problems, indeed, over anything. These individuals were unable to detach themselves from their former spouse and unable to mind their own business. They remained obsessed with their ex. Sometimes their hostilities escalated into protracted legal battles. More commonly, they played "mind games." They would not adhere to agreements, would show up late or not at all, would demand concessions above and beyond the established terms, and would denigrate or sabotage the other parent. Sometimes the former spouses would settle for short periods into a workable routine. But problems would flare up every time they encountered a change—in finances, visitation, new relationships, remarriage, employment locations, and so on. They would make the changes an opportunity to rekindle old conflicts. Transactions regarding the children were particular emotional minefields. One common strategy was to withhold the children from the other parent.

It is noteworthy, that in more than half of the eternal enemy couples, the perpetual hostilities were unilateral. That is, only one parent, like the father in this story, could not forgive and forget and made it his life's mission to make the other parent miserable. The other parent would necessarily be drawn into the conflict because she or he had to raise children with the avenger or was financially dependent.

Sara Krantz

After my dad won custody, he told my mom that she had to give him one week's notice if she wanted to see me. But when she called he would not answer the phone or return her calls. Sometimes he would let her have me, but if she was five minutes late, I would not be there.

If it isn't the children, it is money that is used as a weapon against the other parent.

Sidney Bassett

My father used to write me these horrific letters spewing out his hatred against my mom. Here I quote: "She's a greedy, vengeful bitch who thinks I'm a welfare ATM."

Some men marshal a remarkable armada of resources to convince their ex-wives, the world, and the courts that they cannot possibly afford the ordered payments. One student's father, a multimillionaire who had built his fortune in real estate, spent $75,000 on forensic accountants and $350,000 on attorney's fees to convince the judge that he was penniless.

Women who are financially dependent and economically frustrated after the divorce often feel like victims. And maybe because they are victimized they develop a strange sense of entitlement. "He owes me" was a common slogan. Too often the children are keenly aware of what is going on and deeply hurt by it. Here is one daughter's view:

Deirdre Erin

My dad always claimed he didn't have any money, that he couldn't afford to pay any more support, yet he was living in a brand new house, went on regular gambling sprees to Las Vegas, constantly had some new

toy, jet skis, a boat, a stereo, etc. Last but not least, he
could afford another baby although he already owed my
mother $30,000 in child support. How can the judges, the
courts, the whole system condone this? He felt he could
start a brand new life with a brand new family, although
he couldn't even take care of his previous children. Why
did this new baby take precedence over us? He is still our
father too.

The "eternal enemies" are irrational and reactive. They
see their relationship with the other parent as something that
is happening to them, something out of their control. They
are simply "reacting" to their evil ex's scheming. If things go
badly for eternal enemies, it has nothing to do with them but is
entirely the fault of the other parent. There is no recognition
on their part that their own behavior contributes to the poor
quality of the relationship with the ex-spouse.

Civil Colleagues

Fortunately, not all couples become eternal enemies. Most
people eventually move on, establishing new lives and new
relationships. Although they have their share of conflict and
hostilities they manage in the long run to disentangle their
past business from their present and future objectives and
to make their children a priority. For a minority of couples,
the path seems particularly smooth. Although, like everyone
else, they experience their share of hurt and chaos, most of
the time they remain civil and even considerate toward each
other. Their children's welfare is clearly in the foreground of
their interactions. The following story illustrates some of the
main characteristics of these "civil colleagues."

Jennie Lee Nolan

My mother had a strong attitude; she was nearly
invincible in my eyes. She made a home for us no matter
where we lived. She was incredible about making sure I
was always secure and loved and well taken care of. She

began going to "Parents without Partners" meetings to try to cope with being a single parent. She even dated a little bit but not until a year after the divorce. She also went to a psychologist because she said she wanted to be sure she got her head clear so that she could raise me properly and without any ill-will toward my father. She never made me feel that my father was a "bad guy." As a matter of fact, my father and mother remained friendly after their divorce. My dad was an occasional visitor at our house, and I always felt comfortable talking to them both. They carefully maintained their relationship for my sake and I think this helped me adjust well to the divorce. I can say that my parents worked hard to get along and to raise me—separately, but together.

Civil colleagues were guided in their actions and interactions with their former spouse by their desire to care for their children the best they could. Their strong sense of responsibility toward their children restrained them from making derogatory comments about the other parent. They also maintained open lines of communication about their children and consulted with each other before making major decisions.

Civil colleagues were more likely to stick to agreements, financial and otherwise. They were more likely than other parents to seek out help from friends and family, support groups, and counselors. Like Jennie's mother in the story above, it was important to them to maintain a "clear head" and gain perspective so that their unfinished business with the other parent would not interfere with their responsibilities as parents and with their ability to move on with life.

Also like Jennie's mother, most mothers among the civil colleagues were very resourceful and willing to pursue nontraditional routes to overcome their obstacles. They were more willing to be flexible and share child custody equally with the father. They did not see themselves as victims, and, therefore, they directed less anger toward the father. They also tended to delay dating and other forms of personal gratification.

Civil men's attitudes toward money were drastically different from those of men who were eternal enemies. Their willingness to help their ex-wives out financially set them miles apart from the fathers in most other families. They did not question their financial responsibility toward their children or their responsibility toward their former spouse. They did not waste energy haggling over amounts to be paid but were driven by their objective to provide adequately for the children. Often that meant that fathers were paying more than would be legally required of them in order to help the mother get back on her feet. They did not fall into a depression or throw a temper tantrum when they realized that they had to pay the wife half of all the assets. They understood that their children's well-being was intertwined with their ex-wife's and that it was not possible to leave their ex-wife financially crippled and at the same time be a good father.

Most of the civil colleagues settled their financial affairs out of court and came up with generous arrangements that were tailored to fit the children's needs and each others' circumstances. The following story provides a good example of parents working cooperatively and considerately with each other in order to protect their children.

Amanda Killian

My parents agreed on joint custody and never involved any attorneys or courts in their business. They wanted to do everything in the best interest of the children. An old friend had told my father that there are two things you don't do to a woman after separation. You don't threaten her for the children and you don't undermine her financial ability. My father took that advice and told my mother she could raise the kids but that he wanted a part in it. He told her they would share the expenses. Actually he covered most of the costs because my mother went back to school and could not afford much at the time. For a while, my father took my brother and me on the weekdays and my mother had us on the weekends. It took my mom two or three years to finish school. After that, my parents worked out other arrangements for us. When she was financially able to contribute, she did. Despite the divorce, my parents developed a way of dealing with each other respectfully, which made it easier on both of them. Holidays were spent together at my mother's house—including both sides of the family. A lot of people thought this arrangement was strange, but to me it was normal, the way it should be. Both sides of my family got along very well. My father would even bring his girlfriend over to my mother's house. I didn't realize that the majority of divorced parents couldn't stand each other and made their lives miserable. In the long run my father felt that things turned out to be positive. He believes that if divorce is unavoidable, then parents have a special obligation to be cooperative and supportive so the children's lives aren't marred by the adults' failures. All things considered, I think my parents were able to raise two children that turned out to be pretty normal, happy, and successful.

This story illustrates the flexibility and good will that distinguishes the civil colleagues from other families. Nontraditional arrangements are common. Parents make arrangements that they feel are in the best interest of the children, even if they violate conventional notions of divorce or family life. Among our civil colleagues, it was not uncommon for mothers to go back to school with the financial backing of their ex-husbands. Despite strong social pressure from family and friends, these mothers refused to be their children's exclusive caretakers. Instead they worked flexibly with the father to assure that the children were cared for in the best possible way.

In the preceding story, for example, the mother's circumstances made it better for the children to stay primarily with their father for some time. This kind of arrangement took some courage on the mother's part. She took the risk that her ex-husband would refuse to adjust the arrangement after her circumstances changed. She also disregarded the social stigma mothers often experience when they do not have their children living with them. Unlike other fathers, this one bolstered the mother's economically weaker position and did not use it as a bargaining chip against her in the struggle for child custody. Instead, he supported her and willingly renegotiated the custody arrangement after the mother's situation improved.

The benefits of a civil arrangement are enormous. These children grow up knowing that they have two parents who love them enough to overcome any selfish agendas. They continue to be cared for by both parents and they escape the detriments of ongoing conflict. They learn that the break-up of a marriage does not necessarily jeopardize their bond with either parent, and they see a good role model for constructive coping, problem solving, and parental commitment. The adults, of course, also experience far less stress and pain in the long run and are functioning better in their new lives because they are not stuck in the past; they are not obsessed with hostile thoughts and full of bitterness. Carrying around such dark feelings takes a tremendous toll on one's quality of life and one's ability to grow. Civil parents did not have to pay this toll.

Civil colleagues and eternal enemies differ mainly in their commitment to their children and in their coping skills. Civil colleagues place their children's welfare front and center at all times. Eternal enemies, in contrast, are first and foremost consumed by their own needs, their hurt, and their need for revenge. One mother stated the situation very succinctly: "It seems like he hates me more than he loves our children."

Civil colleagues also have good coping skills. They are able to maintain a realistic perspective on their problems and sustain a positive self-image. Civil colleagues seem to have a greater capacity to compartmentalize their problems. They see their problems as only one aspect of their lives, not as an overriding and all-consuming condition. Rather than ruminating about their problems they view them as something to be dealt with, not as an insurmountable obstacle that will forever determine their behavior toward the other parent.

Civil colleagues are able to attribute the negative aspects of their situation to specific events and to view those events as transitory. Rather than making wholesale claims that their entire life is a mess—caused by the other parent—they will say that they don't have enough money but they expect that this will be temporary. This point of view affords them a sense of control over their circumstances. In general, when problems appear manageable, people are more motivated to improve their situation and take charge of their lives.

It also seems that the civil colleagues were less sensitive to slights and therefore less likely to overreact in response to the other parent. Unlike eternal enemies, they do not immediately interpret the other parent's behavior negatively, and, accordingly, they are less inclined to react hostilely. Civil colleagues also seem to have had a less volatile and violent marital relationship even before the divorce; only few of the dysfunctional couples turned into civil colleagues after the divorce.

Surviving: Children Growing Through Adversity

Although many of our students did suffer severely as a result of their parents' divorce, a substantial number also reported that the anguish and turmoil of the divorce was not all for naught. They said that the adverse experiences from their parents' divorce had made them stronger, better, and more resourceful people. We conclude this book with a sampling of stories showing how these children went through divorce and came out ahead.

Melissa Shipman

My parents' divorce catapulted me into a bad scene. I threw myself into drinking and partying. I was sexually active at fifteen, and pregnant at eighteen. I had to drop out of school and go to work. My husband turned out to be a drug addict. Fortunately, he got help and I managed to go back to school when my son was two years old. I will be graduating this June. Now, I am glad I have had to get through some hard times in my life. I am twenty-three years old, and I have learned a lot at an early age. Although my parents' divorce seemed like a disaster at the time, I have come through it and am getting on with my life.

Christina Chang

I was fourteen when my parents got divorced. At first it was very hard on me. I can't describe the pain I went through. I used to stay up at night and cry and ask God why He was doing this to me. I blamed myself for what happened. In my despair I tried to commit suicide. I got pregnant when I was sixteen and again when I was nineteen. My friends thought it was "uncool" to have a friend with a baby, so I was left to myself with only school, work, and babies to fill my time. I learned that my only chance for a normal life was through education. I knew that it would get me somewhere—and it did. I graduated with honors from high school and came to college. Now I plan to go on to graduate school. Every once in a while I pat myself on the back for changing course. I am proud that I could overcome such dreadful life experiences and learn from them instead of being crushed by them. I have come to terms with my parents' divorce. I have discovered that it is the way you look at things in life that makes your life full of sadness or happiness. Life should never be as hard as it was when my parents were going through a divorce, but I know for a fact that life is what you make of it.

Well put! You can hate the adversities life throws at you, and you can hate your adversaries and in the process become drained and bitter, or you can make the best of the circumstances and move on to a better life. Gaining independence and strength were the positive outcomes most commonly reported by our students. Taking on and mastering unexpected challenges with the support of a caring parent often translated into increased self-confidence and competence for these children of divorce.

Marianne Griffith

By the time high school came around, I was ditching all my classes and experimenting with alcohol. I always came home past curfew, and I constantly fought with my mom. I hated her for alienating me from my father and causing instability in my life. I felt neglected because she was always busy working or taking care of my younger sister and her special needs. When I was caught cheating on a test, they sent me to talk to a school counselor. This was a wake-up call. I spent a lot of time talking things out with the counselor and then with my mother. Most important, I realized that although my mother loved me she could not do much for me because of the demands she was facing. She had to raise six children by herself, one with Down syndrome. So I was forced to become independent. I began to take school seriously and got my life back together. I grew to respect my mother; it takes a strong person to cope with what she did.

One way our students survived was by looking at the benefits of the divorce. And indeed, for some students, there were benefits. Some of them ended up with more resources, such as undivided time and attention from their parent or parents, after the divorce. Others gained from their exposure to new families and new parents. In an ideal remarriage, the children had more adults available, more support, more ideas, and more love, and they benefited.

Megan Hagan

Twenty years have passed since my parents' divorce, and although I still have some pain, there have been positive results. I was forced to become independent at a young age. Because my mother was a single parent working on her graduate degree, my sister and I took on many responsibilities in the household. Visiting my father a thousand miles away created situations that stretched my independence. I also benefited from the opportunity to be exposed to two lifestyles and cultural environments. Living with my mother and stepfather, who are professors, allowed me to experience a liberal environment. Spending time with my stepmother and father, an attorney, exposed me to a more conservative lifestyle. My four parents provided me with four different role models.

Divorce is most successful, if, as this student experienced, the family remains a family. The parents continue to be responsible for the needs of their children; the children stay connected to their parents. This family survived because the parents held no malice and were both concerned for the well-being of their children. They shared the same goal: to maintain their children's family while moving ahead with their separate lives. In these circumstances the children can recover, grow, and even appreciate all the diversity their family members have to offer.

Another student found that maintaining a sense of normalcy in daily life helped her get on with the business of surviving.

Shelly Dennis

My mom and I survived the divorce in a very simple way: we went on with our daily lives and our usual activities. We survived because we didn't give up and kept looking for the positive and for mastering the next step.

Others mentioned new activities that buoyed their survival.

Maggie Farley

My mom and I survived by beginning a whole new life for ourselves. We began doing things that we had wanted to do but that my father never liked to do. We walked and exercised and stopped eating all that red meat my dad loved. In no time, we felt healthier, more energetic, and happier than we had for years.

A common denominator among the students who were survivors was the availability of positive social support. Most commonly, children drew closer to one parent. Coping together in a challenging world and doing this successfully gave them a sense of invincibility. Together they felt strong, and together they could take on and master life's adversities. This close bond boosted their personal growth, their competence, and their confidence in other areas.

Melinda George

For me, there were two positive consequences of my parents' divorce: the development of personal strength and the development of a close relationship with my mother. I discovered my own strength by living through this most difficult experience and surviving the loss of my father. I was helped in this by seeing how my mother handled the loss. I developed a close bond with her from sharing this life experience. She and I have become best friends. In talking with my mom, I also got to know myself better.

Many students mentioned the "special bond" they formed with one of their parents as a result of mastering adversity together.

Leah Frank
I think I survived the divorce pretty well and. I developed a special bond with my mom. I owe her a lot. She always worked hard to give my brother and me the best life possible. We got through the tough times and came out winners. Now I am glad that my parents got divorced. Most people see divorce as a painful and life altering event. I would agree. But there are positive aspects as well, like the inner strength I have developed through the divorce and my mother's support and positive example.

Other students found their solace and strength for survival by separating their well-being from their parents' and taking part in activities with friends outside the family.

Anna Nguyen
I watched my parents suffer, and I suffered with them. But with time, I began to adjust. How? I shifted my focus from my parents' problem to my own life. I realized that, although my parents were important to me, there were other things that were important, too. I worked two jobs. I hung out with my friends. Whenever I had a problem, they were there for me. Through this support I became more self-confident and a stronger and better person.

Some students who searched in their initial despair for a life-saving straw found it in religion.

Tina Hae Kim
My anger, which was directed at my absent father, turned toward men in general. I trusted no one. I refused

to meet new people or to date guys. I was afraid of getting hurt. I was afraid of lies. I was terrified of losing someone I love. When I was at my lowest point, the church saved me. In the church, I discovered that I must fight against my misfortune because otherwise it will damage and imprison me. I now accept the challenges in my life and I know that I can master them.

For other students, education provided the road out of their misery.

Moonja Oh

I wanted to prove that a child from a "broken home" could be a success, so I devoted myself to school. My GPA climbed and I was accepted to college. Since coming to college, I have gained a sense of identity and confidence. I have realized that parental divorce is common and that people can succeed despite their unfortunate family circumstances. My parents' divorce allowed me to become strong, mature, responsible, and persevering. It gave me wisdom, knowledge and empathy, which empower me to remain calm and competent when I encounter life's challenges.

Counseling was another effective support and resource, which helped children work through their problems and improved their coping and communication skills.

Cheryl Wade

My counselor helped me find myself and explore feelings long trapped by pain. It was like I had a tightly tangled ball of yarn inside of me. With therapy, it slowly unraveled, revealing more and more of the consequences of the divorce. I learned to identify my feelings and express them appropriately. It was difficult and emotionally draining to expose my fragile feelings to this stranger, but it was the most beneficial thing I have ever done. Now

I know that there is life after a divorce, so that if it does ever happen to me, I can survive it.

And so can everyone! With compassion, civility, and discipline, divorce does not need to be a total disaster. It can—like other obstacles in life—give rise to a stronger self and better relationships.

Lessons to Be Learned

In this chapter we examined some of the long-term consequences of divorce for children and their parents. We observed four patterns of adjustment—two negative and two positive. One negative pattern was experienced by adults and children who never achieved success and well-being; divorce simply did not fix their problems. A second negative pattern led to parents' becoming eternal enemies; divorce exacerbated their differences. The third pattern involved a positive outcome; parents became civil colleagues and were able to negotiate co-parenting skillfully. The fourth pattern was the most positive: adults and their children found that divorce led them to higher levels of maturity and facilitated their personal growth. Each of these four patterns provides a valuable lesson.

1. Divorce does not fix all problems. Divorce may be a solution to an impossible marriage, but there are many problems that divorce cannot fix. Psychological problems that are not the result of marital difficulties will not disappear when the couple separates, even after a period of adjustment. Problems caused by being the victim of a brutal spouse are also unlikely to be cured by divorce. If emotional problems like these are not resolved, they will eat away at adults' trust and confidence and mental health—forever. Children's problems, too, may last a long time. Although most children are able to overcome the effects of living in an unhappy home and adjust to their parents' divorce within a few years, some experience anxieties, physical symptoms, and lack of trust even years later. They attribute these problems to the breakup of their family. Whether or not the breakup is the sole cause of their problems, these children would have benefited from help at the time of the divorce—and thereafter. With help, children can survive adversity. That help comes in many forms—a family that pulls together, a parent who is strong and with whom the child develops a close bond, a welcoming stepfamily, activities and friends outside the family, a religious faith, higher education, professional counseling. All these can help reach a level of well-being and success after divorce; divorce alone does not heal all their wounds.

2. Individuals who continue to fight are never winners. Eternal enemies hurt themselves and their children. In most situations in life, people who don't like each other can resolve their conflict by severing their relationship. But divorced parents must continue their contact. The mere existence of the other is a constant reminder of their faulty decisions in the past and their continuing dependence on each other in the future. This realization can breed furious resentment. When eternal enemies use their children as pawns and money as a weapon this is especially detrimental. It's a no-win situation, and everyone feels victimized. Irrational enmity damages everyone. Therefore, do all you can not to turn into an "eternal enemy." Reread the stories in this book and find the ways in which you are engaging in enemy actions. Write them down, then review what they have cost you—stress, money, tense relations, lack of cooperation, more stress, damage to the children—and think what you can do to make things better, better for your own sake and for your children's sake.

3. Parents should strive to be civil colleagues. The best most people can hope for after a divorce is not close friendship with their former spouse but a respectful working relationship, a relationship like the kind one would have with a business partner or a neighbor—friendly, respectful, but somewhat reserved. Divorced parents should try to be such civil colleagues. Yes, it is a challenge to achieve a distant yet cooperative relationship with somebody with whom you share a most intimate history. The shared knowledge of past intimacies has a way of luring people into behaviors that are inappropriate for their status as cooperative "business" partners. Even benign remarks or behaviors can shift the tone from cooperation to confrontation. Even worse, ex-spouses have a propensity to make little stabs at each other. His commentary on her ability to handle money, her mood swings, or her tendency to lose her sunglasses, and her commentary on his poor grooming, habitual lying, or lifelong obsession with cars, can only serve to inflame each other. Delivering little jabs that are punctuated with insider knowledge reveals an improper attachment that will thwart a friction-free working relationship. For short moments these hints at past intimacy reestablish a connection that no longer has any currency. Even seemingly innocuous remarks may inflame the emotions, "I miss your great cooking" or "No man understands my jokes like you do" invoke a level of personal involvement that is not conducive to the co-parenting relationship and will stir up emotions about past hurts or longings. It requires great discipline not to keep falling into the intimacy trap and to steer clear of past pain and successfully chart a new course. Nevertheless, that course to a collegial relationship should be the goal.

4. Divorce can lead to personal growth. The best outcome of divorce is when people experience personal growth that they would not have otherwise. If people gain from divorce in terms of increased maturity, they feel like winners. Adults who are winners learn from what went wrong in their marriages, figure out how to avoid it, and go on to success in their futures. Children who are winners gain in strength from meeting challenges and overcoming them. Winners learn to look on the bright side, ask for help, use the resources at their disposal, and appreciate new activities.

It is our hope that the stories and lessons in this book will help every reader achieve personal growth. We are not proponents of divorce. We have presented the stories and lessons about marriage risks and incompatibilities in the early chapters of the book so that readers might make and maintain more successful marriages. But if divorce is necessary, we hope that these stories and lessons about the divorce experience will help readers avoid the worst pitfalls and explore positive possibilities. Divorce *can* lead to happier outcomes for parents and for children. We wish all our readers happiness—whichever road they take.

FOR MORE INFORMATION

Ahrons, C. R. (2004). *We're still family: What grown children have to say about their parents' divorce.* New York: Harper Collins.

Amato, P. R., and Booth, A. (2000). *A generation at risk: Growing up in an era of family upheaval.* Cambridge, MA: Harvard University Press.

Arendell, T. (Ed.) (1997). *Contemporary parenting: Challenges and issues.* Thousand Oaks, CA: Sage Publications.

Booth, A., and Crouter, A. C. (Eds.) (1998). *Men in families: When do they get involved? What difference does it make?* Mahwah, NJ: Erlbaum.

Booth, A., and Dunn, J. (Eds.) (1994). *Stepfamilies: Who benefits? Who does not?* Hillsdale, NJ: Erlbaum.

Booth, A., Crouter, A. C., and Clements, M. (Eds.) (2001). *Couples in conflict.* Mahwah, NJ: Erlbaum.

Bray, J., and Kelly, J. (1998). *Stepfamilies.* New York: Broadway.

Buchanan, C. M., Maccoby, E. E., and Dornbusch, S. M. (1996). *Adolescents after divorce.* Cambridge, MA: Harvard University Press.

Casper, L. M., and Bianchi, S. M. (2002). *Continuity and change in the American family.* Thousand Oaks, CA: Sage Publications.

Clarke-Stewart, A., and Brentano, C. (2006). *Divorce: Causes and consequences.* New Haven, CT: Yale University Press.

Ellis, E. M. (2000). *Divorce wars: Interventions with families in conflict.* Washington, DC: American Psychological Association.

Emery, R. E. (1999). *Marriage, divorce, and children's adjustment* (2nd ed.). Newbury Park, CA: Sage Publications.

Emery, R. E. (2004). *The truth about children and divorce: Dealing with emotions so you and your children can thrive.* New York: Viking/Penguin.

Galatzer-Levy, R. M. and Kraus L. (Eds.), (1999). *The scientific basis of child custody decisions.* New York: Wiley.

Grych, J. H., and Fincham, F. D. (Eds.), (2001). *Interparental conflict and child development: Theory, research, and applications.* New York: Cambridge University Press.

Hetherington, E. M. (Ed.) (1999). *Coping with divorce, single parenting, and remarriage: A risk and resiliency perspective* Mahwah, NJ: Erlbaum.

Hetherington, E. M., and Kelly, J. (2002). *For better or for worse: Divorce reconsidered.* New York: W. W. Norton.

Larson, J. H. (2000). *Should we stay together?* San Francisco: Jossey Bass.

Levin I., and Sussman, M. (Eds.) (1997). *Stepfamilies: History, research, and policy.* New York: Haworth.

McLanahan, S., and Sandefur, G. (1994). *Growing up with a single parent: What hurts, what helps.* Cambridge, MA: Harvard University Press.

Simons, R. L., and Associates (1996). *Understanding differences between divorced and intact families: Stress, interaction, and child outcome.* Thousand Oaks, CA: Sage Publications.

Thompson, R. A., and Amato, P. R. (Eds.). (1999). *The postdivorce family: Children, parenting, and society.* Thousand Oaks, CA: Sage Publications.

Waite, L. J., Bachrach, C., Hindin, M., Thomson, E., and Thornton, A. (Eds.) (2000). *The ties that bind: Perspectives on marriage and cohabitation.* New York: Aldine de Gruyter.

Wallerstein, J. S., & Blakeslee, S. (2003). *What about the kids? Raising your children before, during and after divorce.*

Wallerstein, J. S., Lewis, J. M., and Blakeslee, S. (2000). *The unexpected legacy of divorce: A 25 year landmark study.* New York: Hyperion.

Warshak, R. A. (2003). *Divorce poison: Protecting the parent-child bond from a vindictive ex spouse.* New York: Regan Books.

ON-LINE RESOURCES

www.divorcecentral.com: Links to divorce related resources, organized by state, with an archive of articles and interviews.

www.divorcehelp.com: Information about divorce and referrals to family law attorneys.

www.divorconline.com: Electronic journal providing information and referrals for people facing divorce.

www.divorcecare.com: A divorce recovery support group where you can find help and healing for the hurt and separation of divorce.

www.divorcesupportabout.com: Articles and resources on divorce in a variety of circumstances and from a variety of perspectives.

1692522

Made in the USA